Vanishing Growth in Latin America

Vanishing Growth in Latin America

The Late Twentieth Century Experience

Edited by

Andrés Solimano

Edward Elgar
Cheltenham, UK • Northampton, MA, USA

Published by
Edward Elgar Publishing Limited
Glensanda House
Montpellier Parade
Cheltenham
Glos GL50 1UA
UK

Edward Elgar Publishing, Inc.
136 West Street
Suite 202
Northampton
Massachusetts 01060
USA

A catalogue record for this book
is available from the British Library

Library of Congress Cataloguing in Publication Data
Vanishing growth in Latin America : the late twentieth century experience / edited
   by Andrés Solimano.
        p. cm.
     Includes bibliographical references.
     1. Latin America—Economic conditions—1982– 2. Latin America—Economic
   policy. I. Solimano, Andrés

HC125.V276 2006
330.98'038—dc22

                                                                        2005044198

ISBN–13: 978 1 84542 431 2
ISBN–10: 1 84542 431 X

Typeset by Manton Typesetters, Louth, Lincolnshire, UK
Printed and bound in Great Britain by MPG Books Ltd, Bodmin, Cornwall

Contents

Figures

Tables

Contributors

Manuel R. Agosin, Inter-American Development Bank

Claudio Aravena, United Nations – Economic Commission for Latin America and the Caribbean

Juan S. Blyde, Inter-American Development Bank

Eduardo Fernández-Arias, Inter-American Development Bank

Mario A. Gutiérrez, Georgetown University

André A. Hofman, United Nations – Economic Commission for Latin America and the Caribbean

Roberto Machado, Inter-American Development Bank

Jaime Ros, Department of Economics, Notre Dame University, USA

Andrés Solimano, United Nations – Economic Commission for Latin America and the Caribbean

Raimundo Soto, Department of Economics, Catholic University of Chile

Acknowledgement

This book is mostly based on revised and augmented versions of the papers presented in an international workshop on economic growth in Latin America organized by the Economic Development Division of the Economic Commission for Latin America and the Caribbean of the United Nations in Santiago, Chile. That workshop had the participation of experts in the field from universities, think-tanks, the Inter-American Development Bank, the World Bank, Inter-American Dialogue and UN-ECLAC.

I am also very grateful to the excellent assistant in the preparation of this volume provided by Claudia Allendes of ECLAC and to Alan Sturmer and his team at Edward Elgar Publishing. Finally, we would like to mention that the content of this book represents the views of the authors and not necessarily those of the institutions to which they belong.

Andrés Solimano

1. Introduction and synthesis

Andrés Solimano

1.1 INTRODUCTION

Economic growth is the main source of wealth creation and material welfare to the population. In fact, as an indication of the centrality of the process of wealth creation in economics, Adam Smith entitled his main contribution to economic science, *An Inquiry on the Causes of the Wealth of Nations*, where he investigated the various causes that lead to wealth creation as opposed to the dilapidation of material wealth. The importance of economic growth cannot be overstated. Even relatively small differences in annual growth rates in Gross Domestic Product among countries, when they accumulate over time, can generate large differences in living standards for a country's population. Getting the right (or wrong) policy mix for growth can have far-reaching consequences for the welfare levels (or misery) of its citizens. Nevertheless, in spite of the importance of the topic, our knowledge of the subject is far from complete. The causes that initiate, propagate or stop economic growth are numerous in practice and vary across nations and time. Understanding the causes of growth has important practical implications for the personal fortunes of many people around the world.

Economic growth theory has focused on the relative role of factor accumulation (labor, physical and human capital, natural resources) and productivity growth (due to new knowledge and changes in efficiency with which productive factors are combined) in explaining output growth. This approach is often referred as the 'mechanics of growth' in which factor accumulation and TFP growth constitute the 'proximate' sources of growth on the supply side. In the search of 'ultimate' factors that drive growth we find a long list of variables: incentives, institutions, macroeconomic and political stability, terms of trade and other external shocks, the quality of the political regime, the respect given to property rights, the degree of distributive conflict, geography and others. Pinpointing the specific importance of each of these factors in a given country and time period is one of the tasks of growth analysis.

Two trends have dominated growth economics since the mid-1980s until today: the rise of the endogenous growth theory and the ample use of cross-section growth regressions to test the various propositions of the new growth theory and the effects of macro, trade, financial policies, education and so on, on growth. Most of this analysis is aggregative in nature and focuses on steady-state dynamics. In a sense, this literature has downplayed the concrete factors in specific country experiences that create an impulse to wealth creation and the factors that maintain or stop that impulse. The anatomy of growth at sector and micro levels probably shows a wide variety of growth impulses and contractions operating across the economy with various net effects at aggregate level. Attempted generality (supposedly achieved by cross-section regressions of a large number of countries) is often sought at the cost of missing out the rich concrete experience of countries. Their experiences illuminate concrete factors which boost or impede growth, although those experiences may not lend themselves, in many instances, to easy and mechanical generalizations of the grand factors that drive economic growth.

The global growth experience of the last two to three decades of the twentieth century shows a wide variety of growth paths over time and across countries. This is in contrast with the background of growth economics developed in the 1950s and 1960s that viewed growth as a smooth process around a well-defined trend. Recent empirical evidence shows that growth tends to be a volatile process with little serial correlation in growth rates over time around virtually no trend: past growth is often a poor predictor of future growth. This stylized fact about growth rates is particularly applicable to developing countries and Latin America in particular where growth is more unstable than the growth process of rich industrialized countries (that is the OECD countries).

Models that assume a smooth growth path around a certain mean rate often fail to capture this variety and variability in growth rates. These models are a better approximation for explaining long-run growth trends in countries such as the United States for example where during most of the twentieth century, the economy grew at a smooth rate near 2 per cent per year (except during the Great Depression of the 1930s and the stagflation of the 1970s) or Europe between the late 1940s and early 1970s, during the so-called golden age of capitalism (growth was unstable in the 1914–45 period as Europe witnessed two world wars, high inflation, macroeconomic instability, depression and acute political conflict). In the developing world, global economic performance in the 1980s, 1990s and early 2000s has been affected by shocks and policies that include the debt crises of the 1980s, the reforms of the 1990s, the effect of globalization and financial volatility in the second half of the 1990s. In this period we have seen both success growth stories (that is China, India, Ireland, Chile, Botswana and a few others, although not too many) along with several stories of growth failure, stagnation and even growth implosions (Venezuela, Brazil, Mexico, Argentina after 1980, many Sub-Saharan economies, Russia and former soviet republics during most of the 1990s and others). Much can be learned from these cases in terms of the factors that produce growth, stagnation or growth collapse.

1.2 THE GROWTH RECORD OF LATIN AMERICA

The focus of this book is on the economic growth performance of Latin America in the last two to four decades of the twentieth century. A main message of this volume is that the growth performance of Latin America in the 1980s and 1990s was, on the whole, modest and plagued by cycles that made economic growth also a volatile process. Growth decelerated in most Latin American and Caribbean countries after 1980 with the exception of Chile and Dominican Republic. Average annual growth rates in GDP per capita for the region went down from 3 per cent in 1960–80 to 0.5 per cent in 1980–2002. In addition, the volatility of growth increased in the 1980s and 1990s as compared to previous decades (see Chapter 2 in this volume). Economic growth recovered in the 1990s in Latin America with respect to the 1980s (the decade of the debt crises) although that recovery was again interrupted by the effects of the Asian crises of 1997–8 that sent the region back to a half-decade of sluggish growth. The new hopes for lasting prosperity following the adoption of market-oriented reforms helped by a greater availability of external finance, have been largely disappointed in the critical field of economic growth.

It is apparent that the Latin American region had serious difficulties in adjusting to the global shocks of the last two decades such as the debt crises of the 1980s, the recurrent cycles in capital flows and commodity prices, the various financial crises of the 1990s and early 2000s (Mexico 1994, Asia 1997–8, Russia 1998 and others). At country level, the Latin American region displays also a wide variety of growth experiences in the last four decades. The two economies that grew the fastest in 1960–80, under import substitution and state-dirigisme, Mexico and Brazil, suffered a protracted growth slowdown in the post-1980 period. Incidentally, these are the two largest economies of the region. In turn, two other resource-rich economies of the region, Argentina and Venezuela, experienced sharp growth cycles in the 1980s, 1990s and early 2000s within an overall trend of economic decline with respect to a sustained growth trend. In contrast, Chile managed to grow at more than 7 per cent per year during 1986–97, although growth slowed down for years afterwards, to recover again in 2004–2005 following a boom in copper prices. Also, the Dominican Republic grew very rapidly between 1992 and 2000 although it fell into a crisis in 2002–3.

Other economies of the region suffered various growth cycles but without a noticeable sustained upward trend in growth rates. Macroeconomic instability, inflation, exchange rate volatility, fiscal deficits and external vulnerability have been characteristics of Latin America. The reforms of the 1990s in the region tried to tackle macroeconomic stabilization, the endemic problems of instability and limited growth through policies of external openness, deregulation and privatization. These policies contributed to restore more acceptable levels of macro stability and led to once-and-for-all productivity gains after major distortions were eliminated but their impact on economic growth was neither spectacular nor sustained over time. Investment and savings ratios did not increase significantly and total factor productivity did not accelerate much as we shall see in the different studies included in this book. Public investment declined for most of the 1980s and 1990s and the response of private investment did not compensate for the cut in public investment in most countries of the region (Chile, again, being the exception).

The 'proximate sources' supporting steady growth were simply not there in most of Latin America. Moreover, the region has developed unevenly and conflictive social structure and the quality of its institutions often conspires against steady economic growth. Poverty, inequality and in some countries the exclusion of ethnic groups often lead to social polarization and political instability. In addition, indices of quality of institutions and the costs of doing business put Latin American countries in a modest place in these international rankings. Social consensus is often hard to reach and economic policymaking becomes a difficult process. As a consequence of all this, the socio-political structure of Latin American societies is often not very supportive for capital formation, innovation and growth. Unfortunately the reforms inspired in the Washington consensus have not succeeded in tackling the unequal social structure of the region and its institutions.

In the last four decades or so, Latin American countries have tried various economic models such as import substitution and state dirigisme, socialism, populism and free market reform to solve its endemic economic and social problems and spur economic growth. The political correlates of the economic models have included right-wing dictatorships mainly in the southern cone in the 1970s and part of the 1980s, left-wing governments and various types of democratic and semi-democratic regimes in the 1990s and early 2000s. The outcomes of these experiments has varied depending upon countries and time periods but the robust result is that lasting and sustained growth and prosperity has remained elusive for most of the region as a whole although episodes of growth and prosperity were observed in some individual countries. In some countries those episodes of growth lasted around a decade or more. In turn, relatively long episodes of stagnation and decline are not uncommon in the Latin American region.

1.3 MAIN QUESTIONS

The growth studies of this volume document and analyze the growth performance of various countries in three sub-regions of Latin America: the Southern Cone and Brazil; the Andean countries; Central America and Mexico. The studies in this volume try to ascertain empirically the main determinants of output growth highlighting also the factors that encourage growth and the elements that can impede it. The questions that the contributions of this volume address can be synthesized in the following:

- What has been the growth performance of Latin America in the last four decades, particularly in the 1980s and 1990s following the adoption of market-oriented reforms?
- What has been the contribution of factor accumulation and productivity growth to GDP growth in the different countries and sub-regions of Latin America?
- What is the role of economic shocks, macroeconomic policies and social and institutional structures in explaining the growth performance of the region?
- What starts a growth process? What sustains it? Why can a growth boom run out of steam? Can we provide examples of various growth cycles in Latin America?
- How persistent can a growth boom be? or a growth collapse? Can economic stagnation be a persistent feature in countries of Latin America?
- What is the impact of political economy considerations on growth, in conditions of inequality and through poor quality institutions?
- What is the impact of competitiveness, the trade regime, fiscal policy, education, inequality, economic policy and political instability on the rate of economic growth?

1.4 REGIONAL COUNTRY STUDIES

This book is organized into seven chapters, including this Introduction. Chapter 2 and Chapter 7 are regional growth studies and Chapters 3 to 6 comprise sub-regional growth analysis. The sub-regional growth studies refer to: (1) the 'Southern Cone' composed of Argentina, Brazil, Chile, Paraguay and Uruguay; (2) the Andean countries comprising Bolivia, Colombia, Ecuador, Peru and Venezuela and (3) Mexico and Central America including the Dominican Republic, El Salvador, Guatemala, Honduras, Mexico, Nicaragua and Panama. Most chapters cover the period running roughly from 1960 to

2000 and their methodological approach is a mix of the sources of growth accounting model that separates the roles of factor accumulation and total productivity growth in explaining growth patterns, complemented with a structural approach of the 'ultimate' determinants of growth as specified by the different authors for their specific set of countries.

The book also tries to identify, at a regional level, patterns and cycles of growth, detecting episodes of rapid growth, of the collapse of growth (growth crises) and stagnation. A common theme across the different chapters is the impact of external shocks, domestic policies, structural reform and the under-lying economic and political structure on the mean rate and variability of growth rates.

Chapter 2 by Andrés Solimano and Raimundo Soto considers 12 Latin American and Caribbean economies (Argentina, Bolivia, Brazil, Colombia, Chile, Costa Rica, Ecuador, Mexico, Peru, the Dominican Republic, Uruguay and Venezuela) in the period 1960–2002. The chapter presents several stylized facts of the growth performance of the 12 countries in 1960–80 compared with 1980–2002, showing that the distribution of growth rates of 1980–2002 exhibits a lower mean and higher standard deviation than the distribution of growth rates in the period 1960–80. The chapter also shows that there is great hetero-geneity in growth performance across countries and over time in Latin America.

Also there is a change in the countries that were growing rapidly before and after 1980. Under import substitution strategies, Brazil and Mexico were fast growers before 1980. In contrast, under market-oriented policies, Chile and the Dominican Republic were fast growers after 1980. The chapter per-forms growth decompositions to assess the role of factor accumulation versus total factor productivity growth in explaining growth in the region; in general total factor productivity (TFP) growth (also reflecting cyclical elements) explain most of the variation in growth rates between the 1960s and 1970s and the 1980s and 1990s. The authors also show that in the post-1980 period, public investment has been more volatile than private investment in Latin America and that the reduction in public investment in the last two decades has not been compensated by an offsetting increase in private investment (except in Chile).

The chapter also focuses on the dynamics of growth in time spans of one to two decades for the group of 12 Latin American economies compared to a reference (or control group) outside the region, identifying episodes of rapid growth and of growth crises that last between five to ten years. In trying to explain the behavior of TFP growth, the chapter finds a high correlation between various measures of macro stability and TFP growth but no persist-ent correlation between external shocks and TFP growth.

Chapter 3 by Juan Blyde and Eduardo Fernández-Arias, looks at the growth record of Argentina, Brazil, Chile, Paraguay and Uruguay (referred as the

'Southern Cone' countries, SC) in the 1960–2000 period. The chapter evaluates their growth performance taking as a benchmark a sample of 68 countries, of which 15 are from Latin America and 53 from the rest of the world (20 of them belong to developing countries). Southern Cone countries exhibited medium to strong growth in the 1960s and 1970s, deceleration in the 1980s, and recovery in the 1990s until the Asian crisis and then a growth slowdown or crisis (in Argentina and Uruguay growth collapsed following serious exchange rate and financial crises in each of the two countries in the early 2000s). Since 2003 Argentina, and Uruguay started a strong recovery. Argentina, Chile and Uruguay performed best in the 1990s (up to 1998) whereas Brazil and Paraguay saw better times in the 1970s. Brazil, for example, went from high to low growth during the 1960–2000 period and Chile followed the opposite path, going from moderate average growth in the 1960s and 1970s to faster average growth in 1980–2000 (although punctuated by growth cycles of different intensity). On average, the SC group grew slower than the rest of the world in the period 1960–2000 and experienced higher instability in growth rates than the overall sample of 68 countries.

The growth experience of the southern cone countries confirms our previous observation on the lack of correlation between growth rates over time that characterizes the growth process in many developing countries. The lagging growth performance of the SC group in recent decades is reflected in lack of convergence of per capita income with the rest of the world. The sources of growth calculation for the SC countries show that TFP growth is key to explaining the variability of GDP per capita growth in the sample period. Also the lack of TFP growth, except in Chile, accounts for most of the slower growth of the Southern Cone countries relative to the rest of the world. However, TFP growth is higher in the SC group than in the rest of Latin America, largely because of the weak growth in TFP of the rest of the region. The authors estimate a panel model and find that the degree of external openness and the quality of institutions are the main determinants of the growth in total factor productivity growth. Also the authors find that the share of imports of machinery and equipment in GDP, as a proxy for technology diffusion, is also an important determinant of TFP growth, a finding similar to the one found in Central America by Agosin and Machado in Chapter 5.

Chapter 4, by Claudio Aravena, André Hofman and Andrés Solimano, explores economic growth in the Andean countries (Bolivia, Colombia, Ecuador, Peru and Venezuela) for the whole twentieth century and for the 1950–2002 period. A main focus of the chapter is to distinguish between the effect of economic determinants and the impact of governance-related factors in explaining economic growth in the Andean region. In a long-run perspective, the data shows that the Andean countries grew faster in the first half of the twentieth century than in the second with a marked deceleration in growth rates after the mid-1970s. This trend was particularly noticeable in Venezuela, a rapid grower from the 1920s to the 1970s. In contrast, Colombia experienced a less severe decline in GDP and productivity growth with respect to the rest of the world, although since the mid-1990s growth slowed down. The chapter performs a source-of-growth decomposition between factor accumulation (labor, capital and land, adjusting for the quality of the factors of production) and total productivity growth for the period 1950 to 2002 and various sub-periods. The sources-of-growth analysis show a declining trend in TFP growth since 1973 when compared to the 1950–73 period. For 1950–2002 the average annual rate of TFP growth was below 1 per cent. Colombia experienced the highest TFP growth and Peru the lowest in this period. The chapter complements the sources of growth analysis with estimates of empirical growth equations using panel regressions for the five countries in the period 1950–2002. The analysis considers the effects of a set of economic and governance factors on growth such as initial per capita GDP, the investment ratio, inflation, exchange rate variability, degree of external openness, the ratio of government consumption on GDP, the type of political regime and degree of political instability. The empirical analysis shows that conditional convergence holds in the sample period, the investment ratio and the degree of external openness have a significant positive effect on GDP growth, and inflation has a negative effect on growth. Regarding governance variables the chapter finds that political instability (measured as frequency of presidential crises) has a negative effect on growth and democracy (with a lag) has a positive effect on growth, after controlling for other determinants of growth. Then growth regressions are run for each Andean country. The estimates tend to confirm the previous results on the effects of economic factors on growth but finds insignificant effects for the political regime variable on the growth rate of GDP.

Chapter 5, by Manuel Agosín and Roberto Machado, studies the process of economic growth in Costa Rica, El Salvador, Guatemala, Honduras, Nicaragua, Panama and the Dominican Republic in the period 1960–2000. The average income per capita level of the group is below U$1500, and they specialize in tropical products, light manufacturing and tourism, and suffered the effects of the oil shocks of the 1970s, the debt crises of the 1980s and the financial instability of the second half of the 1990s and early 2000s. In the 1980s Nicaragua, El Salvador and Guatemala also experienced civil wars. In addition, several of these economies suffered natural disasters such as earthquakes and hurricanes that led to a loss of human life and the destruction of physical assets. They all started economic reforms in the early to mid-1990s. The growth performance of the group in the last 25 years has been moderate with little absolute convergence in per capita income to the levels of advanced countries; moreover, there is a variety in the growth performance of countries within the Central America group. Nicaragua has been a faltering economy since the 1980s although experiencing a modest and fragile recovery in the 1990s. In contrast, Costa Rica, the Dominican Republic, and Panama have had a better growth performance in this period.

The chapter identifies both 'proximate and ultimate' determinants of economic growth, highlighting the role of natural resources and history, integration to the world economy and institutions, in explaining growth patterns in Central America. A growth accounting exercise correcting for changes in quality of labor and capital inputs shows that around 85 per cent of total output growth in the 1991–99 period is due to capital accumulation and the rest to TFP growth. The results also show different contributions of TFP growth to GDP expansion through the seven countries with a higher contribution in Costa Rica, the Dominican Republic and El Salvador and a lower contribution in the other countries. In Nicaragua, TFP growth was virtually zero in that period. In general, physical capital accumulation was low in Central America although advances were made in the education area in the 1990s. The chapter also estimates a multi-equation model in which growth of GDP, investment in machinery and equipment; human capital and the degree of institutional development (rule of law) are simultaneously determined. The model is estimated with panel data of seven countries for 1971–2000. A strong effect is found for investment in machinery and equipment as a prime determinant of GDP growth. The degree of external openness, capital inflows and financial deepening, affect growth. The rule of law variable has a significant effect on GDP growth and on investment in machinery and equipment. Also the authors emphasize the double causality between growth, education and institutional development, noting that higher GDP growth and better education improve the rule of law.

Chapter 6 by Jaime Ros examines growth constraints in northern Latin America (NLA) namely Mexico and Central America (the same set of countries of Chapter 5 besides Mexico). The author notes the importance of tourism and export processing zones as new sources of growth in these countries. He also examines the recovery of growth in the 1990s in NLA following internal reforms, macroeconomic stabilization, increased US growth and the end of the armed conflict in El Salvador, Nicaragua and Guatemala. The author also explores the main factors affecting competitiveness and growth in the NLA countries such as the real exchange rate, the macroeconomic environment and the business climate. Ros also identifies some key constraints for growth in the NLA group: lagging competitiveness, inequality in income distribution, dependence on commodity exports with volatile prices in international markets, limited internal linkages and the weak productivity effects of newly dynamic export products. Using catching-up growth models to project potential growth and income convergence of the NLA countries the corresponding simulations do not yield very encouraging results for the medium run in those two dimensions (growth potential and convergence in income per capita levels). Finally the author provides calculations of required investment ratios, required export growth and savings gaps for the group of northern Latin American countries.

Chapter 7 by Mario Gutiérrez produces evidence about the contribution of the level and composition of investment and other sources to the growth process of Latin America during the period 1960–2002. The combined growth accounting and regression analysis used data for the six largest Latin American countries: Argentina, Brazil, Chile, Colombia, Mexico and Venezuela. These countries produce nearly 90 per cent of Latin America's GDP. Alternative growth accounting methodologies were used to measure the contributions of the sources of growth to GDP growth in this period. The study also provides evidence of the effects of investments in machinery and equipment and construction, and the effects of private and public investment on per capita GDP growth.

The research found evidence of the primary role played by total factor productivity in explaining the difference between fast and slow growth experiences. Extending the traditional growth accounting approach did not change this conclusion. It also found that investment in machinery and equipment, and private investment, were most effective in raising per capita GDP growth, but that key policy related variables, including education, were essential ingredients contributing to per capita GDP growth. Evidence of mutual causality between private investment and growth, and inconclusive evidence regarding the incidence of FDI and infrastructure on private investment were also found in this chapter.

2. Economic growth in Latin America in the late twentieth century: evidence and interpretation*

Andrés Solimano and Raimundo Soto

2.1 INTRODUCTION

Economic growth in Latin America in the last 30 years or so has been, on average, modest (in per capita terms) and volatile. This period has witnessed cycles of prosperity, stagnation, and negative growth. The last third of the twentieth century was also characterized by shifting patterns of capital flows, recurrent terms of trade shocks, substantial economic reforms and a rapidly changing global economy. In this context understanding economic growth as a smooth process around a secular trend is a departure far from reality. On the contrary, the growth process of Latin America in this period is better characterized by a complex interaction of shifting growth trends, alternating with complex cycles of variable intensity and duration. Besides, at a national level, a wide variety of growth stories are detected. It is not uncommon to find in the last 30–40 years, several episodes of prosperity lasting for a decade followed by protracted stagnation or outright growth collapse in several countries of the region.

The growth regimes of recent decades have in the background the large shocks of the 1970s, 1980s and 1990s and the early twenty-first century. In the 1970s, the region was able to recover from the global shocks of the 1970s (the collapse of Bretton Woods exchange rate parities and the two oil price shocks) through abundant and cheap external borrowing that proved to be temporary; then came the debt crises of the 1980s followed by a period of slow and unstable growth and macroeconomic instability. In the early to mid-1990s the region adopted market-oriented policies and enjoyed a new cycle of easy external borrowing. In spite of a cyclical recovery and one-time efficiency gains, sustained growth proved again to be elusive. After the Asian and Russian crises of the late 1990s, Latin America entered a cycle of sluggish growth that started to recover in 2004. Thus, large external shocks, important changes in the global economy and internal policy transformations have dominated the growth process of the last 30 or 40 years in Latin America.

The 1980s and 1990s were decades of instability and slow growth for most of the Latin American region. There are exceptions, however. Chile and the Dominican Republic grew rapidly in the last decade or so, although after the Asian crises hit both economies, they experienced cycles of more sluggish growth. Chile, however, recently started to approach its pre-Asian crisis growth rates.

The purpose of this chapter is to advance our understanding of the growth patterns of the Latin American economy in the final decades of the twentieth century. We focus on the analysis of medium-to-long run growth, as opposed to the standard discussion of the determinants of high frequency fluctuations (business cycles), and disentangle the contribution of factor accumulation and total factor productivity to output growth. While business cycles are of interest for stabilization policies, growth cycles tend to be related to different variables from those that determine short-run growth, such as investment, human capital formation and the adoption of technology.

We also want to understand the spells of prosperity and stagnation in several important economies of the region, as well as to identify cases of growth decline and divergence in recent decades. The role of factor accumulation and total factor productivity growth performance are investigated in the chapter, as well as the role of terms of trade shocks and capital inflows, changes in the quality of the labor force and macroeconomic instability on total factor productivity growth (TFP) and GDP growth.

The chapter is organized in six sections. Section 2.2 analyzes the main stylized facts of economic growth in the last 40 years in Latin America. Section 2.3 identifies medium-term growth cycles as deviations from trend growth that can cumulate for decades. Section 2.3 examines growth cycles in Latin America. Section 2.4 carries out a source of growth exercise for 12 Latin American economies discussing the behavior of TFP growth and factor accumulation and comparing them to a reference group of six economies in Asia and Europe. Section 2.5 constructs several episodes of 'sustained growth' and 'sustained decline' in Latin America in the 1960–2003 period. Section 2.6 analyzes the role of several external variables, macroeconomic factors and factor quality in driving TFP and GDP growth. Section 2.7 concludes.

2.2 THE EMPIRICAL EVIDENCE AND STYLIZED FACTS ON ECONOMIC GROWTH

We study the growth record of 12 Latin American economies (representing in 2001 nearly 86 per cent of Latin American GDP (World Bank, 2003)) over a period of 43 years, running from 1960 to 2003. In Table 2.1 we present the main indicators of long-run growth for these countries. From this evidence, we highlight three stylized facts.

Table 2.1   Average annual per capita GDP growth rates

	Average annual GDP growth rates (%)		
	1960–2003	1960–1980	1981–2003
Argentina	1.1	2.6	–0.3
Bolivia	0.9	2.3	–0.3
Brazil	2.1	4.4	0.1
Chile	2.3	1.6	3.0
Colombia	1.7	2.6	1.0
Costa Rica	1.9	3.0	1.0
Dominican Republic	3.0	3.3	2.7
Ecuador	1.7	3.5	0.1
Mexico	2.0	3.7	0.6
Peru	0.7	1.7	–0.1
Uruguay	0.8	1.5	0.2
Venezuela	–0.2	1.5	–1.7
Unweighted average	1.5	2.6	0.5

Source: Authors' elaboration based on data by ECLAC (2004).

Stylized fact 1   There is substantial heterogeneity and volatility in long-run growth.

What is remarkable about the Latin American growth experience in this period is the variability and volatility in growth patterns, across countries and over time. In fact, the average rate of growth of per capita GDP for the 12 countries in the 1960–2003 period was 1.5 per cent. This rate is similar to the 1.7 per cent level computed for the world in the twentieth century by Maddison (2003), but below the 2 per cent average rate of growth of the USA docu-mented in Kehoe and Prescott (2002). This suggests that in the last four decades, Latin America has lagged behind world economic growth.[1] Given the unequal distribution of income in Latin American economies, an average rate of growth of GDP per capita of 1.5 per cent in the last 43 years makes the pace of poverty reduction very slow.

In addition, there is substantial heterogeneity in growth experiences across Latin American economies. As depicted in Table 2.1, five of these economies have grown well below the 2 per cent benchmark in the 1960–2003 period. The dismal performance of Argentina, Bolivia, Peru, Uruguay and Venezuela is apparent. Only one economy exhibits a vigorous and sustained growth rate – the Dominican Republic – while the remaining six countries show that they have merely kept the pace of growth of the more developed economies (Brazil, Chile, Colombia, Costa Rica, Ecuador and Mexico).

Stylized fact 2   There was a substantial slowdown in economic growth after 1980.

In terms of growth patterns, we should distinguish two sub-periods in the sample: 1960–80 and 1981–2003.[2] The (unweighted) average rate of growth of per capita GDP in the 1960–80 period was 2.6 per cent for the 12 countries (see Table 2.1), significantly higher than that in the period 1981–2003 of 0.5 per cent. In turn, the standard deviation of growth rates was 3.5 in the period 1960–80 and 4.5 in 1981–2003. This shows an important result: since 1980, economic growth has become slower and more volatile than in the two previous decades. This change in the growth pattern of the Latin American region is verified at any growth rate, as displayed in the histogram of growth rates for the 12 countries in the 1960–80 and 1981–2003 periods in Figure 2.1. The modest growth performance of Latin America in the period 1981–2003 can be appreciated in the shifting of the distribution to the left. It also shows when comparing the cumulative densities of growth rates for both sub-periods. These cumulative densities show that the probability of having less than zero growth for any given country in the period 1960–80 is close to 30 per cent compared to close to 50 per cent in the period 1981–2003. The figure also shows that there is stochastic dominance: economic growth was slower in the 1981–2003 period, for any level of GDP growth observed in the 1960–80 period.

Two caveats are in order here. First, the deceleration in per capita growth rates observed in Latin America in the 1980–2003 period also coincides with slower per capita growth in the world economy in the same period. Yet, the decline in per capita GDP growth in Latin America is much larger than that of developed economies: per capita GDP growth in the world economy declined from 3.4 per cent per year in the 1960–80 period to 2.0 per cent in the 1981–2003 period (Loayza and Soto, 2002, updated). Second, the growth deceleration

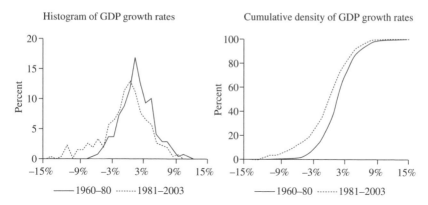

Histogram of GDP growth rates   Cumulative density of GDP growth rates

Source: Authors' elaboration.

Figure 2.1   Histograms of annual GDP growth rates

is not uniform across countries. Although growth rates in all Latin American economies in the 1981–2003 period were lower than that of the 1960–80 period, in Chile they accelerated from a mediocre 1.6 per cent per year to a robust 3 per cent.[3] In some countries the rapid growth of the 1960s and 1970s was followed by a period of very slow growth or complete stagnation. For example, in Brazil and Ecuador, economic growth disappeared, while in Mexico growth rates in the 1981–2003 were one-sixth of their 1960–80 levels. In five countries average per capita GDP growth rates have been negative for the last 20 years (Argentina, Bolivia, Ecuador, Peru and Venezuela), leading to outright decline. Other economies saw a marked reduction in their growth rates but managed to expand per capita GDP, albeit modestly (Colombia and Costa Rica).

Stylized fact 3   There are important changes in the relative growth performance between countries.

It is interesting to note that there was an important change in the growth performance across countries in the 1981–2003 and 1960–80 periods. Relatively rapid growers, defined as those countries with annual rates of growth in per capita GDP above 3 per cent in the period 1960–80, included five countries: Brazil, Mexico, Costa Rica, the Dominican Republic and Ecuador (see Table 2.2).[4] In contrast, the most rapid growers in the 1960–80 period, Mexico and Brazil, also the largest Latin American economies, became slow growers in the 1981–2003 period, registering annual rates of growth of GDP per capita between 0 and 1 per cent in that period. Interestingly these results are

Table 2.2   *Changes in economic performance in Latin American economies*

	Countries where real per capita income grew				
	less than zero	0% to 1%	1% to 2%	2% to 3%	above 3%
1960–1980			Chile Peru Uruguay Venezuela	Argentina Bolivia Colombia	Brazil Costa Rica Dominican Republic Ecuador Mexico
1981–2003	Argentina Bolivia Peru Venezuela	Brazil Colombia Costa Rica Ecuador Mexico Uruguay		Dominican Republic	Chile

Source: Authors' elaboration based on data by ECLAC (2004).

not driven only by their record during the 'lost decade' of the 1980s: Brazil's average rate of growth per capita in the 1981–2003 period was 0.3 per cent. The rate of growth of GDP per capita of Mexico was 0.8 per cent, higher than that in Brazil in the same period.

Modest growers in 1960–80 (with annual rates of growth of GDP per capita in the range 1 to 2 per cent) were Chile, Peru, Venezuela and Uruguay. In contrast, Chile in the period 1981–2003 became the only 'rapid grower', according to our definition, registering annual rates of growth in GDP per capita of 3 per cent.[5] In the period 1981–2003 a handful of economies shrunk, experiencing average negative growth rates per capita. These economies were Argentina, Bolivia, Peru, and Venezuela (see Table 2.2).

In summary, while the overall growth performance of Latin America in the last 40 years has been disappointing, the successful experiences of Chile and to some extent the Dominican Republic suggest that slow growth is not an exogenous phenomenon. Latin American countries hold the key to their development but, as some cases sadly show, they do not know how to make use of it.

2.3 GROWTH CYCLES

Let us turn now to growth cycles. Defining a growth cycle is not a simple matter. Analytically, the study of economic growth processes has been conducted at three levels: (1) long-run or steady-state growth, this is a time span of 50 years or more; (2) medium-run growth dynamics, comprising periods of 10 to 30 years and (3) short-run (high frequency) fluctuations of growth, say business cycles of up to four years.[6]

The actual time series of GDP growth, in turn, reflect a complex interaction of trend and cyclical growth of different frequencies. We will be interested here in detecting cycles of prosperity and cycles (or phases) of slow growth or stagnation that last a substantial time period, say a decade or more. Again our focus is on growth cycles rather than on business cycles, although high frequency cycles may be correlated with medium-run growth cycles (see Fatás, 2002).

We will use a criterion for identifying growth cycles based on comparing the dynamics of actual per capita GDP growth relative to a long-run growth trend. Abstracting from changes in the capital–output ratio, we shall assume that trend growth in GDP per working age person is driven by the evolution of knowledge useful in production (see Solow, 1956; Kehoe and Prescott, 2002). Trend growth will be assumed to be exogenous.

Also knowledge is postulated to grow smoothly over time at a constant rate given by the rate of the GDP per capita of the industrial leader, the United States, which as said before, grew at 2 per cent per year in the twentieth century.[7] Of course an individual country's trend growth may differ from that rate but it is still a good reference point to judge long-run growth performance and also deviations from the trend. In a subsequent section we will identify 'growth episodes' of persistent or sustained growth. We will also compare the growth performance of the Latin American economies with a reference group of economies outside the region.

For the time being, we will assume that if actual GDP growth per capita (or per working age person) is above its trend rate of growth for a decade we shall identify it as a boom or a period of prosperity. Conversely if growth is below trend for at least decade we shall identify it as a period of growth slowdown or a stagnation phase. Large deviations from trend can occur and be persistent over time. Some authors have even defined as 'great depressions' – in a modern meaning of the term, different from the classical definitions used to describe 1930s type of depressions – as a period in which output per working age adult fell 20 per cent below trend (with at least 15 per cent taking place in a decade: see Kehoe and Prescott, 2002).

Figure 2.2 shows the evolution of GDP per capita for each of the 12 countries considered, normalizing the data using 1960 = 100. There are a

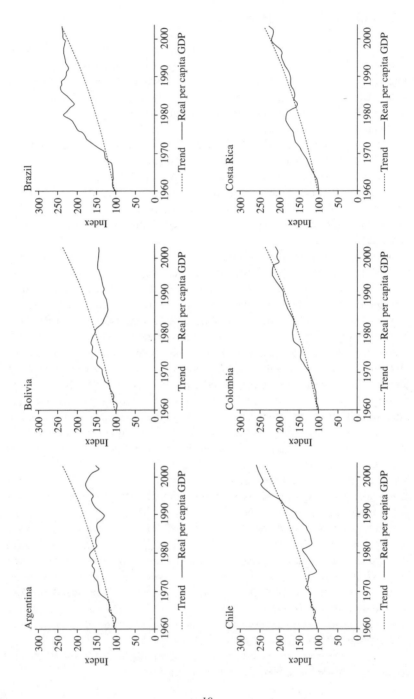

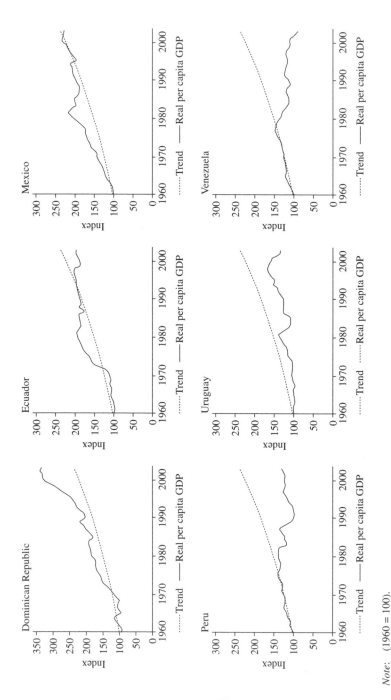

Note: (1960 = 100).

Source: Authors' elaboration based on data from the World Bank and ECLAC.

Figure 2.2 Real GDP per capita and long-run trends: Latin American countries

wide variety of paths in per capita GDP in the last 40 years for different countries. Countries such as Brazil, Mexico and the Dominican Republic grew above the 2 per cent trend for several years. However, Mexico and Brazil started a protracted period of slow GDP per capita growth in the early 1980s. The Dominican Republic has accelerated its growth rate above trend more sharply since the early 1990s.

A country that was above the trend of 2 per cent growth for a decade (or more) was Ecuador in the 1970s when the country experienced a boom of very rapid growth, led essentially by the oil sector. Chile's GDP per capita fell below the line of trend growth for almost 20 years from the early 1970s to the early 1990s; however, due to the rapid growth process initiated in the late 1980s, Chile's growth surpassed the 2 per cent trend line in the early 1990s.

A group of five Latin American countries experienced a long cumulative slowdown in which actual GDP per capita deviated from trend growth. That cumulative deviation from trend lasted for a quarter century. These economies have suffered 'great depressions' in the Kehoe and Prescott (2002) definitions. The group includes Argentina, Bolivia, Peru, Uruguay, and Venezuela. We had already shown that these economies experienced negative average GDP growth per capita in the 1980–2003 period.

Argentina's GDP per capita started to fall below trend growth in the late 1970s, and there were cyclical growth accelerations (for example in the first half of the 1990s) without returning to the trend in a sustained way. Uruguay, in turn, has diverged from the international trend since the early 1960s, with growth accelerations in the mid-1970s and early 1990s followed by a sharp decline in the early 2000s.[8] Bolivia's growth started to decline relative to trend since the late 1970s. Economic growth in Venezuela, an oil exporter, started to fall relative to international trends since the mid 1970s, as did Peru. Clearly, the growth record of these countries is very meager as measured relative to trend growth, accumulating a cycle of growth slowdown for more than two decades in a few cases.

The empirical evidence shows also a high frequency of 'growth crises' in Latin America, particularly in the 1981–2003 period. A 'growth crisis' is defined here as any year in which the rate of growth of GDP per capita is negative. Table 2.3 presents the crisis accounting results. It is striking that in the 12 Latin American countries the average number of years of growth crisis was 12 years (12.3) in the period 1960–2003. That is, one crisis every three to four years. In turn, the frequency of growth crisis was more than twice as much in the 1981–2003 than in the 1960–80 period. The higher simultaneous concentration of growth crises in several Latin American countries took place in 1981–3, the years of the onset of the debt crisis of the 1980s.

Also in 2000–02 there is a high concentration of growth crises. The country with the highest frequency of per capita growth crises in the last four

Table 2.3   Growth crises in Latin America and reference group

	Number of years with negative GDP per capita growth rates			Percentage of crisis in total period:
	1960–1980	1981–2003	1960–2003	1960–2003
Argentina	6	11	17	38.6
Bolivia	4	9	13	29.5
Brazil	2	11	13	29.5
Chile	4	3	7	15.9
Colombia	2	5	7	15.9
Costa Rica	3	8	11	25.0
Dominican Republic	4	6	10	22.7
Ecuador	3	8	11	25.0
Mexico	0	8	8	18.2
Peru	4	10	14	31.8
Uruguay	5	9	14	31.8
Venezuela	10	13	23	52.3
Average	3.9	8.4	12.3	28.0
Korea	2	1	3	6.8
Thailand	0	2	2	4.5
Philippines	0	7	7	15.9
Ireland	2	2	4	9.1
Spain	2	2	4	9.1
Turkey	5	6	11	25.0
Average	1.8	3.3	5.2	11.7

Source: Authors' elaboration based on ECLAC (2004) and IMF data (2004).

decades is Venezuela (23 years) followed by Argentina (17 years), Uruguay (14 years) and Peru (14 years). The countries with the lowest number of growth crises in the sample are Chile and Colombia (seven years). This evidence points out the volatility of the growth process in Latin America, particularly since 1981. Some of these crisis episodes were triggered by common external shocks like the debt crisis of the early 1980s. However, internal policies and country-specific volatility (inflation, fiscal deficits, currency volatility) are ingredients observed in certain periods in several economies, especially in Argentina and Venezuela. These developments have to be correlated with the growth record of these two economies.

Summing up, the evidence presented here indicates that the growth slowdown of the last two decades in Latin America has been accompanied by a high frequency of growth crises around a low mean growth rate. Of course the defining parameters of the contours of growth paths (mean and variance) vary from country to country.

Comparison with Reference Group

The growth performance of Latin America can be seen in comparative perspective to a reference group of six European and Asian economies: South Korea, Thailand, Spain, Ireland, the Philippines and Turkey (see Figure 2.3). Using the 2 per cent benchmark of trend growth for GDP per capita starting in 1960, it is noteworthy that several of these countries had already surpassed the trend by the 1960s, and grew much faster over sustained periods of time. This was the case in South Korea, Thailand, Spain and Ireland, although the different countries have their own growth cycles. Still the tendency in these economies was to depart in a sustained way from the international growth trend. However, it is fair to say that the Philippines and Turkey have growth paths that resemble more the Latin American record. The Philippines stays above trend in the 1960s until the mid 1970s when growth accelerated briefly only to decline and stagnate after the early 1980s when the country was hit by the debt crisis. Turkey in turn, shows a highly cyclical path of growth (at high frequencies) around the trend, punctuated by crises in the late 1970s and in the early 2000s.

Differences in growth performance between Latin America and these economies can be gauged by the following simple calculation. It took over four decades for the Latin American economies to double their initial per capita GDP level in the 1960–2003 period. In contrast, doubling initial income in South Korea and Spain took only 13 years, 16 years in Thailand, 20 years in Ireland and 30 years in Turkey. The Philippines has been unable to double per capita income in the last 43 years.

To put in perspective the high frequency of growth crises in Latin America we replicate the crisis accounting exercise for the reference group. In these countries the average number of years with negative growth rates is five years, less than half as much the average number of growth crises in the 12 Latin American countries in the 1960–2003 period. The countries with the highest incidence of growth crises are Turkey and the Philippines, again with the highest number of growth crises taking place in the 1981–2003 period.

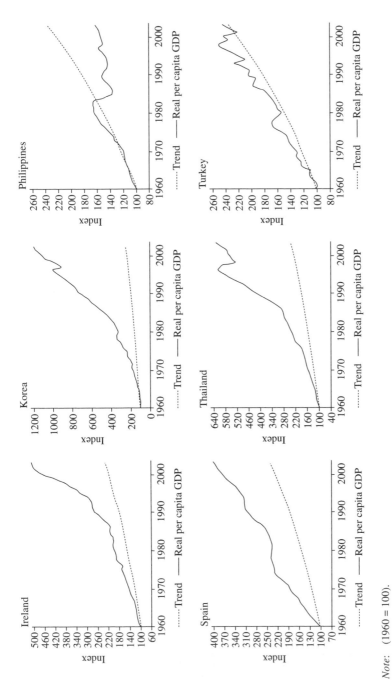

Note: (1960 = 100).

Source: Authors' elaboration.

Figure 2.3   Real GDP per capita and long-run trends: reference group

23

2.4   SOURCES OF GROWTH

In this section we compute the sources of growth for the 12 Latin American economies as well as for the six other economies that we use as a reference group. We decompose GDP growth into factor accumulation and TFP growth.

The Measurement of Total Factor Productivity

In order to measure total factor productivity (TFP) in each country we assume that GDP is produced according to the following Cobb–Douglas production function:

$$GDP_t = A_t \mu_t K_t^\alpha e_t L_t^{1-\alpha} \tag{2.1}$$

where e_t is an indicator of the efficiency of hours worked, L_t and μ_t is the occupation rate of capital, K_t. Parameter A_t is an indicator of the technical efficiency in the use of factors. In this chapter we define TFP to encompass not only technical efficiency but also the efficiency of labor and the degree of use of the capital stock. Consequently, in our view several elements could affect factor productivity beyond the technical ability to mix inputs and generate goods. For example, government regulations leading to lower production with same use of inputs is interpreted as declining TFP.

To compute TFP we need to build capital series. For eight countries – Argentina, Bolivia, Chile, Colombia, Costa Rica, Mexico, Peru and Venezuela – we use and update the capital series provided by Hofman (2003). For all other countries, we cumulate investment, I_t, according to the perpetual inventory method and an annual depreciation rate, δ, of 5 per cent:[9]

$$K_{t+1} = (1-\delta)K_t + I_t \tag{2.2}$$

In addition, we need an estimate for the share of capital in GDP, α. National income accounts indicate that the share of labor compensation in GDP valued at factor prices (GDP at market prices minus indirect taxes) is small in Latin American economies relative to, say, that in the OECD countries. We choose a higher value of the labor share for growth accounting 0.65 – corresponding to $\alpha = 0.35$ – for two reasons. First, measured labor compensation in developing countries fails to account for the income of most self-employed and family workers, who make up a large fraction of the labor force. Gollin (2002) shows that, for countries where there is sufficient data to adjust for this measurement problem, the resulting labor shares tend to be close to the value in the United States, at 0.70. Second, a high capital share implies implausibly high rates of return on capital in the long run.[10] The results are largely unaffected by the choice of this parameter.

Given our choice of α and the computed capital series, we calculate TFP, as follows:

$$TFP_t = \frac{GDP_t}{K_t^\alpha L_t^{1-\alpha}} \tag{2.3}$$

In order to eliminate transient phenomena, we focus on long-run changes in TFP and GDP and, hence, concentrate on decades rather than year-to-year variations. Table 2.4 presents the results of this growth accounting exercise for our sample of 12 Latin American economies.

The decline in growth is to some extent the result of changes in factor accumulation. The evidence in Table 2.4 suggests there was a decline in capital accumulation in the last 20 years in all Latin American economies except Chile, but the magnitude of the effect is relatively small and, hence, cannot be the driving force for the differences in the growth performance of Latin American economies. On average, lower capital accumulation accounts for only 0.6 percentage points or roughly one-third of the drop in GDP growth. Nevertheless, the impact in some countries has been much larger: in Brazil and Venezuela it accounts for over 1.5 percentage points, while in Argentina and Mexico it accounts for around 1 percentage point. Yet, in these cases lower capital accumulation still represents only one-third of the total fall in GDP growth. On the other hand, the contribution of capital accumulation in more successful economies (such as Chile and the Dominican Republic) remained unchanged in the entire period, suggesting also a minor role for capital accumulation in determining the differences in long run growth.

An additional look at the role of capital accumulation is provided in Table 2.5. It can be seen that the decline in the contribution of capital to growth is, in general, not the result of lower investment rates in the private sector.[11] Only in Bolivia and Ecuador is there a 1 percentage point drop in private investment as share of GDP. Public investment, on the other hand, fell in seven of the 12 countries, in particular in Argentina.

This evidence, which suggests that there may be an important role for public investment as a source of growth, is consistent with the results of Calderón and Servén (2002) derived from standard growth regressions. Nevertheless, the mechanics of the contribution of public investment to growth may not be easy to disentangle: a lower public investment rate is not always associated with slow growth, while a higher one does not signal faster growth. In Chile, public investment declined by 2.5 percentage points in the last 20 years, but this was amply compensated by a substantial increase in private investment. On the other hand, in Colombia public investment expanded by

Table 2.4 *Growth accounting for Latin American economies*

		GDP	Average annual contribution to GDP growth (%)		
			Labor	Capital	TFP
Argentina	1960–2003	2.6	0.7	1.1	0.7
	1960–1980	4.2	0.8	1.6	1.8
	1981–2003	1.1	0.7	0.7	-0.3
Brazil	1960–2003	4.2	1.7	2.1	0.4
	1960–1980	7.2	2.1	3.1	2.0
	1981–2003	1.7	1.5	1.3	-1.1
Bolivia	1960–2003	3.3	1.5	1.1	0.7
	1960–1980	4.7	1.3	1.2	2.2
	1981–2003	2.0	1.8	0.9	-0.7
Chile	1960–2003	4.1	1.4	1.3	1.4
	1960–1980	3.5	1.1	1.1	1.3
	1981–2003	4.6	1.6	1.4	1.5
Colombia	1960–2003	4.1	1.6	1.4	1.1
	1960–1980	5.3	2.1	1.4	1.8
	1981–2003	3.0	1.2	1.4	0.4
Costa Rica	1960–2003	4.9	2.2	1.9	0.8
	1960–1980	6.2	2.4	2.4	1.4
	1981–2003	3.8	2.1	1.5	0.3

		GDP	Average annual contribution to GDP growth (%)		
			Labor	Capital	TFP
Dominican Republic	1970–2003	5.4	2.2	1.1	2.1
	1970–1980	7.3	2.3	1.7	3.4
	1981–2003	4.6	2.2	1.6	0.8
Ecuador	1965–2003	4.7	1.9	1.4	1.3
	1965–1980	8.4	1.8	1.7	4.8
	1981–2003	2.1	2.0	1.3	-1.2
Mexico	1960–2003	4.5	1.9	2.1	0.6
	1960–1980	6.8	2.0	2.7	2.1
	1981–2003	2.4	1.7	1.5	-0.8
Peru	1960–2003	3.1	1.7	1.4	0.0
	1960–1980	4.6	1.6	1.8	1.1
	1981–2003	1.8	1.9	1.1	-1.1
Uruguay	1960–2003	1.5	0.3	0.3	0.9
	1960–1980	2.2	0.8	0.3	1.1
	1981–2003	0.9	-0.1	0.3	0.8
Venezuela	1960–2003	2.7	2.2	1.3	-0.8
	1960–1980	5.1	2.7	2.1	0.3
	1981–2003	0.6	1.8	0.6	-1.8

Source: Author's elaboration based on the methodology in text and data from ECLAC (2004).

Table 2.5 Private and public investment in Latin America (as percentage of GDP)

		Private investment	Public investment	Total investment			Private investment	Public investment	Total investment
Argentina	1970–2000	14.8	5.2	20.0	Dominican Republic	1970–2000	15.4	6.6	21.9
	1970–1980	14.1	8.8	23.0		1970–1980	15.2	6.5	21.8
	1981–2000	15.2	3.2	18.4		1981–2000	15.4	6.6	22.0
Brazil	1970–2000	7.1	7.5	14.6	Ecuador	1970–2000	12.3	7.5	19.8
	1970–1980	7.9	8.9	16.7		1970–1980	13.0	8.3	21.3
	1981–2000	6.7	6.7	13.4		1981–2000	11.8	7.1	18.9
Bolivia	1970–2000	15.5	5.7	21.2	Mexico	1970–2000	13.8	6.0	19.9
	1970–1980	14.8	7.0	21.8		1970–1980	12.8	7.9	20.7
	1981–2000	15.9	5.1	21.0		1981–2000	14.4	5.0	19.4
Chile	1970–2000	12.5	6.1	18.6	Peru	1970–2000	15.6	5.3	20.9
	1970–1980	7.4	7.7	15.1		1970–1980	15.3	5.5	20.8
	1981–2000	15.3	5.2	20.6		1981–2000	15.8	5.2	21.0
Colombia	1970–2000	10.2	7.0	17.2	Uruguay	1970–2000	8.9	4.4	13.3
	1970–1980	10.3	5.8	16.1		1970–1980	8.6	4.6	13.2
	1981–2000	10.2	7.6	17.8		1981–2000	9.1	4.3	13.4
Costa Rica	1970–2000	15.0	6.0	21.0	Venezuela	1970–2000	na	na	na
	1970–1980	15.3	7.0	22.3		1970–1980	na	na	na
	1981–2000	14.8	5.5	20.3		1981–2000	9.1	8.9	18.0

Source: Authors' elaboration based on data from IFC (2002) and IMF (2004) 'International Financial Statistics' (various issues).

almost 2 percentage points, yet the rate of growth in per capita GDP declined from 5.3 per cent in the 1960–80 period to less than 3 per cent in the 1981–2003 period.

The contribution of labor to GDP growth has been quite stable in almost all countries and, as such, cannot be an important explanation for either the slower growth of the last two decades, nor for the different growth path of Latin American economies. On average, changes in labor account for just 0.3 per cent of the decline. Nevertheless, for some economies (notably Brazil and Colombia) the demographic transition induced a significant reduction in GDP growth. Uruguay is the only extreme case where the absolute reduction in employment implied a negative contribution of labor to economic growth.

Given that changes in the contribution of labor and capital do not seem to be an important source of changes in growth rates, one has to conclude that most of the decline in GDP growth rates should be linked to declining TFP. In fact, in every period and country TFP has been the main determinant of GDP growth.[12] In the 1960–80 period, TFP grew at roughly the same path of developed economies (1.5 to 2 per year) in most countries, with the only exceptions of Chile, Peru, and Uruguay, where productivity grew somewhat more slowly. Two economies, Ecuador and the Dominican Republic, exhibit very high TFP growth rates. In the 1981–2003 period, however, productivity growth disappeared in almost all economies. TFP growth was negative in seven of the 12 countries (Argentina, Bolivia, Brazil, Ecuador, Mexico, Peru and Venezuela) and close to zero in Colombia and Costa Rica. Only in Chile and the Dominican Republic has TFP growth been positive and significant, leading to rising per capita GDP.

Our results are consistent with those obtained a decade ago by Elías (1992). In a comparative study of the sources of growth for seven Latin American economies, he estimated an average rate of growth of TFP of 1.4 per cent and an average rate of growth of GDP of 5 per cent in the 1940–80 period.[13] At that time, less than 30 per cent of GDP growth in that period could be explained by TFP growth. In addition, his decade-average calculations of TFP growth by country from the 1940s to the 1980s show a pattern of declining TFP growth over time in that period in each of the seven countries.

The study by Hofman (2000) calculated TFP growth rates in the sub-periods 1950–73 and 1973–80, 1980–89 and 1989–94 for six Latin American economies (Argentina, Brazil, Chile, Colombia, Mexico and Venezuela). This study also shows decreasing average TFP growth rates for the six Latin American countries through these several sub-periods. On average, TFP growth was 2.5 per cent in 1950–73, 1.1 per cent in 1973–80, –0.9 per cent in 1980–89 to recover to 1.8 per cent in 1989–94.

The substantial impact of TFP on economic growth does not only occur in the very long run. Figure 2.4 shows that changes in TFP have a striking similarity with those of GDP per working-age person in the short run. Thus, it is safe to conclude that most of the evolution of GDP growth is the result of changes in the efficiency and rate of utilization in the use of capital and labor. From Figure 2.4 the dissimilar path of TFP changes between countries in the last four decades is also noticeable. In most of the economies, TFP and GDP per working-age person increased markedly between 1960 and the late 1970s. The only exceptions were Chile, the Dominican Republic, and Uruguay, where growth was only moderate. After 1980, there was remarkable recovery in TFP and GDP growth in Chile and the Dominican Republic, while in Uruguay growth came to an abrupt end in the late 1990s. On the contrary, in Bolivia, Ecuador, Peru and Venezuela TFP and GDP per working-age person plummeted: by 2000, TFP levels were as low as in the mid 1960s if not much lower. In this sense, the last four decades have been almost lost in these countries. Two countries deserve special attention for the contrasting experience before and after 1980: growth was vigorous and substantial in the 1960s and 1970s in both Mexico and Brazil. In contrast, in the last two decades both economies stagnated.

Are Latin American Countries Different from Other Economies?

The above growth accounting exercise suggests that, if one is to model long-term growth in Latin America, TFP ought to be a very important part of the analysis. This is also the case for other economies in the world, as suggested when computing TFP changes in our reference group in the 1960–2003 period. These countries are at different stages of development, located in very different areas of the world (and thus facing different business opportunities), and endowed with dissimilar amounts of factors and resources. Hence, they provide an adequate counterpoint to the experience of Latin American countries.

Figure 2.5 presents the evolution of per capita GDP and TFP computed using the same methodology we employed for the analysis of Latin American economies. It can be seen that TFP closely resembles the evolution of per capita GDP in the long run in all economies, independent of whether countries have grown at high rates (for example, South Korea) or quite slow (for example, the Philippines).

Table 2.6 presents the corresponding growth decomposition. It can be seen that in both East Asian and European economies, growth experiences have been quite different between countries, but in all of them long-run growth is largely determined by TFP. The so-called East Asian 'miracles' (represented here by South Korea and Thailand) show that where GDP increases substantially, factor productivity accounts for around 40 per cent. This also occurs in Ireland and Spain, where TFP largely determines economic growth even when one takes into account the significant contribution of employment to

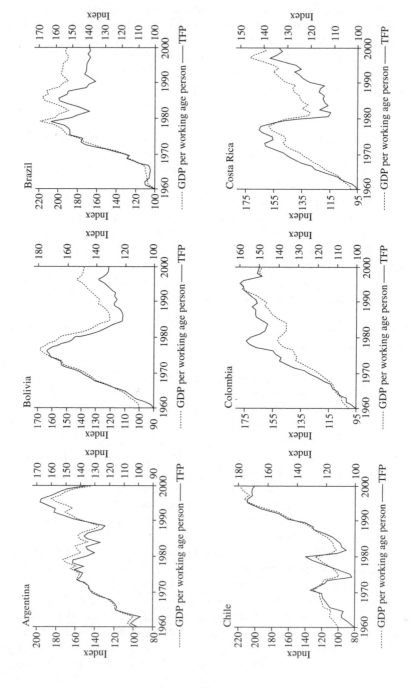

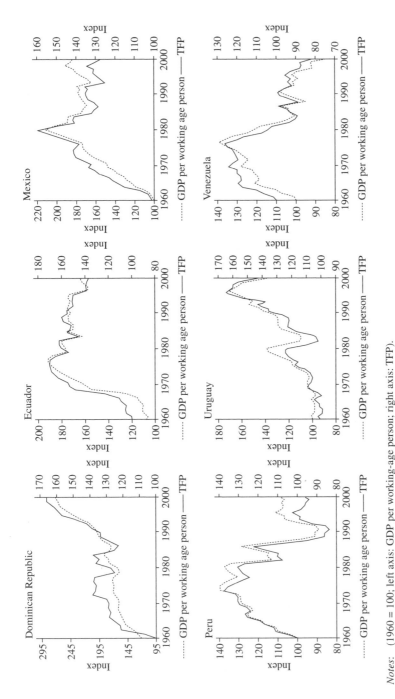

Notes: (1960 = 100; left axis: GDP per working-age person; right axis: TFP).

Source: Authors' elaboration.

Figure 2.4 Real GDP per working-age person and TFP: Latin American countries

31

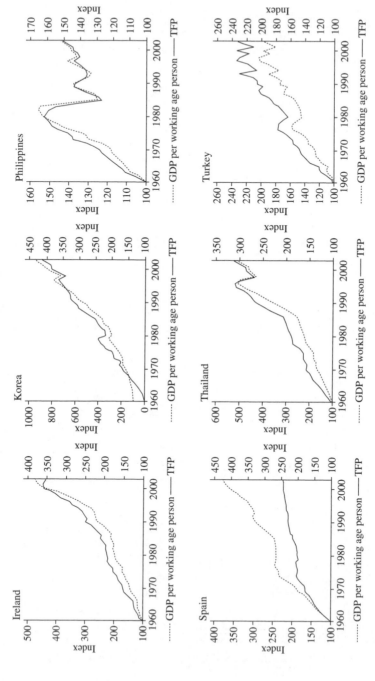

Source: Author's elaboration based on data from the World Bank and the Statistics Office in each country.

Figure 2.5 GDP per working-age person and TFP: reference group

Table 2.6   Growth accounting for reference group economies

		GDP growth (%)	Average annual contribution to GDP growth (%)		
			Labor	Capital	TFP
Korea	1960–2003	7.6	1.5	2.6	3.4
	1960–80	8.7	1.8	2.3	4.6
	1981–2003	6.7	1.3	2.9	2.4
Philippines	1960–2003	3.8	1.6	1.2	1.0
	1960–80	5.2	1.6	1.1	2.4
	1981–2003	2.7	1.6	1.3	−0.2
Thailand	1960–2003	6.7	1.6	2.4	2.8
	1960–80	7.5	1.9	2.3	3.3
	1981–2003	6.0	1.3	2.4	2.3
Ireland	1960–2003	4.8	0.5	1.4	3.0
	1960–80	4.3	−0.1	1.2	3.2
	1981–2003	5.2	1.0	1.5	2.7
Spain	1960–2003	4.0	0.5	1.3	2.1
	1960–80	5.5	0.3	1.5	3.6
	1981–2003	2.7	0.7	1.2	0.9
Turkey	1960–2003	4.4	0.9	1.5	2.1
	1960–80	4.8	1.1	1.2	2.5
	1981–2003	4.2	0.7	1.7	1.7

Source: Author's elaboration based on IMF (2004) data.

fueling growth. The remaining two reference countries are cases of sluggish economic growth and, to a large extent, closely resemble the Latin American experience. In Turkey and the Philippines, GDP growth was faster in the 1960–80 period than afterwards and, in both countries, economic growth was largely determined by changes in TFP. The experience of both successful and unsuccessful economies suggests that, in terms of economic growth, Latin American economies are not different from other countries.

Our results are in line with those from other studies. A recent IMF study of TFP growth in nine Asian economies (Iwata, Khan and Murao, 2003) shows a range of estimates of annual values of TFP growth rates from 3.4 per cent in South Korea to 1.7 per cent in the Philippines. Thailand has a TFP growth rate of 3.7 per cent.[14] In general, most of these Asian economies show a higher TFP growth rate than for the Latin American economies. In turn, the Philippines is 'closer' to Latin American values for TFP growth. For East Asian economies in general, TFP explains between 44 and 47 per cent of total output growth in the period 1960–95. This shows the importance of productivity growth, rather than capital accumulation, in driving economic growth, although this may not be the story for other Asian economies.

Economic Growth in Latin America Compared with Developed Economies

The more important comparison of the growth record of Latin America is against developed economies. Average productivity levels in developed economies can be considered as reflecting the economic 'frontier' that describes the most efficient transformation of factors and resources into goods and services. Less-developed economies, on the other hand, operate with lower productivity levels and, hence, locate in interior points within that frontier. Increases in productivity can be attained in two ways: (1) by allowing the economy to move towards the economic frontier, and (2) by the continuous displacement of this frontier. The latter is largely determined by technological progress and human knowledge. In Figure 2.6 there is a schematic representation of the mechanism.

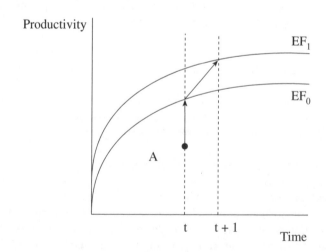

Source: Authors' elaboration.

Figure 2.6   Movements towards efficiency frontiers

At time t, an economy is located at point A. The line EF_0 represents the expected balanced growth path for a given technology and knowledge level. A movement from A towards a point in the EF_0 frontier is an improvement in productivity that can be obtained by relocating resources from less productive toward more efficient uses. The line EF_1 represents a new, more efficient balanced expected growth path. Moving from any point in EF_0 towards a point in the EF_1 curve is a net improvement in productivity.

We proxy the movements of the economic frontier in developed economies using TFP in the USA. This eliminates aggregation and comparability problems that would otherwise appear when dealing with the group of OECD countries. In the 1960–2003 period, TFP growth in the USA has been around 1.4 per cent per year and per capita GDP around 2 per cent. This is consistent with a balanced growth path. We thus de-trend GDP per working-age person and TFP by these two values.

The results are presented in Figure 2.7. A gloomy picture emerges. The evolution of GDP per-working age person and TFP for Latin America shows that the region is being left increasingly behind. Only two economies, Chile and the Dominican Republic, manage to keep track of the expansion in the economic frontier, while the rest of the economies present a continuous decline. While this suggests an especially bad record of growth in Latin America, another important implication is that it is relatively easy to increase per capita GDP and productivity if the necessary conditions for growth are implemented. Returning to Figure 2.6, productivity gains are probably easier to obtain when moving from an inefficient point within the efficient frontier than when following the displacement of such a frontier.

2.5 GROWTH EPISODES

Despite the negative picture of low growth that emerges from Latin American economies in the last four decades, an additional feature of the data holds out hope for renewed growth in the region. Over the years, several Latin American countries have undergone phases of sustained growth. Likewise, other economies have gone for periods of protracted slow growth. Studying these episodes from a comparative point of view may provide evidence with regard to the main patterns of sustained growth. This, in turn, can help to identify factors that can create an impulse and sustain economic growth.

In this chapter, we define an *episode of sustained growth* as one in which the rate of growth of per capita GDP is above 2 per cent every year for at least six consecutive years (to avoid pure spending booms, we couple this definition with a similar one for TFP at the 1.4 per cent benchmark). Note that this definition does not consider sustained growth as a period in which

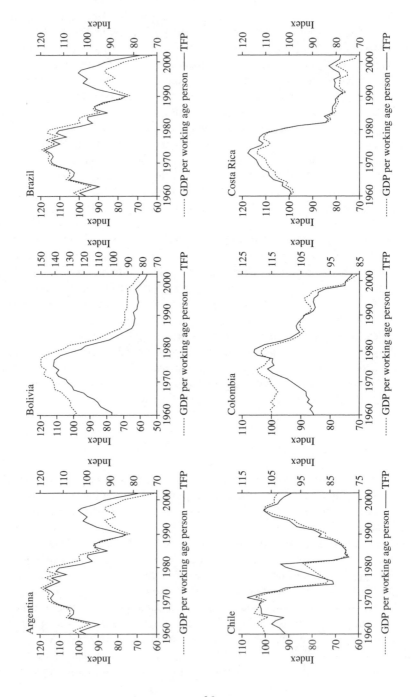

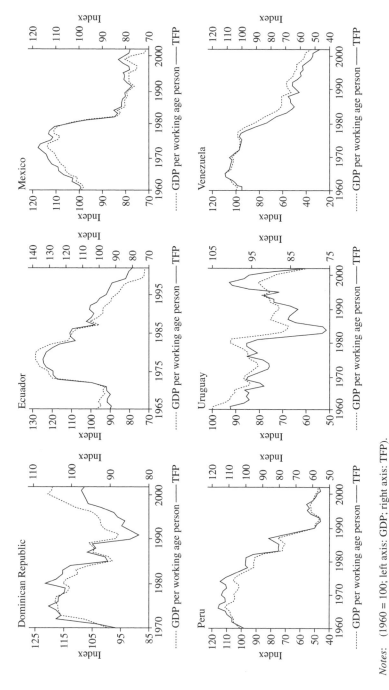

Notes: (1960 = 100; left axis: GDP; right axis: TFP).

Source: Author's elaboration.

Figure 2.7 Detrended real GDP per working-age person and TFP

Table 2.7   Growth episodes in Latin America and other countries

		Sustained growth per-capita GDP growth rates above 2 per cent per year for six continuous years or more			
		Length of the cycle (years)	Cumulative growth in per capita GDP growth (%)	Contribution of total factor productivity (%)	Contribution of capital and labor (%)
Bolivia	1965–73	9	34.8	36.7	–1.9
Brazil	1971–80	10	67.7	32.5	35.2
Chile	1986–97	11	91.1	55.0	46.5
Colombia	1968–74	7	24.9	20.0	4.9
Costa Rica	1965–74	10	41.9	23.0	18.9
Dominican Republic	1992–2000	9	51.1	29.0	22.1
Ecuador	1972–80	9	53.6	40.1	23.5
Mexico	1963–70	8	33.5	25.0	8.3
Korea	1963–71	9	67.7	42.1	25.6
	1982–91	10	56.5	35.9	26.6
Ireland	1994–2001	8	64.5	39.6	34.9
Spain	1961–74	14	112.4	81.9	40.5
Thailand	1986–96	11	124.5	54.7	69.8

Source: Authors' elaboration.

the average rate of growth of per capita GDP is 2 per cent. Sustained growth requires per capita GDP to grow at least 2 per cent per year. Using this definition we identify eight sustained growth episodes in Latin America in the past four decades (see Table 2.7). Likewise, we identify five episodes in our reference group, two of them in South Korea.

It can be seen that the growth cycles share some common characteristics. The average duration of the cycle in all economies (9.6 years) is much higher than the cutoff level of six years. In Latin America the duration is slightly less, reaching nine years. Thus, growth episodes come in decades. However, the growth decades are concentrated in the 1960s and 1970s. Only two economies benefited from growth decades after 1980: Chile and the Dominican Republic. All other Latin American economies experienced growth cycles ending either in the mid-1970s or by 1980. In the reference group of countries, Ireland and Thailand have had growth cycles recently while the Spanish boom was very long, covering the 1961–74 period. Interestingly, episodes of sustained growth take place in the 1960s (Mexico) and in the 1970s (Brazil) under import substitution regimes as well as in the 1990s after market-oriented regimes were implemented (the Dominican Republic and Chile) (see Solimano, 1996, 1999).

The intensity of these growth cycles differs notoriously among countries. Among Latin American economies, the Chilean cycle brought about the highest cumulative per capita GDP growth with an index of 91 in 11 years. On the other hand, the growth cycles of Bolivia, Costa Rica and Mexico were among the mildest. Likewise in the reference group, the growth episodes in Spain and Thailand induced higher cumulative growth than the one in Ireland.

A second distinctive feature shared by most of these growth cycles is that roughly 50 per cent of the cumulative growth in GDP is due to equal increases in TFP and factor accumulation (for example, Brazil, Chile, Costa Rica, Dominican Republic and all countries in the reference group except Spain). This type of growth cycle reflects a movement along the balanced growth path. On the contrary, the growth episodes in Bolivia and Colombia suggest that growth was largely due to TFP, which would be consistent with a movement from an interior point towards the efficient frontier more than with a movement of such a frontier.

2.6 ON THE DETERMINANTS OF TFP GROWTH IN LATIN AMERICA

The determinants of TFP are quite difficult to grasp. As discussed in Prescott (1997), and also as shown in this chapter, differences in physical and intangible capital cannot account for the large international income differences that characterize the world economy. As shown in the sections above, private saving and investment rates do not seem to be strongly correlated with such differences[15] and differences in TFP and GDP growth across countries seem to be the rule rather than the exception. We lack a theory that can account for differences in TFP arising for reasons other than growth in the stock of technical knowledge. Nevertheless from an empirical point of view we can explore the role of variables that, according to other researchers, may have been important in determining the slow growth of Latin American economies.

We use our panel of the 12 Latin American countries in the 1960–2003 period and compute the sample correlation (and the standard deviations) of the first difference of the log of TFP in each country as calculated by equation (2.2) and its potential determinants. It is important to use the rate of growth of TFP since it is a non-stationary variable; using its actual value might lead to a spurious correlation. Table 2.8 provides the results.

We first correlate TFP growth with transient phenomena, such as the business cycle, where we expect a significant correlation, as suggested by Figure

Table 2.8   Correlation of TFP growth and other variables in Latin
American countries

	1960–2002	1960–80	1981–2002
Business cycles (Growth in consumption of electricity per capita)	0.152** (0.032)	0.198** (0.043)	0.116** (0.044)
Quality of the labor force (Growth in secondary education achievement)	0.157** (0.079)	0.314** (0.087)	–0.188 (0.150)
International trade shocks (Changes in terms of trade)	0.032 (0.014)	0.031 (0.017)	0.033 (0.022)
International financial flows (Changes in external debt as share of labor productivity)	0.006 (0.017)	0.035 (0.021)	–0.045 (0.029)
Economic instability I (Monthly inflation rate)	–0.0925** (0.026)	0.148* (0.075)	–0.122** (0.029)
Economic instability II (Standard deviation of the monthly inflation rate)	0.006 (0.027)	0.210** (0.097)	–0.008 (0.030)
Economic instability III (Standard deviation of the real exchange rate)	–0.029 (0.017)	0.014 (0.030)	–0.047** (0.022)

Note: * and ** are statistically significant at 90% and 95%, respectively.

Source: Author's elaboration using data from ECLAC (2004).

2.4. We use as an instrumental variable of the business cycle the consumption of electricity per capita: given that this is a non-storable good, it is less likely to suffer from spurious correlation. Table 2.8 confirms the correlation in the entire sample and for the two sub-periods. However, the size of correlations also suggests that transient phenomena cannot account for a significant fraction of the movements in TFP.

Second, we consider the role of changes in the quality of labor. Since the latter are unobservable, they are included in our measure of TFP. We proxy such changes using formal education measures: primary education will unlikely be correlated to TFP because it varies little in the sample of Latin

American economies in the 1960–2003 period. Hence we use secondary education achievement and find a significant correlation for the first half of the sample but no correlation after 1980. One possible explanation for this result is that most countries have achieved already a similar level of achievement in secondary education so that differences among them cannot account for the differences in TFP growth.

A small digression at this point seems to be necessary. We focus on zero correlations, rather than significant ones, to derive our conclusions because significant correlations can be spurious. On the contrary, lack of correlation cannot be a spurious result.

Third, we turn to foreign shocks as a major source of long-run differences in TFP growth and find no evidence of a significant impact of either the terms of trade shocks or of capital flows.[16] This does not mean that these variables do not play a role, only that they are not correlated with TFP growth in medium- to long-run horizons. Most certainly, these variables have short-lived effects on TFP, but they cannot account for the long-run differences observed among different economies.

Fourth, given that external fluctuations do not seem to play a significant role, we turn to domestic sources of fluctuations. We use an indicator of fiscal imbalances (the inflation rate) and two indicators of macroeconomic instability (the intra annual standard deviation of inflation and the real exchange rate). Inflation is a measure of the inability of the government to obtain direct financing for its expenditures. The results in Table 2.8 are somewhat surprising. In the 1981–2002 period we obtain the expected negative relationship between TFP and the inflation rate. For the 1960–80 period we obtain a positive sign. An interpretation of this result is that in this period nominal interest rates were fixed at rather low levels in most countries: hence, higher inflation rates led to negative real interest rates that might have induced a lower cost of financing capital.

The two measures of macroeconomic instability also provide some interesting results. In the 1981–2002 there is no evidence of a negative relationship between TFP growth and the volatility of inflation, despite the fact that a number of high-inflation and hyper-inflationary processes occurred in the region. In the 1960–2003 period, there is no evidence of a negative relationship between TFP growth and the volatility of the real exchange rate. This could reflect the fact that in that period Latin American economies were less open to foreign competition and the importance of the real exchange rate was smaller in resource allocation. After reforms in the 1980s and 1990s, the expected negative correlation appears and the magnitude of the coefficient suggests that this could be an important determinant of TFP and GDP growth.

2.7   CONCLUSIONS AND FINAL REMARKS

Economic growth in Latin America in the last 40 years has been modest and unstable. The rate of growth of GDP per capita in this period has been 1.6 per cent (for the main 12 economies), a meager performance by international standards.

Economic growth decelerated and become more volatile in the 1980–2003 period compared to the two previous decades. After the poor performance of the 1980s there was a recovery in growth in the early to mid-1990s in the region but that proved to be transient. In the half decade since the Asian and Russian crises of the late 1990s there has been another growth slowdown in the region.

Certainly the Latin American region has had serious problems in adjusting to the more competitive but also more volatile global economy of the last two decades. The internal policy reforms of the 1990s did not lead to more rapid growth in a sustained way for the region as a whole. Growth performance after 1980 became more sluggish in all countries, in particular in the fast growers of the 1960s and 1970s, Brazil and Mexico. The stories of persistent decline in per capita growth in 1980–2003 are Argentina, Bolivia, Peru and Venezuela. This performance has delayed economic progress and poverty reduction. Chile and the Dominican Republic have been the only two economies that managed to grow at fast rates in the post-reform period, although, currently, both economies are growing at less than their average 1990s' rates.

The 1981–2003 period is characterized not only by lower average growth but also by a dramatic increase in the frequency of growth crises (years of negative growth) with respect to preceding decades. The countries with the highest frequency of growth crises are Venezuela (13 years in 22) and Argentina (11 years in 22). Internal instability and external factors married to drive these countries to repeated growth crises with very negative welfare consequences for their citizens.

The sources-of-growth analysis conducted in the chapter shows that deceleration in capital formation explains around one-third of the deceleration in GDP growth since 1980 on average in Latin America. This percentage is higher, though, for Mexico, Brazil and Venezuela. However, the acceleration in growth in the Dominican Republic and Chile in the 1990s is explained by accelerations in TFP growth and by faster capital accumulation.

The data shows that public investment has been more volatile than private investment in the 1980–2003 period. This may have been the consequence of recurrent fiscal crises that were 'adjusted' by repeated cuts in public investment that, save for the case of Chile, were not followed by a compensating increase in private investment rates.

Episodes of 'sustained growth' and 'sustained decline' identified in this chapter highlight the variety of impulses to sustained growth as well as of factors that halt growth and send the economies into a downward spiral of negative growth. We identified eight cases of GDP growth per capita above 2 per cent per year for at least six consecutive years (on average these episodes lasted nine years). Interestingly, these growth episodes were accompanied by sustained increases in TFP. These episodes occurred both in the 1960s and 1970s (for example in Brazil and Mexico) under import substitution, but also in the 1990s under more market-oriented policy regimes (in Chile and the Dominican Republic). In turn, we also computed four cases of 'sustained decline' in which GDP per capita grew at rates below 1 per cent (often GDP growth was negative) for five consecutive years. These episodes of protracted growth collapse have reduced living standards in substantial ways in the affected countries.

In the 1980–2003 period, TFP grew at negative rates in seven out of 12 economies. TFP growth was close to zero in Colombia and Costa Rica and positive in the two most dynamic economies of that period: the Dominican Republic and Chile.

Historically, factor productivity has been following a decreasing trend in Latin America, particularly since the 1960s (although TFP growth is quite pro-cyclical: it goes up in periods of rapid growth and declines in slowdowns and recessions). Still across cycles, various empirical studies show a downward trend in TFP growth in several economies of the region. This is consistent with the modest rates of increases in GDP per capita registered in Latin America in the last 40 years.

International comparisons of TFP growth rates indicate much higher TFP growth in dynamic Asian economies such as South Korea, Hong Kong, Singapore and Thailand as well as in Ireland and Spain, part of our reference group. These economies, in turn, have had a more steady growth process than Latin America and have experienced a much lower frequency of growth crises than the Latin American countries. In our reference group, only Turkey and the Philippines have frequencies of growth crises comparable to the Latin American averages in the 1980–2003 period.

NOTES

* Comments by F. Rosende, A. Hofman and C. Aravena are gratefully acknowledged. We thank C. de Camino, A. Hofman, and C. Aravena for the data and M. Larraín for able research assistantship. All remaining errors are ours.

1. Using the median for comparison, instead of the average, does not change the results.

2. Setting the break at 1980 is to some extent arbitrary but practical for comparison. In some countries, GDP decline started slightly before 1980 (as early as 1975). For no country did the break occur after 1981.

3. The 1981–2003 period is also quite heterogeneous: average per capita GDP grew at 1.1 per cent in the 1990s while it was negative in the 1981–90 period (–0.3 per cent).
4. See ECLAC (2002) for an analysis of the Latin American economy in a longer perspective.
5. See Solimano (1999), Loayza and Soto (2002), Schmidt-Hebbel (1999) for analyses of the growth process in Chile in the 1990s and before.
6. See Pritchett (2000) and Comin and Gertler (2003) on volatility of growth and decomposition of growth series. Earlier literature dealt with overlapping of cycles of different frequency and duration. Schumpeter (1939) for example identified at least three cycles: a short-term cycle of no more than four years (Kitchen cycle), a medium-run cycle of over 10 years (Juglar cycle) and long-run cycle of approximately 50 or 70 years (Kondratieff cycle).
7. The actual trend in per capita GDP in the USA and other developing economies in the 1960–2003 period is sometimes depicted as comprising two regimes: one for the 1960–80 period of around 2.3 per cent per year and one for the remaining period of 1.7 per cent per year. For the purposes of our study, this break is inconsequential and so we, use a 2 per cent benchmark.
8. Our evidence matches that of Kydland and Zarazaga (2002) for Argentina and Casacuberta et al. (2004) for Uruguay.
9. For these counties, we assume the capital–output ratio to be 3 in 1950. This assumption is inconsequential for the qualitative results of the analysis.
10. With $\alpha = 0.65$ as suggested by national accounts and a capital–GDP ratio of 2.8 (the mean for all Latin American economies in the 1960–2003 period), the equilibrium real interest rate should be above 23 per cent per year.
11. Private investment figures are taken from IFC (2002) and include investment by decentralized, public firms.
12. This need not be the case. From equation (2.1) GDP growth per working-age person can be expressed as $\hat{GDP}_t = \hat{N}_t = \hat{A}_t + \alpha\hat{K}_t + (1-\alpha)\hat{L}_t - \hat{N}_t$, where N_t is working-age population (that is, between 15 and 65 years of age). Hence GDP per working-age person grows as a result of increases in productivity, capital utilization, capital accumulation, more efficient workers and more hours worked, and it decreases with higher working-age population growth.
13. Countries are Argentina, Brazil, Chile, Colombia, Mexico, Peru and Venezuela.
14. Countries are Hong Kong, Indonesia, South Korea, Malaysia, the Philippines, Singapore, Taiwan, Thailand and China for the period 1960–95 (Iwata et al., 2003).
15. In a world of integrated capital markets the correlation between savings and investment is weaker as individuals can allocate savings beyond national boundaries. Domestic investment is not the only opportunity to allocate national savings in an open economy.
16. Since the data of capital flows is of low quality (scarce and inconsistently defined among countries), we use as a proxy the change in the end of period stock of external debt, including both public and private foreign liabilities. To avoid scale problems we de-trend the values by average labor productivity. Similar results obtain if de-trended by GDP.

REFERENCES

Calderón, C. and L. Servén (2002), 'The output cost of Latin America's infrastructure gap', Central Bank of Chile, working papers 186.

Casacuberta, C., N. Gandelman and R. Soto (2004), 'Long run growth and productivity changes in Uruguay: evidence from aggregate and plant level data', mimeo, Instituto de Economía, Pontificia Universidad Católica de Chile.

Comin, D. and P. Gertler (2003), 'Medium term business cycles,' *National Bureau of Economic Research working papers series* 10003, September.

Economic Commission for Latin America and the Caribbean (ECLAC) (2004), *Anuario Estadístico de America Latina y el Caribe*, Santiago, Chile: ECLAC.

Elías, V. (1992), *Sources of Growth. A Study of Seven Latin American Economies*, San Francisco: ICS Press.

Fatás, A. (2002), 'The effects of business cycles on growth' in Norman Loayza and Raimundo Soto (eds), *Economic Growth: Sources, Trends, and Cycles*, Santiago: Banco Central de Chile.

Gollin, D (2002), 'Getting income shares right', *Journal of Political Economy*, **110** (2), 458–74, April.

Hofman, A. (ed.) (2000), *The Economic Development of Latin America in the Twentieth Century*, Cheltenham, UK and Northampton, MA, USA: Edward Elgar.

Hofman, A. (2003), database of *The Economic Development of Latin America in the Twentieth Century*, Cheltenham, UK and Northampton, MA, USA: Edward Elgar.

International Finance Corporation (IFC) (2002), 'Trends in private investment in developing countries' statistics for 1970–2000 and the impact on private investment of corruption and the quality of public investment', *IFC discussion papers number 44*, Washington, DC: World Bank.

International Monetary Fund (IMF) (2004), *International Financial Statistics*, Washington, DC: IMF.

Iwata, S., M. Khan and H. Murao (2003), 'Sources of economic growth in East Asia: a non parametric approach', *IMF staff papers* **50** (2), 157–77.

Kehoe, T. and E. Prescott (2002), 'Great depressions of the twentieth century', *Review of Economic Dynamics*, **5** (1), 1–19.

Kydland, F. and C. Zarazaga (2002), 'Argentina's lost decade', *Review of Economic Dynamics*, **5** (1), 166–205.

Loayza, N. and R. Soto (eds) (2002), *Economic Growth: Sources, Trends, and Cycles*, Central Bank of Chile, Santiago, Chile.

Maddison, A. (2003), *The World Economy: Historical Statistical*, OECD Development Centre Studies.

Prescott, E. (1997), 'Needed: a theory of total factor productivity', Federal Reserve Bank of Minneapolis staff report number 242.

Pritchett, L. (2000), 'Understanding patterns of economic growth: searching for hills among plateaus, mountains and plains', *World Bank Economic Review*, **14** (2), May.

Schmidt-Hebbel, K. (1999), 'Chile's takeoff: facts, challenges, lessons', in Danny Leipziger and Guillermo Perry (eds), *Chile: Recent Policy Lessons and Emerging Challenges*, WBI development studies, Washington, DC: World Bank.

Schumpeter, J. (1939), *Business Cycles. A Theoretical, Historical, and Statistical Analysis of the Capitalist Process*, vol I, New York and London: McGraw-Hill.

Solimano, A. (ed.) (1996), *Roadmaps to Prosperity. Essays on Growth and Development*, Ann Arbor, MI: University of Michigan Press.

Solimano, A. (1999), 'The Chilean economy in the 1990s: on a "golden age" and beyond', in Lance Taylor (ed.), *After Neoliberalism. What Next for Latin America?*, Ann Arbor, MI: University of Michigan Press, 113–26.

Solow, R. (1956), 'Technical change and the aggregate production function', *Review of Economics and Statistics* **39**, 312–20, August.

World Bank (2003), *The Little Data Book*, Washington, DC: World Bank.

3. Economic growth in the southern countries*

Juan S. Blyde and Eduardo Fernández-Arias

3.1 INTRODUCTION

This chapter examines the growth experiences of Argentina, Brazil, Chile, Paraguay and Uruguay (in the rest of the chapter referred as 'southern countries'). The analysis sheds light on the strengths and weaknesses of long-run growth of these countries by identifying similarities and differences with other countries and assesses their economic performance on that comparative basis.

During the past four decades, the southern countries, like many other countries in Latin America, went through several episodes of economic crisis, political instability, external shocks and social unrest. In the same period, they also experienced episodes of economic stabilization, political reorganization and structural reforms. A cursory look at some basic development indicators suggests a positive net result (see Table 3.1). Generally speaking, income per capita increased as well as health and education indicators, while the underlying economic structure turned in a more integrated way to global trade and there were improvements in institutional quality and macroeconomic management (as measured by a composite index of institutions and inflation levels, respectively). However, how satisfactory are these achievements?

In order to analyze how satisfactory the development process in the southern countries has been over the past 40 years it is important to make relevant comparisons with other countries. To tackle this issue, we focus on the per capita economic growth rate and its contributing factors, comparing the experience in southern countries with that of benchmark countries, namely a country typical of the rest of Latin America (LAC), of the rest of the world outside Latin America (ROW) and of its subset of developed countries (DEV).

We found that, in the period 1960–99, southern countries experienced faster growth than the typical LAC country. However the favorable comparisons end here. In fact, their growth was slower than that of the typical ROW country, and in particular of the typical DEV country, thus producing a

Table 3.1 *Basic indicators (averages over decades)*

	Real GDP per capita in 1985 international dollars				Real GDP growth (%)				Real GDP per capita growth				Life expectancy at birth (total years)			
	1960s	1970s	1980s	1990s	1960s	1970s	1980s	1990s	1960s	1970s	1980s	1990s	1960s	1970s	1980s	1990s
Argentina	4831	5952	5617	5864	4.0	3.1	-0.9	4.3	2.5	1.4	-2.3	3.0	66	68	70	72
Brazil	1946	3335	4091	4204	5.5	8.8	2.6	1.8	2.6	6.3	0.6	0.4	56	60	64	66
Chile	3240	3461	3705	5541	4.7	2.3	3.6	6.0	2.4	0.7	1.9	4.3	59	65	71	75
Paraguay	1273	1670	2183	2200	4.3	6.9	3.5	3.6	1.8	4.0	0.4	0.8	65	66	67	69
Uruguay	3831	4281	4514	5435	0.9	2.5	0.6	3.2	-0.1	2.2	0.0	2.5	68	69	71	73
Latin America	2125	2706	2777	2835	5.2	4.9	1.3	3.1	2.4	2.4	-0.8	1.1	56	61	65	68
Developed	6958	9794	11948	14250	5.1	3.6	2.6	2.3	4.0	2.9	2.1	1.7	71	73	75	77
Rest of the World	2437	3426	4147	4791	5.7	5.0	3.2	3.2	3.7	3.2	1.5	1.6	58	61	65	67

	Years of education in population of age 15 and over				Trade volume (% of GDP)				Inflation (%)				1st principal component of ICRG variables			
	1960s	1970s	1980s	1990s	1960s	1970s	1980s	1990s	1960s	1970s	1980s	1990s	1960s	1970s	1980s	1990s
Argentina	5.5	6.4	7.3	8.5	13	13	15	17	22	133	566	253	–	–	-1.1	0.6
Brazil	3.0	3.1	3.5	4.4	13	17	18	18	49	34	321	824	–	–	0.5	1.1
Chile	5.2	5.8	6.7	7.2	28	38	52	59	27	175	21	12	–	–	0.3	1.0
Paraguay	3.7	4.4	5.3	6.1	30	34	48	84	4	11	20	16	–	–	-1.7	0.0
Uruguay	5.3	6.0	6.7	7.3	28	34	42	43	51	59	58	49	–	–	-0.6	0.2
Latin America	3.1	3.8	4.7	5.4	37	44	48	57	11	30	240	164	–	–	-1.3	-0.2
Developed	7.1	7.8	8.7	9.4	47	55	61	64	4	10	10	7	–	–	3.0	3.4
Rest of the World	3.3	4.3	5.3	6.3	55	67	72	78	4	11	14	10	–	–	1.0	1.6

Note: ICRG variables: rule of law, corruption, bureaucratic quality, risk of expropiation and risk of repudiation of contracts.

Sources: Penn World Tables, World Development Indicators (WB), International Country Risk Guide (ICRG).

widening of the income per capita gap between southern countries and developed countries. The key to these differences is productivity, not factor accumulation. Productivity growth was the driver that contributed the most to the better performance of the southern countries relative to the rest of Latin America, but, paradoxically, it was also productivity growth that accounts for their slower growth relative to countries outside Latin America. Concerning productivity growth, one-eyed southern countries are kings in the land of blind Latin America. Finally, we provide some econometric evidence suggesting that the better (worse) institutional quality of the southern countries relative to LAC (ROW) has been an important factor behind these differences in productivity growth.

The rest of the chapter is organized as follows. Section 3.2 describes the economic performance of the southern countries during the last four decades and compares these performances with the experience of the benchmark countries and Section 3.3 conducts accounting exercises in order to examine the contributions of various factors to the differences in performance observed in Section 3.2. Section 3.4 develops an econometric model to explore the role of policy and institutional variables as drivers of these contributions. Finally, Section 3.5 concludes.

3.2   PERFORMANCE

In order to compare the southern countries with benchmark countries we use a sample of 68 countries,[1] of which 15 are from LAC and 53 from ROW (20 of them belong to DEV). In constructing the benchmarks, we use simple (unweighted) averages across countries in the control group to account for the growth experience of the typical country in it. A detailed list of the country groupings is shown in Appendix 3.A. Our summary measure of economic performance is the growth rate of real (PPP-adjusted) GDP per capita. The data is taken from the Penn World Table 5.6 and supplemented by other sources described in Appendix 3.A.

Growth rates of GDP per capita for the southern countries during the last four decades shown in Figure 3.1 reveal a number of features. First, all the southern countries experienced progress overall during the period and, with the exception of Argentina during the 1980s, none of them exhibited significant regress in any of the four decades. Second, the patterns of performance over time were similar across countries: medium to strong economic growth during the 1960s and 1970s, deceleration during the 1980s, and recovery during the 1990s. However, one remarkable difference is that while Argentina, Chile and Uruguay experienced their best growth performance in the 1990s, Brazil and Paraguay saw their best performance in the 1970s. In other

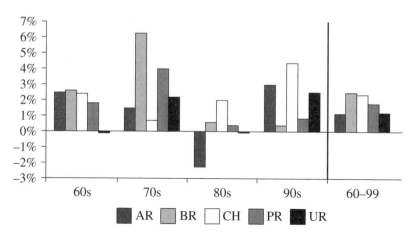

Source: Authors' calculations.

Figure 3.1   GDP per capita growth

words, Argentina, Chile and Uruguay have done better over time while Brazil and Paraguay have done worse.[2]

The ample swings in per capita growth rates across decades are indications that growth performance was unstable in the southern countries. How does it compare to the well known low persistence of country growth performance that has been established by Easterly et al. (1993) as a general feature in the world over a similar period (and throughout history)? Using our sample, we find that the experience of southern countries is significantly more unstable. For example, the correlation coefficient of growth per worker in southern countries between the first two decades (1960–79) and the last two (1980–99) is –0.7; in other words, for the countries in this group, higher-than-average growth in one period would predict lower-than-average growth in the other period. This compares to a solid positive correlation of 0.55 for the rest of Latin America and a respectable correlation of 0.45 for our full sample of 73 countries. In the next section we analyze the role of the different sources of growth in accounting for this extraordinary instability in southern countries.[3]

Southern countries compare favorably with the rest of Latin America in terms of trends in per capita growth performance (as measured by decade averages); see Figure 3.2. Southern countries performed significantly better than the typical country in the rest of Latin America during the 1980s and 1990s (with the exception of Argentina during the 1980s) and did not do significantly worse during the 1960s and 1970s (with the exception of Uruguay during the 1960s). Accordingly, relative to LAC, all of the southern countries ended up in a better position by the late 1990s than where they

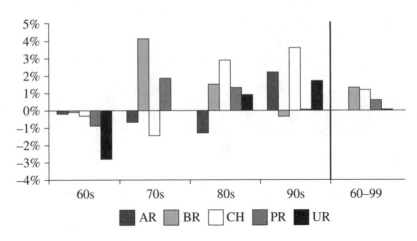

Source: Authors' calculations.

Figure 3.2   Difference in GDP per capita growth with respect to rest of LAC

Table 3.2   Income per capita with respect to rest of LAC

	1960–62	1997–99
Argentina	2.58	2.59
Brazil	1.05	1.75
Chile	1.68	2.62
Paraguay	0.68	0.87
Uruguay	2.21	2.37

Note: Based on real GDP per capita in 1985 international dollars purchasing power parity (PPP).

Source: Authors' calculations

started at the beginning of the 1960s (see Table 3.2). (Nevertheless, as of today this is no longer true for Argentina and Uruguay due to the recessions they experienced in the early 2000s despite the strong growth recovery currently taking place.)

Growth performance relative to countries outside the Latin American region, however, is very different. Compared to ROW (Figure 3.3), most of the relative growth rates are negative. The exceptions essentially coincide with the very best decades of each one of the southern countries identified above:

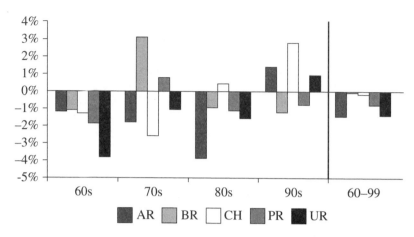

Source: Authors' calculations.

Figure 3.3   *Difference in GDP per capita growth with respect to ROW*

the 1970s for Brazil and Paraguay, and the 1990s for Argentina, Chile and
Uruguay. Overall, when we consider the entire 1960–99 period, each and
every one of the southern countries saw its income per capita decline with
respect to ROW, including Brazil and Chile despite their stellar performances
in the 1970s and 1990s, respectively. In particular, the substantial income per
capita gap of southern countries with respect to the USA and to the typical
developed country (shown in Table 3.3) widened further in all of them during
the past 40 years. It is worth noting that this trend has also continued during
the 2000s for all the countries in this group. The southern countries have
become relatively poorer by international standards.

Table 3.3   *Income per capita with respect to DEV*

	1960–62	1997–99
Argentina	0.76	0.43
Brazil	0.31	0.29
Chile	0.49	0.43
Paraguay	0.20	0.14
Uruguay	0.65	0.39

Note: Based on real GDP per capita in 1985 international dollars (PPP).

Source: Authors' calculations.

What were the main factors accounting for the better performance of the southern countries relative to Latin America and their worse performance relative to the rest of the world? Do southern countries differ in this respect or they all tell the same story? In fact, despite their similarities in comparative performance relative to benchmarks over the entire period there are remarkable differences in their growth patterns over time which may reveal important underlying differences, especially in the cases of Brazil and Chile. While Brazil exhibited spectacular growth rates during the 1960s and 1970s and saw these rates plummet during the 1980s and 1990s, Chile went from low rates during the 1960s and 1970s to medium and very high rates during the 1980s and 1990s respectively. In the next section we perform growth accounting exercises to help answer these questions.

3.3   ACCOUNTING FOR PERFORMANCE

In this section we perform growth accounting exercises based on a Cobb–Douglas production function. Let Y represent domestic output, K physical capital, L labor force, h the average quality of the labor force (scaled in such a way that hL measures human capital in units of unskilled labor), and A total factor productivity or TFP (that is the combined productivity of physical and human capital):[4]

$$Y = K^{\alpha} \cdot (h \cdot L)^{1-\alpha} \cdot A. \qquad (3.1)$$

The production function can be written in terms of number of workers as follows:

$$\frac{Y}{L} = \left(\frac{K}{L}\right)^{\alpha} \cdot h^{1-\alpha} \cdot A. \qquad (3.2)$$

In order to account for the growth rate in per capita terms, we can express (3.2) in terms of the entire population, rather than labor force. Let P be total population. We can use the following relationship:

$$\frac{Y}{P} = \frac{L}{P} \cdot \frac{Y}{L} \qquad (3.3)$$

to express (3.2) in income per capita terms:

$$\frac{Y}{P} = \frac{L}{P} \cdot \left(\frac{K}{L}\right)^{\alpha} \cdot h^{1-\alpha} \cdot A. \qquad (3.4)$$

In terms of growth rates this is expressed as follows:

$$\left(\frac{\hat{Y}}{P}\right)=\left(\frac{\hat{L}}{P}\right)+\alpha\cdot\left(\frac{\hat{K}}{L}\right)+(1-\alpha)\cdot\hat{h}+\hat{A}. \qquad (3.5)$$

The output and population data are taken from the Penn World Table 5.6. The capital stock series are taken from Easterly and Levine (2001) which in turn the authors updated from the Penn World Table 5.6. The labor input is measured by the labor force. This data is taken from the World Development Indicators of the World Bank. (Alternatively, factor inputs could be measured by the extent to which they are actually utilized in production, that is labor input could be measured by employment, excluding the unemployed, and capital input could be measured according to its actual utilization rate. Appendix 3.B describes how this alternative choice of measurement would amount to a more narrow definition of productivity and shows that the use of employment as labor input would not qualitatively change the interpretation of our findings.)

We follow Hall and Jones (1999) and consider h to be relative efficiency of a unit of labor with E years of schooling. Specifically, the function takes the form:

$$h = e^{\phi'(E)} \qquad (3.6)$$

where the derivative $\phi'(E)$ is the return to schooling estimated in a Mincerian wage regression. We take Hall and Jones's approach and assume the following rates of return for all the countries: 13.4 per cent for the first four years, 10.1 per cent for the next four years, and 6.8 per cent for education beyond the eighth year. The average quality of the labor force h results from applying (3.6) to the average years of schooling of the labor force. Finally, we consider a capital share α of one-third. Sensitivity analysis, however, showed no qualitative differences in the comparative results when we use capital shares of 0.4 or 0.5.

The contributions of the various components in (3.5) to account for the overall effects on income per capita Y/P help identify the proximate drivers of growth. The first component, L/P, measures the labor participation rate, that is the labor force as a proportion of total population.[5] The second component refers to capital intensity K/L and measures the effect of physical capital accumulation. The third component refers to labor skills h and measures the effect of human capital accumulation. The combined effect of these three components can be interpreted as the effect of factor accumulation, respectively of labor force size, physical capital intensity, and skill level of the labor force. Finally, the last component A is obtained as a residual once the effect of the rest of the observable variables on to income per capita *Y/P*, that is the effect of factor accumulation, is accounted for. This last component thus measures the effect of total factor productivity or TFP.

TFP turns out to be key to explain some of the observed trends in the evolution of income per capita, so it is important to be precise about how to interpret our estimations of it. Evidently, our measure of TFP in part reflects available technology. However, this is not the interesting aspect of the interpretation of this measure because our main findings are based on gaps resulting from comparisons across countries, which in principle could benefit equally from technological progress thus making these gaps disappear. Apart from technology, our measure of TFP also incorporates the degree to which available factors of production, both physical and human capital, are utilized. This is so because we chose to account for all available capital, that is including unutilized physical capital and unemployed labor, so that any waste in these resources available to market forces due to partial utilization is reflected in a lower TFP. The use of this more encompassing measure of TFP is very important to explain cyclical variations driven by factor utilization rates, but once again is unimportant in the long run (see Appendix 3.B). In the long run our preferred interpretation of TFP to explain gaps between countries, especially changes in these gaps, is that of distortions in the workings of the economy that drives aggregate efficiency below the technological frontier even if each firm is technologically efficient at the micro level (for an elaboration on this interpretation see Parente and Prescott, 2002).

In all the southern countries TFP explains a large portion of the annual variability of per capita GDP. Table 3.4 reports the variance decomposition

Table 3.4   Variance decomposition over time

	Percentage contribution of:		
1960–99	TFP growth	Factors growth	Covariance [g(TFP), g(f)]
ROW	93.28	14.34	−7.62
DEV	88.63	11.89	−0.52
Argentina	98.17	1.92	−0.10
Brazil	98.17	3.60	−1.77
Chile	89.78	4.26	5.96
Paraguay	87.32	7.82	4.86
Uruguay	112.37	6.21	−18.58

Source: Authors' calculations.

over time for each of the countries. The measure indicates what parts of the annual variation in the rate of economic growth are accounted for by variations in TFP growth and variations in everything else, referred to as factor growth.[6] For all the countries, TFP growth accounts for most of the variability in the growth of per capita output. In the case of Uruguay, the contribution of TFP actually exceeds 100 per cent which implies that TFP was more volatile than output during this period. These results are in line with previous findings for other regions in that factor growth is much more stable than productivity and output growth (see Table 3.4 and also Easterly and Levine, 2001).

The instability of TFP growth is also high over lower frequencies. For example, the correlation coefficient of TFP growth rates between the first two decades (1960–79) and the last two (1980–99) is actually negative (–0.50). This compares to a solid 0.57 for the rest of Latin America. This remarkable feature of southern countries matches the negative persistence of their overall growth performance discussed in the previous section but is not the only explanation: the correlation coefficient of human capital accumulation is similarly negative, again in contrast to benchmarks. This is in part a reflection of the extraordinary instability of the southern countries in this 40-year period: physical capital accumulation, highly correlated across time in the benchmark countries, is uncorrelated within this group.[7]

Although TFP variability is the dominant driver underlying the variability of growth rates in all the southern countries, its importance is minor or null for explaining the level of long-run growth rates over the entire period. As shown in Figure 3.4, factor accumulation (resulting from labor participation rates, workers' skills and physical capital intensity) is the main driver explaining growth in all the southern countries during the 1960–99 period. Average TFP growth during the period was somewhat substantial only in Chile and Brazil, but even in these countries its contribution relative to factor accumulation was quite minor. Nevertheless, averaging over decades does leave an important role for TFP growth rates in explaining overall growth in some decades for some countries, for example relatively fast TFP growth in Argentina and Uruguay underpinning overall growth in the 1990s despite its overall irrelevance over the 40-year period (see Figure 3.5).

The fact that all the southern countries (except Chile) experienced negative growth rates of TFP during the 1980s may appear puzzling. This is very hard to explain as a technology reversal. In Appendix 3.B we argue that our measure of productivity is associated with a broad definition of efficiency because it also captures changes in input utilization. Figure 3.B.1 shows, however, that the reductions in the utilization of labor account only for a small part of the fall in productivity during the 1980s. Still a very large portion of the decline in productivity remains unexplained. As we argued

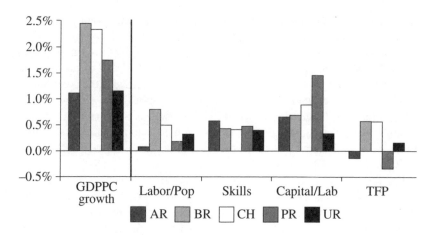

Source: Authors' calculations.

Figure 3.4   Growth accounting: period (1960–99)

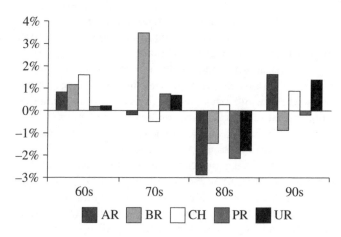

Source: Authors' calculations.

Figure 3.5   TFP growth

previously, an alternative interpretation of the slump of the 1980s is to consider that a rise in the level of distortions hindered the level of efficiency with
which the economy operated, perhaps due to lack of financing and forced
fiscal adjustment. In fact, such a decrease in aggregate efficiency goes directly into the productivity measure because this is calculated as a residual
from the aggregate production function.

*Table 3.5   Difference in growth with respect to rest of LAC (1960–99)
(percentage)*

	GDP per capita growth	Labor/pop	Skills	Capital/labor	TFP
Argentina	0.02	−0.40	0.04	0.16	0.23
Brazil	1.36	0.33	−0.12	0.21	0.94
Chile	1.25	0.03	−0.13	0.41	0.94
Paraguay	0.65	−0.29	−0.08	0.98	0.04
Uruguay	0.07	−0.15	−0.16	−0.14	0.53

Source: Authors' calculations.

In order to examine the factors that could account for faster growth of the southern countries relative to the rest of Latin America during the 1960–99 period we compare their underlying contributing factors to growth performance (Table 3.5). Here the rest of Latin America refers to the non-weighted average (of the growth rates of output and the growth rates of the contributing factors) of the additional 15 Latin American countries of the sample, which we interpret as a country typical of the rest of Latin America. In all cases the productivity growth gap is positive. In fact, it was precisely productivity growth that was the main advantage in the southern countries relative to the rest of Latin America over this period (except Paraguay where it was the accumulation of capital). Besides faster productivity growth, the southern countries gained ground in Latin America in physical capital deepening (except Uruguay) and lost ground in skills (except Argentina).

Next we examine the factors underlying the slower growth of the southern countries relative to the rest of the world (Table 3.6). Here the rest of the

Table 3.6   Difference in growth respect to ROW (1960–99) (percentage)

	GDP per capita growth	Labor/pop	Skills	Capital/labor	TFP
Argentina	−1.39	−0.19	0.05	−0.27	−0.98
Brazil	−0.06	0.54	−0.11	−0.22	−0.27
Chile	−0.17	0.24	−0.12	−0.02	−0.27
Paraguay	−0.77	−0.07	−0.07	0.55	−1.17
Uruguay	−1.35	0.06	−0.15	−0.58	−0.68

Source: Authors' calculations.

world refers to the non-weighted averages of the 53 non-Latin American countries of the sample (see Appendix 3.A for a detailed list of countries). The lack of TFP growth was very important in accounting for the slower growth of the southern countries with respect to the rest of the world during the 1960–99 period. In fact, it was the dominant factor in accounting for the growth gap in all the countries.

What appeared to be a strong point in the performance of southern countries within Latin America turns out to be a weak one in a world perspective. Total factor productivity growth in the southern countries compared favorably to the rest of Latin America only because of the dismal productivity performance in the rest of the region. The southern countries fell behind in the world because of low total productivity growth. Leaving aside higher labor participation in Brazil and Chile, the only important gain relative to the rest of the world in this group of countries appears to be in Paraguay, due to physical investment (in hydroelectric dams). When we compare the southern countries with developed countries (Table 3.7) the findings are similar: the growth gap opens mainly due to the opening of the productivity gap, despite some closing of the workers' skill gap.

Table 3.7   Difference in growth with respect to DEV (1960–99) (percentage)

	GDP per capita growth	Labor/pop	Skills	Capital/labor	TFP
Argentina	−1.52	−0.36	0.20	−0.30	−1.07
Brazil	−0.19	0.37	0.05	−0.25	−0.35
Chile	−0.30	0.07	0.03	−0.05	−0.35
Paraguay	−0.90	−0.25	0.09	0.51	−1.25
Uruguay	−1.48	−0.11	0.01	−0.61	−0.77

Source: Authors' calculations.

3.4   EXPLAINING PRODUCTIVITY GROWTH

We found that productivity is the main factor accounting for the slower growth of the southern countries relative to the rest of the world and, at the same time, it is also the factor that accounted for the faster growth of these countries relative to the rest of Latin America. Therefore, we are interested in explaining what drives productivity. For this reason, we performed Barro-style regressions not only to the growth rate of per capita output, as is customary, but also to its components: factor growth and TFP growth. The econometric model in this section is explained in more detail in Blyde and Fernández-Arias (2005).

The explanatory variables used for all the regressions are: education (log of average years of secondary schooling in the male population over age 25); life expectancy (log of average years of life expectancy at birth); infrastructure (log of electricity produced); openness (structure-adjusted trade volume as percentage of GDP);[8] inflation (log of inflation rate); overvaluation of exchange rate (overvaluation of the real effective exchange rate); credit to private sector (log of credit to private sector as percentage of GDP); government consumption (log of government expenditure as percentage of GDP); terms of trade shocks (growth rate of terms of trade); institutions (first principal components of the International Country Risk Guide variables). We also control for cyclical reversion to the long run trend (see Loayza et al., 2002). Finally, we proxy technology diffusion by including the imports of machinery and equipment (log of machinery and equipment as percentage of GDP). Tables 3.8 and 3.9 provide a complete definition of all the variables as well as their descriptive statistics and correlations for the sample of 73 countries during the period 1985–99 for which relevant information is available.

The results from the econometric exercises are shown in Table 3.10. Potential endogeneity is controlled using instrumental variable (IV) estimation based on lagged values. The main result from the statistical analysis is that long-run productivity growth is affected by trade policy and by institutions (as measured by the International Country Risk Guide, ICRG, which combines risk of repudiation of contracts by government, risk of expropriation, corruption, rule of law and bureaucratic quality). More open economies and economies with good institutions seem to experience faster productivity growth (besides the short-run cyclical factor). We did not find statistically significant evidence that economic policies other than those related to openness have an effect on productivity growth in the long run for a given institutional setting.[9]

Finally, we use the estimated equation of TFP to determine the role of the explanatory variables in explaining the TFP growth gap of southern countries relative to the typical country inside and outside Latin America, which was shown to be the key for its relative performance in growth per capita over the past forty years (see Figures 3.6 and 3.7). In these simulations we re-estimated the TFP growth equation retaining only the statistically significant explanatory variables (cycle, openness and institutions).

Figure 3.6 shows the differences in the contributions of openness and institutions to TFP between the southern countries and the rest of Latin America during the 1985–99 period. According to the model, during this period southern countries made gains in productivity over the rest of Latin America mainly

Table 3.8 Descriptive statistics (1985–99)

Variable	Description	Obs	Mean	Std. Dev	Min	Max
GRGDPPC	Growth rate of GDP per capita	219	0.015	0.026	-0.083	0.089
GRA	Growth rate of TFP	219	0.002	0.021	-0.071	0.061
GFAC	Growth rate of factors	219	0.013	0.011	-0.017	0.057
LGDPPC	Initial GDP per capita (in logs)	219	8.275	1.015	6.233	9.854
LGAPA	Initial productivity level (in logs)	219	5.442	0.401	4.313	6.156
LFAC	Initial factor level (in logs)	219	2.833	0.692	1.180	3.948
CYCLEY	Cyclical reversion in output: initial GDP per capita gap relative to trend (in logs)	219	-0.023	0.066	-0.240	0.276
CYCLEA	Cyclical reversion in productivity: initial productivity gap relative to trend (in logs)	219	-0.022	0.058	-0.217	0.230
CYCLEF	Cyclical reversion in factors: initial factor gap relative to trend (in logs)	219	0.000	0.030	-0.080	0.117
LSHYRM	Education: ave. years of sec. and higher schooling in male population age 25+ (in logs)	210	0.653	0.718	-1.370	1.895
LLIFEE	Life expectancy at birth, years (in logs of [years/100])	219	-0.405	0.164	-1.058	-0.220
LELEC	Infrastructure: electricity produced – kwh per capita – (in logs)	201	7.357	1.658	1.695	10.208
OPEN	Openness: structure-adjusted	216	0.078	0.417	-0.511	2.400
LINFLA	Inflation (in log of [1 + infla/100])	220	0.212	0.528	0.003	3.543
LOXR	Overvaluation of the real exchange rate (log of index)	207	4.592	0.372	3.561	5.561
LCREDIT	Credit to private sector / GDP (in logs)	217	-0.977	0.848	-3.631	0.712
LGOV	Government consumption / GDP (in logs)	218	-1.965	0.390	-3.133	-1.113
LMACHIN	Imports of machinery and equipment / GDP (in logs)	219	-2.925	0.677	-5.171	-0.346
GTOT	Growth rate of terms of trade	211	0.002	0.047	-0.328	0.301
ICRG	First principal components of ICRG variables	213	0.333	1.849	-4.121	3.075

Source: Authors' calculations.

Table 3.9   Correlations (1985–1999)

	GRGDPPC	GRA	GFAC	LGDPPC	LGAPA	LFAC	CYCLEY	CYCLEA	CYCLEF	LSHYRM	LLIFEE	LELEC	OPEN	LINFLA	LOXR	LCREDIT	LGOV	ICRG	GTOT	LMACHIN
GRGDPPC	1																			
GRA	0.888	1																		
GFAC	0.596	0.159	1																	
LGDPPC	0.273	0.233	0.180	1																
LGAPA	0.256	0.192	0.215	0.901	1															
LFAC	0.257	0.235	0.140	0.964	0.752	1														
CYCLEY	−0.271	−0.426	0.161	0.175	0.203	0.141	1													
CYCLEA	−0.089	−0.295	0.324	0.152	0.180	0.120	0.827	1												
CYCLEF	−0.366	−0.297	−0.267	0.035	0.042	0.027	0.494	0.029	1											
LSHYRM	0.288	0.264	0.157	0.838	0.665	0.864	0.100	0.081	−0.008	1										
LLIFEE	0.322	0.208	0.327	0.869	0.775	0.841	0.046	0.083	−0.067	0.741	1									
LELEC	0.239	0.203	0.159	0.922	0.803	0.906	0.120	0.110	0.012	0.797	0.826	1								
OPEN	0.280	0.192	0.265	−0.001	0.016	−0.011	0.036	0.041	−0.013	−0.033	0.014	−0.023	1							
LINFLA	−0.232	−0.196	−0.155	−0.163	−0.128	−0.169	−0.234	−0.224	−0.041	−0.170	−0.134	−0.156	−0.202	1						
LOXR	−0.187	−0.117	−0.196	0.172	0.159	0.164	0.049	0.008	0.057	0.083	0.087	0.136	−0.208	0.116	1					
LCREDIT	0.230	0.134	0.259	0.681	0.531	0.707	0.232	0.238	0.010	0.571	0.560	0.634	0.219	−0.238	0.179	1				
LGOV	0.003	0.100	−0.169	0.479	0.392	0.486	0.150	0.137	0.035	0.419	0.324	0.459	−0.067	−0.197	0.250	0.460	1			
ICRG	0.325	0.307	0.162	0.855	0.700	0.868	0.210	0.224	−0.044	0.767	0.702	0.829	0.101	−0.302	0.181	0.702	0.561	1		
GTOT	−0.108	−0.107	−0.046	−0.093	−0.115	−0.071	−0.091	−0.059	−0.055	−0.127	−0.012	−0.076	0.002	0.031	0.089	−0.029	−0.076	−0.064	1	
LMACHIN	0.283	0.193	0.269	0.172	0.144	0.172	−0.003	0.040	−0.059	0.166	0.209	0.177	0.741	−0.239	−0.125	0.242	0.181	0.249	0.002	1

Source: Authors' calculations.

Table 3.10   Dependent variable in growth rates

	5-year period (1985–1999)		
	GDPPC	Factors	TFP
Log of initial level	–0.0098	–0.0191	–0.0059
	(1.44)	(3.93)**	(0.89)
Cyclical reversion	–0.1218	–0.0545	–0.1285
	(4.91)**	(2.31)**	(5.16)**
Education	0.0071	0.0034	0.0049
	(1.51)	(1.41)	(1.26)
Life expectancy	0.0780	0.0664	0.0230
	(2.87)**	(5.53)**	(1.10)
Infrastructure	–0.0028	–0.0011	–0.0016
	(0.98)	(0.87)	(0.66)
Openness	0.0113	–0.0025	0.0116
	(1.66)*	(0.78)	(1.90)*
Inflation	0.0006	0.0050	–0.0033
	(0.08)	(1.37)	(0.52)
Overvaluation of exchange rate	–0.0116	–0.0068	–0.0044
	(2.22)**	(2.67)**	(0.97)
Credit to private sector	0.0030	0.0075	–0.0027
	(0.88)	(4.23)	(0.91)
Government consumption	–0.0076	–0.0110	0.0030
	(1.21)	(3.62)**	(0.54)
Imports of machinery and equipment	–0.0006	0.0037	–0.0034
	(0.17)	(1.94)	(0.99)
Terms of trade shocks	–0.0582	–0.0191	–0.0351
	(1.87)*	(0.42)	(1.29)
First principal components of	0.0054	0.0026	0.0035
institutional variables	(2.04)**	(1.91)*	(1.71)*
Observations	173	173	173
R-squared	0.41	0.38	0.32

Notes:
t-statistics in parentheses.
Year controls not shown.
* Significant at 10 per cent level.
** Significant at 5 per cent level.

Source: Authors' calculations.

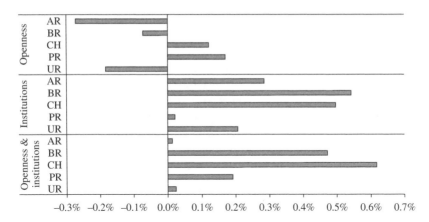

Source: Authors' calculations.

Figure 3.6   Difference in the contributions of openness and institutions to annual TFP growth with respect to LAC (1985–99)

as a result of better institutions. The exception is Paraguay, in which the main contributing factor was openness. In Chile there was a relatively large contribution from openness, but the main contributing factor was still institutions.

In Figure 3.7 we make the same comparison with respect to the rest of the world. According to the model, the performance of southern countries with

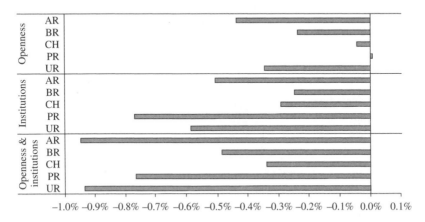

Source: Authors' calculations.

Figure 3.7   Difference in the contributions of openness and institutions to annual TFP growth with respect to ROW (1985–99)

respect to the rest of the world was depressed by insufficient openness and inferior institutions. Although lack of openness contributed to the relatively poor performance (the exception is Paraguay), the main factor was the lower institutional quality in the southern countries.

The above results are averages over the period. However, how is the situation evolving over time? In order to answer this question, we repeat the exercises shown in Figures 3.6 and 3.7 using two sub-periods: 1985–90 and 1995–99. Figure 3.8 shows the case in which Latin America is the benchmark. The average result applies to both sub-periods, but it is interesting to note that the relative disadvantage arising from the lack of openness is more pronounced in the second period (except for Paraguay) while the relative advantage arising from the better institutions is less pronounced in the second period (except for Argentina and Paraguay).

Figure 3.9 shows the case with respect to the rest of the world. Again, the previous average still applies to both sub-periods, but the relative disadvantage from the lack of openness increased in the second period (except for Paraguay) and the relative disadvantage from the inferior institutions decreased in the second period (except for Brazil).

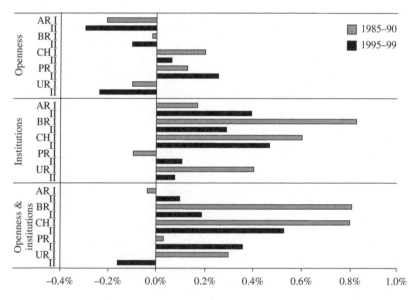

Source: Authors' calculations.

Figure 3.8   Difference in the contributions of openness and institutions to annual TFP growth with respect to LAC (1985–90 and 1995–99)

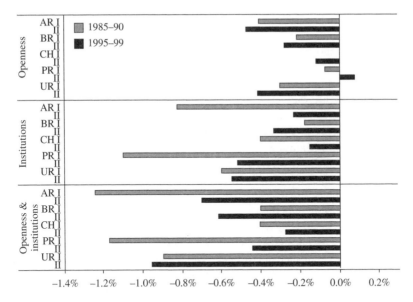

Source: Authors' calculations.

Figure 3.9 *Difference in the contributions of openness and institutions to annual TFP growth with respect to ROW (1985–90 and 1995–99)*

Therefore, between 1985–90 and 1995–99, there is convergence in terms of institutions and divergence in terms of openness. In fact, on the one hand, the institutions of the typical Latin American country moved closer to those the southern countries while the institutions of the southern countries moved closer to those of the typical country from the rest of the world. The institutional gap narrowed somewhat. On the other hand, the relative disadvantage in terms of openness of the southern countries increased, both with respect to the typical Latin American country and also with respect to the typical country from the rest of the world. The openness gap widened.

Before concluding, it is worthwhile to reflect on the peculiar time patterns of growth in Brazil and Chile previously mentioned and see how this information can be integrated into this analysis. In what follows we borrow from country studies included in Fernández-Arias et al. (2005) to enrich the discussion. The findings of these studies are richer in detail but largely consistent with the general results of our work.

As noted, Brazil's top growth performance three and four decades ago plummeted. Pinhero et al. (2005) offer an analysis of this experience. At first look, the growth experience in Brazil during the last four decades seems paradoxical in two ways. First, Brazil managed to exhibit high rates of growth during the 1960s and 1970s despite a mix of policies that are not favored by orthodox economists. And second, after the debt crisis of the 1980s, the recovery during the 1990s was met with limited success despite Brazil's efforts to integrate itself into the world economy, establish macro-economic stability, and rely on private enterprise rather than state planning as the engine of economic growth.

However, according to these authors, the growth performance observed in Brazil during this time was less paradoxical than it seems. High growth rates of the 1960s and 1970s were based on policies that were remarkably ortho-dox when set against the economic debates alive at the time (a stabilization program to lower inflation, reduce the public deficit, and correct relative prices; an exchange rate devaluation followed by a crawling peg regime, and tax reform, greatly reducing tax distortions, raising revenues dramatically, and improving the current account; monetary and capital market reforms with establishment of an indexation mechanism). These policies eventually suc-ceeded in fostering investment in the 1960s, a process which continued into the 1970s fueled by external borrowing that eventually led to the debt crisis of the 1980s.

Consistent with the main findings of our chapter, Pinhero et al. (2005) argue that TFP growth during the 1960s and 1970s appears to have been systematically associated with growth in the stock of machinery and equip-ment. This suggests another reason for the eventual faltering of Brazil's high growth performance after the 1970s since part of the government response to external imbalances early in the decade had been to increase import barriers on capital goods. The subsequent drop in capital goods imports created negative effects by decreasing embodied technological progress. This expla-nation goes in line with the high TFP growth rate observed during the 1970s and its subsequent decline during the 1980s (see Figure 3.5).

During the 1990s Brazil embarked on a series of market reforms. The authors argue that the acceleration of GDP growth after the price stability reform in 1994 was entirely due to higher TFP growth (using our data set, annual TFP growth went from –2.6 per cent during the 1990–93 period to 1.6 per cent during the 1994–99 period). However, the reason low inflation and the 1990s' market reforms have failed to bring output growth back to pre-1980 levels has been the failure of those reforms to generate factor accumulation, with the contributions of both labor and capital to output growth actually declining in comparison to the 1981–93 period, a result that is confirmed in our data set.

Chile presented a growth performance almost opposite to the one observed in Brazil: while the 1960s and the 1970s showed low rates of growth, output accelerated greatly during the 1980s and 1990s (see Figure 3.1). Particularly remarkable was the behavior of TFP, which exhibited positive rates during the 1980s and continued its acceleration during the 1990s (see Figure 3.5). The interesting question in Chile is then, how did it manage to achieve output growth and, especially, TFP growth during the 1980s, when almost all other countries in Latin America were experiencing a crisis, and continue with higher rates during the 1990s? Chumacero and Fuentes (2005) provide an answer to this question that centers on the evolution of TFP.

Using an econometric model to explain the behavior of TFP, the authors find that distortions (as measured by the participation of government expenditures to GDP) were among the main factors that help to explain the periods of slow TFP growth in Chile. They argue that the reforms initiated in the mid-1970s that moved the economy from a highly regulated towards a market-oriented economy were strongly associated with this reduction of distortions. In fact, given that these reforms were kept in place even during the international debt crisis of the 1980s, an environment that was relatively free of distortions would have helped to explain why TFP in Chile did not collapse during this decade, like in the other Southern Cone countries, and kept rising through the 1990s.

3.5 FINAL REMARKS

In this chapter we have provided an overview of the growth experience of the southern countries during the last four decades. When comparing the southern countries with the rest of Latin America, we found that these countries performed better than the rest of the region on the basis of higher total factor productivity growth. However, given the dismal performance of Latin America's productivity, the latter comparison would be profoundly misleading and would hide the Achilles' heel of growth in the southern countries. Among the main findings of the chapter is that it is precisely lower TFP growth, not lower investment, that is the main factor in accounting for the slower growth of the southern countries with respect to the rest of the world during the 1960–99 period.

Superior productivity performance is behind the Brazilian miracle of the 1970s and Chile's growth during the lost decade of the 1980s and its stellar performance afterwards. By and large, however, in the southern countries TFP growth has failed to meet international standards in a sustainable fashion over the long run and has led to the gradual opening of the income gap with respect to the rest of the world (including Brazil and Chile, despite their growth spurts). Our econometric results suggest that limited openness and, especially, poor institutions are important factors explaining the shortfall of TFP growth in the southern countries relative to the rest of the world.

What to expect in the future? If recent performance over the 1985–99 period is an indication of trends, we note that only Chile has been able to increase its productivity at and beyond international standards supported by an equally robust achievement in factor accumulation. Uruguay has seen an equally impressive improvement in productivity growth but without any reaction in factor accumulation, which coupled with the prolonged and deep recession of the early 2000s opens serious doubts about sustainability. As to the rest of the southern countries, they have exhibited consistent regress by international standards during the period. Nevertheless, there is a discernible tendency to improvements in institutional quality within the period that, if continued, bodes well for the prospect of closing the TFP gap.

APPENDIX 3.A

Groups of Countries

Southern countries   Argentina, Brazil, Chile, Paraguay, Uruguay.

Rest of Latin America   Bolivia, Colombia, Costa Rica, the Dominican Republic, Ecuador, El Salvador, Guatemala, Haiti, Honduras, Jamaica, Mexico, Nicaragua, Panama, Peru, Venezuela.

Rest of the world   Australia, Austria, Belgium, Benin, Botswana, Cameroon, Canada, Côte d'Ivoire, Cyprus, Denmark, Egypt, Fiji, Finland, France, Germany, Ghana, Greece, Hong Kong, Hungary, Iceland, India, Ireland, Israel, Italy, Japan, Kenya, Korea, Madagascar, Malawi, Malaysia, Morocco, Netherlands, New Zealand, Norway, Pakistan, Papua New Guinea, Philippines, Portugal, Senegal, Sierra Leone, Singapore, South Africa, Spain, Sri Lanka, Sweden, Switzerland, Syria, Thailand, Togo, Tunisia, United Kingdom, United States, Zimbabwe.

Developed countries   Australia, Austria, Belgium, Canada, Denmark, Finland, France, Germany, Iceland, Ireland, Italy, Japan, Netherlands, New Zealand, Norway, Spain, Sweden, Switzerland, United Kingdom, United States.

Data Sources

GDP indicators: Penn World Table 5.6, Easterly and Levine (2001), and World Development Indicators
Capital indicators: Penn World Table 5.6, Easterly and Levine (2001), and World Development Indicators

Labor force: World Development Indicators
Years of education: Barro and Lee (2001) database
Life expectancy: World Development Indicators
Electricity consumption: World Development Indicators
Openness: Authors' construction using WDI data
Inflation: Global Development Finance and World Development Indicators
Overvaluation of exchange rate: Easterly and Levine (2001)
Credit to private sector: World Development Indicators
Government consumption: World Development Indicators
Imports of machinery: UN Commodity Trade Statistics Database
Terms of trade: Global Development Finance and World Development Indicators
Institutional variables: International Country Risk Guide

APPENDIX 3.B

The labor and capital data employed in the growth accounting exercises of this chapter refer to the inputs that are 'available' in the marketplace rather than the inputs 'effectively used' in the economy. In this Appendix we explain how this is consistent with a broad definition of total factor productivity. Consider the following production function:

$$Y = K_u^\alpha \cdot (h_u \cdot L_u)^{1-\alpha} \cdot A_u \qquad (3.B.1)$$

where K_U and $h_U L_U$ are the capital and labor inputs effectively utilized in the production process and A_U the corresponding observed productivity. Denoting the levels of available capital and labor inputs as K and hL respectively (L being unskilled labor and h its average skill level), we can use the following expressions:

$$K_u = K \cdot \frac{K_u}{K}; L_u = L \cdot \frac{L_u}{L}; h_u = h \cdot \frac{h_u}{h}$$

to rewrite equation (3.B.1) as follows:

$$Y = \left(K \cdot \frac{K_u}{K} \right)^\alpha \cdot \left(h \cdot \frac{h_u}{h} \cdot L \cdot \frac{L_u}{L} \right)^{1-\alpha} \cdot A_u. \qquad (3.B.2)$$

In growth rates, equation (3.B.2) becomes:

$$(\hat{Y}) = \alpha \cdot (\hat{K}) + \alpha \cdot \left(\frac{\hat{K}_u}{K}\right) + (1-\alpha) \cdot (\hat{h}) + (1-\alpha) \cdot \left(\frac{\hat{h}_u}{h}\right)$$
$$+ (1-\alpha) \cdot (\hat{L}) + (1-\alpha) \cdot \left(\frac{\hat{L}_u}{L}\right) + (\hat{A}_u).$$

(3.B.3)

From this expression, it can be seen that the growth rate of output depends on the growth rate of the available inputs and skills $(\hat{K}), (\hat{L}), (\hat{h})$, the growth rate of the utilization of these inputs and skills $(K_u\hat{/}K), (L_u\hat{/}L), (h_u\hat{/}h)$, and the growth rate of productivity $(\hat{A}_u)$.

The productivity variable in this specification is not affected by changes in factor utilization rates. This productivity variable only reflects changes in aggregate 'technology' springing either from changes in efficiency at the micro level or from changes in the efficiency of the overall economic environment in which the production takes place. We like to think about efficiency, however, in a broader sense, taking into account the additional output that would be obtained if available inputs that are not channeled into the production process were utilized. We view idle input resources as a form of inefficiency and want to measure it accordingly. To achieve this, we want to measure total factor productivity relative to potential output under full utilization of inputs available in the marketplace.

For example, consider two economies, A and B, with the same endowments and technology. Country A, however, exhibits a larger unemployment rate. We like to think country A as being less efficient than country B because it produces less with the same amount of available resources. Growth accounting exercises based on the amount of inputs used (rather than the amount of inputs available) will conclude that the productivity of both countries is the same, therefore, failing to capture this type of inefficiency. The productivity variable will only capture this inefficiency if the growth accounting exercises are based on the amount of inputs available. To see this, consider the following production function:

$$Y = K^\alpha \cdot (h \cdot L)^{1-\alpha} \cdot A. \qquad (3.B.4)$$

Here, K and hL represent the levels of inputs of capital and labor 'available' in the economy. Expressing equation (3.B.4) in growth terms and solving for the growth rate of productivity gives:

$$(\hat{A}^*) = (\hat{Y}) - \alpha \cdot (\hat{K}) - (1-\alpha) \cdot (\hat{h}) - (1-\alpha) \cdot (\hat{L}). \qquad (3.B.5)$$

Finally, using equation (3.B.3) to substitute for $(\hat{Y})$ in this expression gives:

$$(\hat{A}) = (\hat{A}_u) + \alpha \cdot \left(\frac{\hat{K}_u}{K}\right) + (1-\alpha) \cdot \left(\frac{\hat{h}_u}{h}\right) + (1-\alpha) \cdot \left(\frac{\hat{L}_u}{L}\right). \qquad (3.B.6)$$

Expression (3.B.6) shows that the growth rate of productivity $(\hat{A})$, depends on the growth rate of 'technological' change $(\hat{A}_u)$, and the growth rates of factor utilization of capital $(\hat{K}_u/K)$, labor $(\hat{L}_u/L)$, and skills $(\hat{h}_u/h)$. Therefore, for example, if an economy exhibits an increase in the rate of unemployment, that is $(\hat{L}_u/L < 0)$, this will be captured as a lower productivity growth $(\hat{A})$.

Understandably, there are changes in the utilization of inputs along the economic cycle. Economies tend to use more or less inputs depending on which phase of the cycle they are in. Therefore, it would be misleading to judge an economy as less efficient just because it is in a lower part of the cycle. The issue of factor utilization becomes important only if there are differences in long-run trends. Consequently, in our growth accounting exercises we use 10-year averages to smooth out changes in the utilization of inputs due to the cycle.

Following equation (3.B.6), we used data on employment and labor force to measure the size of the contribution of the utilization of labor $(1 - \alpha) \cdot (\hat{L}_u/L)$, on the growth rate of productivity $(\hat{A})$. We show that in general this contribution is rather small (see Figure 3.B.1). An immediate

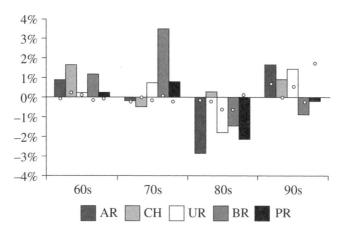

Note: Contributions from labor utilization indicated by a dot.

Source: Author's calculations.

Figure 3.B.1 *TFP growth and contributions from changes in labor utilization*

implication of the smallness of these contributions is that the results and conclusions of this chapter, which is based on the analysis of decade averages, do not change qualitatively if we adjust for the rate of unemployment.

NOTES

* We would like to thank Daniel Oks and Andrés Solimano for useful comments and suggestions. We would also like to thank participants at the ECLAC–UN Workshop 'Latin America Growth: why so slow?' held at ECLAC in Santiago. The authors are solely responsible for the contents of the study. The conclusions and opinions expressed in this chapter do not necessarily coincide with the policies and opinions of the Inter-American Development Bank.
1. Maximum set for which complete information was available.
2. This trend was drastically interrupted in Argentina and Uruguay during the early 2000s, which casts doubts about the sustainability of observed growth acceleration in the previous decade.
3. These relatively high correlation coefficients significantly differ from the uncorrelation found by Easterly and Levine (2001) over a similar period for a larger sample of countries. Our analysis with our sample reveals that their uncorrelation results change significantly when periods are updated and are also dependent on including countries we chose to discard from our sample because of low informational value.
4. In this specification, total factor productivity excludes the effect of changes in the skill level of the labor force, which is captured by h and accounted as factor accumulation of human capital.
5. A more detailed analysis can decompose this component into a demographic factor, dealing with the fraction of the population of working age, and a behavioral factor concerning their participation rate in the labor force (that is, the fraction of the able who are willing to work).
6. $VAR(\hat{y}) = VAR(\hat{TFP}) + VAR(\widehat{factors}) + 2\{COV(\hat{TFP}, \widehat{factors})\}$.
7. Although as noted in the previous section our numbers differ considerably from those in Easterly and Levine (2001), their key result that persistence in physical capital accumulation is higher than that of GDP growth remains true for all of the country groupings.
8. The idea of adjusted trade volume is taken from Pritchett (1996) and is measured as the residual of the following equation: $TRADE ((M+X)/Y)_i = a + b^*LPOB_i + c^*LAREA_i + d^*LGDPPC_i + e^*LGDPPC_i^*LGDPPC_i + f^* OIL_i + g^*LANDLOCK_i + E_i$. The measure indicates the amount by which a country's trade intensity exceed (or falls short) of that expected for a country with similar characteristics.
9. It is worth noting that the results of these econometric exercises are only informative, in the sense that they describe broad trends that may inform the comparison of alternative economic policies but clearly cannot substitute for detailed country analysis. In particular, institutions that work in one country might not work in another country if certain idiosyncratic aspects are not taken into account.

REFERENCES

Barro, R. and J.W. Lee (2001), 'International data on educational attainment: updates and implications', *Oxford Economic Papers*, **53** (3).
Blyde, J. and E. Fernández-Arias (2005), 'Why Latin America is falling behind', in E. Fernández-Arias, R. Manuelli and J. Blyde (eds), *Sources of Growth in Latin*

America: What is Missing?, Washington, DC: Inter-American Development Bank (forthcoming).

Chumacero, R. and R. Fuentes (2005), 'On the determinants of Chilean economic growth', in E. Fernández-Arias, R. Manuelli and J. Blyde (eds), *Sources of Growth in Latin America: What is Missing?* Washington, DC: Inter-American Development Bank (forthcoming).

Easterly, W., M. Kremer, L. Pritchett and L. Summers (1993), 'Good policy or good luck? country growth performance and temporary shocks', *Journal of Monetary Economics*, **32**, December.

Easterly, W. and R. Levine (2001), 'It is not factor accumulation: stylized facts and growth models', Central Bank of Chile working paper.

Fernández-Arias, E., R. Manuelli and J. Blyde (eds) (2005), *Sources of Growth in Latin America: What is Missing?* Washington, DC: Inter-American Development Bank (forthcoming).

Hall, J. and C. Jones (1999), 'Why do some countries produce so much more output per worker than others?', *Quarterly Journal of Economics*, February.

Loayza, N., P. Fajnzylber and C. Calderón (2002), 'Economic growth in Latin America and the Caribbean, stylized facts, explanations, and forecasts', World Bank working paper.

Parente, S. and E. Prescott (2002), *Barriers to Riches*, Cambridge, MA: MIT Press.

Pinhero, A.C., I.S. Gill, L. Servén and M.R. Thomas (2005), 'Brazilian economic growth, 1900–2000: lessons and policy implications', in E. Fernández-Arias, R. Manuelli and J. Blyde (eds), *Sources of Growth in Latin America: What is Missing?*, Washington, DC: Inter-American Development Bank (forthcoming).

Pritchett, L. (1996), 'Measuring outward orientation in LDCs: can it be done?', *Journal of Development Economics*, **49** (2).

Summers, R. and A. Heston (1991), 'The Penn World Table (Mark 5): an expanded set of international comparisons, 1950–88', *Quarterly Journal of Economics*, **106** (2).

4. Economic growth in the Andean region: the role of economic and governance factors*

Claudio Aravena, André A. Hofman and Andrés Solimano

4.1 INTRODUCTION

This chapter analyzes the growth performance of Bolivia, Colombia, Ecuador, Peru and Venezuela – the so-called Andean region – in the last decades of the twentieth century. Economic growth is a main vehicle to improve living standards, reduce poverty and provide resources to the state for the financing of social policy. The Andean countries are a diverse group in terms of economic characteristics, policies and socio-political conditions. Several Andean countries exhibited in the last three decades high indices of Presidential crises, regime changes and above average frequencies of constitutional changes (see Solimano, 2003 and 2005). Growth in the Andean region has to be understood in a context of chronic political instability, and governance problems that have characterized this region.

In terms of natural resource endowments Venezuela and Ecuador are oil exporters while Bolivia, Peru and Colombia are net oil importers. Ethnic diversity is far greater in Peru, Bolivia and Ecuador than in Colombia and Venezuela. Colombia was, historically, a country of mild growth cycles and prudent macroeconomic management, although a deterioration of economic conditions started in the mid-1990s. Ecuador experienced very rapid rates of economic growth in the 1970s led by the oil sector but fell down into a protracted period of sluggish economic growth and macroeconomic instability in the 1980s and 1990s. This culminated with a severe economic and financial crisis in 1998–99. In 2000 the country officially dollarized the economy, starting a process of stabilization and resumption of growth with ups and downs.[1] Bolivia suffered extreme economic instability in the mid-1980s, including an episode of hyperinflation in 1985, but the economy started to recuperate in the 1990s. Peru suffered severe instability in the late 1980s, undertook reforms in the 1990s but sustained growth has been difficult to consolidate. Venezuela, in spite of its large oil resources, grew at a sluggish and erratic pace in the last two decades.

This chapter looks at the record of economic growth in the Andean region from several perspectives. First, it takes a comparative and historical perspective, for different sub-periods in the twentieth century, comparing the growth performance of the Andean region with the average of Latin America, the rest of the world and with the productivity leader of the twentieth century: the USA.

Second, we identify cycles of economic growth in the Andean countries in the last two to three decades, highlighting tendencies for divergence and convergence of growth paths and reflecting the diversity in stories of economic growth within the Andean group.

Third, we undertake an analysis of sources of growth for each Andean country for the period 1950–2002, ascertaining the role of factor accumulation (labor and capital) and total factor productivity growth on the rate of growth of GDP and the evolution of total factor productivity over time in the five Andean countries.

Fourth, for the period 1950–2002 an econometric analysis of empirical growth equations is made for a panel of the five Andean countries and individual growth equations for each Andean country. We investigate the role of external openness, government consumption, terms of trade changes, political instability and political regimes on the rate of economic growth. We will attempt to measure quantitatively the effect of governance conditions on the growth record of these economies.

4.2   GROWTH PERFORMANCE IN THE TWENTIETH CENTURY

Table 4.1 shows overall economic growth in the Andean region in a comparative perspective. Several surprising facts are to be noted. Although over the whole twentieth century growth in Latin America was better than the world average there are clear signs of deteriorating growth rates towards the end of the century. Also in comparison with the USA, the world productivity leader for the great part of the twentieth century, Latin America's growth performance is not as impressive. The relatively good growth performances over the century are heavily influenced by the first half of the twentieth century when Latin America was sheltered from the two world wars and did not experience their devastating effects as much as the rest of the world (see also ECLAC, 2002).

Surprisingly, Andean growth over the century was somewhat higher then the average for Latin America again especially in the first half of the century when Ecuador and Venezuela show impressive growth records. Within the

Table 4.1   *Rate of growth of GDP in the world, USA, Latin America and the Andean region, 1900–2002*

	Annual rate of change, %						
	1900– 2002	1900– 50	1950– 2002	1950– 73	1973– 80	1980– 90	1990– 2002
World	2.9	2.0	3.8	4.9	3.6	3.0	2.6
United States	3.2	3.1	3.3	3.9	2.4	2.8	2.9
Latin America	3.7	3.5	3.9	5.3	5.4	1.7	2.5
Andean region	4.1	4.3	3.9	5.6	4.4	1.4	2.3
Bolivia	2.6	2.5	2.7	3.3	2.9	0.2	3.5
Colombia	4.1	4.0	4.2	5.1	5.0	3.4	2.5
Ecuador	4.5	4.5	4.4	6.1	6.4	2.1	2.2
Peru	3.7	3.9	3.5	5.3	3.6	–1.2	3.9
Venezuela	4.8	5.8	3.8	6.4	4.1	0.6	1.1

Sources: Hofman (2000) and Maddison (2003).

Andean region, and taking averages for the twentieth century (1900–2002), Venezuela had the best growth performance and Bolivia the worst. However, in the second part of the century, and especially in the last decades Venezuela lost a great part of the advances made in the period 1900–50.

The Andean countries' performance has gone from better to worse in the twentieth century. Overall growth performance was better than in Latin America and the rest of the world in the first half of the century when the Andean countries, and especially Venezuela,[2] outperformed the rest of Latin America and the average of the world. From 1950 to1973 growth was already sluggish and from 1973 onwards Andean performance has been dismal, with the exception of Ecuador and Colombia between 1973 and 1980.

However, it is crucial to include demographics in our analysis. Table 4.2, presenting GDP per capita, shows that population growth was fairly fast in Latin America as compared to the rest of the world. Again it becomes very clear that the growth performance since the 1970s has been very weak. The real effects of the demographic transition in the Andean countries are very recent. Therefore, one of the most appropriate measures of economic performance, GDP per capita, shows a much less favorable outcome for the Andean region as well as Latin America as a whole.

Figure 4.1 shows the evolution of GDP per capita and here it becomes clear that the level of GDP per capita shows a far more unfavorable performance for the Andean countries since 1950, compared to the rest of Latin

Table 4.2   *Rate of growth of GDP per capita in the world, USA, Latin*
              America and the Andean region, 1900–2002

	Annual rate of change, %						
	1900– 2002	1900– 50	1950– 2002	1950– 73	1973– 80	1980– 90	1990– 2002
World	1.5	1.0	2.1	2.9	1.4	1.3	1.4
United States	1.9	1.7	2.0	2.4	1.4	1.8	1.9
Latin America	1.6	1.6	1.6	2.5	2.6	−0.7	1.0
Andean region	1.8	2.6	1.1	2.4	1.4	−1.3	0.3
Bolivia	0.9	1.5	0.4	1.1	0.5	−2.0	1.1
Colombia	1.7	1.8	1.7	2.2	2.6	1.3	0.6
Ecuador	1.9	2.0	1.7	3.1	3.4	−0.5	0.1
Peru	1.8	2.5	1.0	2.5	0.9	−3.4	2.1
Venezuela	2.5	4.5	0.6	2.6	0.5	−1.9	−1.0

Sources: Hofman (2000) and Maddison (2003).

America and the world. From the middle of the 1970s the Andean region, on average, has not increased its GDP per capita. The world GDP per capita has made a steady improvement. However the sharp fall in the 1980s has placed Latin America below the average world level.

The average GDP per capita of the Andean countries in 2002, as a share of the GDP per capita of the USA, is below its level of 1950. This is corroborated with Figures 4.2 and 4.3, which shows the evolution of GDP per capita in each Andean country compared to a trend growth rate of 2 per cent per year.[3]

Here it becomes clear that four of our five countries (Bolivia, Ecuador, Peru and Venezuela) are below the level of around the mid-1970s. In Bolivia, GDP per capita reached its peak in 1977 and the level in 2002 was still more than 10 per cent below this peak level. Since 1986 Bolivia experienced some recovery until the end of the 1990s when GDP per capita stagnated again. In Ecuador, the growth spurt of the 1970s ended in 1981 and in 2002 the country was still 5 per cent below the 1981 level. Peru experienced relatively fast growth until 1975 when a peak GDP per capita was reached; in 2002 GDP per capita was still 10 per cent below the level. Finally, economic growth in Venezuela's GDP reached its peak in 1977 and its 2002 GDP per capita was more than 30 per cent below the 1977 level (it recovered again in 2003 and 2004).

In terms of convergence towards the world productivity leader the Andean region has lost ground since the 1970s. From 1900 to 1950 the region

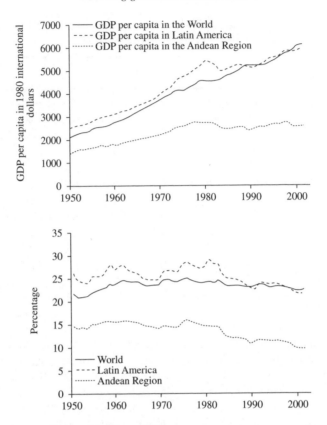

Source: Hofman (2000) and Maddison (2003).

Figure 4.1   GDP per capita in 1980 international dollars (top) and relative to USA (bottom) for the world, Latin America and the Andean region, 1950–2001

increased its GDP per capita as compared with the USA by 50 per cent (from roughly 10 per cent to 15 per cent, see Table 4.3). Their relative GDP per capita level remained constant until 1973 and since then the Andean countries have lost almost all the terrain gained before 1950 (their average level of GDP fell from 15 per cent in 1973 to 9 per cent in 2002). The most severe deterioration has been observed in the last quarter-century in Venezuela: its GDP per capita fell from 27 per cent of US GDP per capita in 1973 to 13 per cent in 2002. Large relative declines are observed also in Bolivia, Ecuador and Peru. The country with the lowest relative decline in GDP per head is Colombia. This fall in relative position for the Andean group in the last

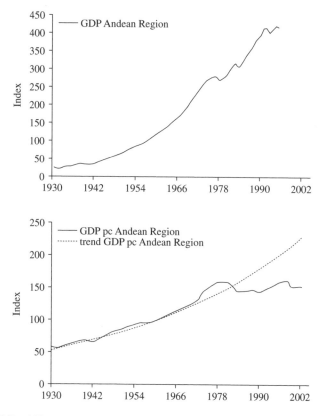

Note: 1960 = 100.

Source: Hofman (2000) and Maddison (2003).

Figure 4.2   Andean region GDP (top) and GDP per capita (bottom) 1930–2002

quarter century is a direct consequence of their modest growth performance in that period (although of course the growth stories are not uniform across the group).

4.3   A GROWTH ACCOUNTING EXERCISE

In this section we perform a sources of growth exercise in which GDP growth is decomposed in factor accumulation (labor, capital and natural resources) and total factor productivity growth. This provides a useful framework for

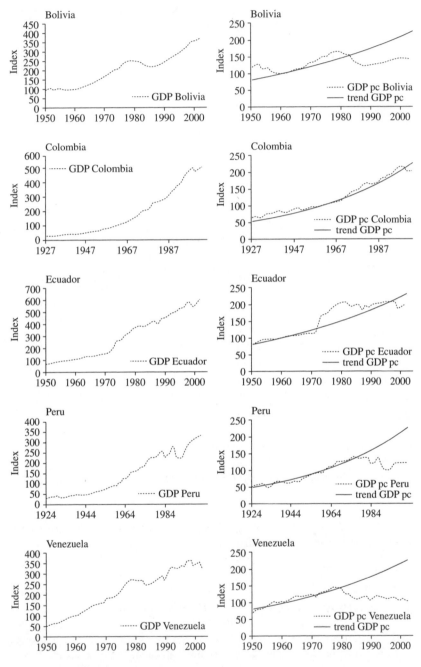

Note: 1960 = 100.

Sources: Hofman (2000) and Maddison (2003).

*Figure 4.3   Evolution of GDP in each Andean country (left) compared to
             evolution of GDP per capita with trend growth rate of 2 per
             cent per year (right)*

Table 4.3 *GDP per capita in the world, Latin America and the Andean region relative to USA, 1900–2002*

	1900	1950	1973	1980	1990	2002
World	31.9	22.1	24.7	24.7	23.6	22.1
United States	100.0	100.0	100.0	100.0	100.0	100.0
Latin America	27.7	26.7	27.3	29.6	23.1	20.7
Andean region	9.8	14.8	14.8	14.8	10.9	9.0
Bolivia	10.7	9.7	7.1	6.7	4.5	4.1
Colombia	12.4	12.8	12.1	13.2	12.5	10.6
Ecuador	9.3	10.7	12.5	14.3	11.4	9.2
Peru	10.0	15.0	15.1	14.6	8.6	8.8
Venezuela	6.8	25.9	27.1	25.5	17.6	12.4

Note: USA = 100.

Source: Hofman (2000) and Maddison (2003).

assembling quantitative 'facts' and qualified hypotheses about growth causality in a coherent way (Maddison, 1987). The growth accounts start in 1950 as data inadequacy prevents systematic analysis of previous periods. Growth accounting exercises are important because they can serve many different purposes: explaining differences in growth rates and levels between countries, illuminating processes of convergence and divergence, assessing the role of technical progress and calculating potential output losses. We present the results with respect to the most traditional explanatory factors, that is changes in the quantity and quality of labor inputs and changes in the quantity and quality of capital inputs. We also include natural resources as an explanatory factor.

In this growth accounting exercise, a simple Cobb–Douglas function was applied.

$$Y = A \; L^{\alpha} K^{\beta} N^{(1-\alpha-\beta)} \tag{4.1}$$

where Y represents GDP, L labor, K capital, N natural resources, A technical progress, α the factor share of labor and β the factor share of capital. In its logarithmic version (ln stands for natural logarithm):

$$\ln Y = \alpha \ln L + \beta \ln K + (1-\alpha-\beta) \ln N + A. \tag{4.2}$$

In the case of the capital and labor production factors, the quantity and quality of inputs were considered. The physical increase in labor was estimated by the increase in the amount of hours worked and the quantity increase in capital by fixed capital formation. The increase in the quality of labor was estimated through the educational level of the population, measured as the growth rate of the years of education, in the case of the capital stock, increased quality was measured through a vintage effect.

Having incorporated these effects, five different measures of total factor productivity (TFP) can be differentiated (see equation (4.3)). In turn, equation (4.4) presents the most elaborate version in which L represents labor quantity (hours), l labor quality (education), K physical capital stock, k the vintage effect of capital and N natural resource stock.

The two TFP estimates are as follows (in a simplified annotation with growth rates, g): The first version includes only the physical increases in capital and labor:

$$TFP_1 = g_Y - \alpha g_L - (1 - \alpha) g_K. \qquad (4.3)$$

The second version includes physical effects plus the quality effects of both labor and capital (doubly augmented joint factor productivity) and changes in factor N.

$$TFP_2 = g_Y - \alpha g_{(L+l)} - \beta g_{(K+k)} - (1 - \alpha - \beta) g_N. \qquad (4.4)$$

Labor Input

Labor input was estimated in terms of hours worked rather than employment rates because average annual hours worked per employee year vary substantially between countries and over time.[4] It is important to adjust for changes in the quality of labor input. In this study, this is represented by changes in the level of education of the population aged between 15 and 64 years. Our estimate consists of equivalent years of education per person. The quality effect of labor results from the growth of equivalent years of education, and is based on the assumption that a 1 per cent increase in education causes a 0.5 per cent proportionate gain in labor quality[5] (see Table 4.4).

Capital Input

Growth accounting only becomes possible if reliable estimates of the flow of services from physical capital are available. Making an analogy with labor, one would like to know the amount of machine hours used in production during the period of reference. However, the lack of available data normally does not permit this procedure, so we used the general accepted proxy for this calculation, that is, the estimation of the capital stock based upon the

Table 4.4 Andean region: rate of growth of labor inputs (quantity and quality), 1950–2002

	Labor quantity (hours worked)					Labor quality (level of education)				
	1951–73	1973–80	1980–90	1990–2002	1951–2002	1951–73	1973–80	1980–90	1990–2002	1951–2002
Bolivia	0.57	2.82	2.85	2.89	1.85	2.97	2.97	2.97	2.97	2.97
Colombia	2.03	3.03	1.77	1.31	1.97	2.78	2.39	3.64	2.28	2.76
Ecuador	1.24	2.78	4.19	3.37	2.48	1.87	1.96	2.09	1.41	1.80
Peru	1.74	2.72	2.70	2.83	2.31	0.26	6.77	4.12	2.25	2.45
Venezuela	2.87	5.02	2.11	2.86	2.98	3.37	5.10	4.32	2.56	3.56
Andean region	1.69	3.27	2.73	2.65	2.32	2.25	3.84	3.43	2.30	2.71

Source: Hofman (2000).

Table 4.5   Andean region: rate of growth of capital inputs (quantity and quality), 1950–2002

	Capital quantity					Capital quality				
	1951–73	1973–80	1980–90	1990–2002	1951–2002	1951–73	1973–80	1980–90	1990–2002	1951–2002
Bolivia	2.43	4.56	1.80	3.46	2.84	3.18	5.58	2.33	4.37	3.63
Colombia	3.79	5.14	4.73	3.24	4.01	4.53	6.03	5.56	4.15	4.82
Ecuador	5.51	7.57	5.19	2.46	5.01	6.90	9.13	5.75	3.12	6.08
Peru	5.11	6.29	3.11	2.58	4.29	5.86	6.94	3.61	2.98	4.89
Venezuela	6.19	7.53	3.13	0.05	4.36	7.06	8.84	3.91	0.59	5.20
Andean region	4.61	6.22	3.60	2.36	4.10	5.50	7.30	4.23	3.04	4.92

Source: Hofman (2000).

'perpetual inventory model' developed by Raymond Goldsmith (1952).[6] The capital stock was disaggregated into machinery and equipment, structures and dwellings with service lives of 15, 40 and 50 years, respectively. The 'perpetual inventory model' provides an indication of productive capacity (see Table 4.5).

Natural Resources

Land was used as a proxy indicator of natural resource endowment for the countries, using for the land respective weights of 1 for arable and permanent crop land, 0.3 for permanent pasture and 0.1 for forest land. The factor share used for weighting land was 0.10 for all countries (see next section). Table 4.6 shows clearly that the movement of the agricultural frontier has slowed down since 1950. In some cases land has been increasingly diverted from agricultural uses since 1973.

Table 4.6   Andean region: rate of growth of the land in use, 1960–2001

	1960–73	1973–80	1980–90	1990–2001	1960–2001
Bolivia	0.17	0.69	0.38	0.46	0.43
Colombia	0.50	0.03	−0.10	−0.18	0.08
Ecuador	−0.17	0.84	1.34	0.25	0.50
Peru	0.40	0.26	0.19	0.16	0.24
Venezuela	−0.04	0.21	1.12	−0.10	0.25
Andean region	0.17	0.40	0.58	0.12	0.30

Source: FAO, *Production Yearbook*, various issues.

Factor Shares

Factor shares in output are necessary for calculating total factor productivity, as each factor input has to be weighted by its respective factor share. The factor weights used in growth accounting affect the results of the exercises substantially, because rather big differences exist in growth rates of labor and capital stocks. The three main components of GDP are fixed capital consumption, compensation of employees and operating surplus. This last component must be divided between capital, labor and land income.

In Latin America an important part of the operating surplus, much more than in the advanced countries, consists of labor compensation for the self-employed and these earnings have to be attributed to labor's share. The total capital share has been disaggregated into the capital shares of its three components, residential and non-residential capital and machinery and equipment. In some growth accounting exercises, the individual items in the capital stock are weighted at their total stock value. However, the service flow per unit of capital in machinery and equipment is much higher than from a unit of residential capital. Therefore, the components of the capital stock have been weighted by their asset life, and the resulting disaggregated capital stock shares were multiplied by the national accounts total capital share. For land income, used as a proxy for natural resource endowment, a 10 per cent share was assumed for the whole period based on national accounts estimates.

Results

The exercise allows a quantitative interpretation of economic growth in the Andean countries in the post-war period. The interpretation of total factor productivity is still a matter of debate; here, a step-by step approach has been followed, starting with measurement of total factor productivity, including quantities of factor inputs and doubly augmented total factor productivity, which includes also the quality improvement of the factor inputs.

The finally remaining 'residual' includes advances of knowledge, and it also picks up the net error (positive or negative) in the other estimates as well as the net contribution of other sources of growth for which no estimation was attempted (Denison, 1967). Changes in capital utilization rates can also account for the pro-cyclical behavior of TFP.

Table 4.7 presents the rate of growth of labor, capital and TFP and their relative contribution to GDP growth. The contributions of factor inputs and TFP to output growth vary significantly across countries and, within each country, between periods. Capital inputs are consistently an important source of economic growth while the contribution of labor and especially total factor productivity is more volatile.

The sources-of-growth analysis shows that total factor productivity growth has been in a declining trend since 1973. From a relatively high level during the period 1950–73, total factor productivity growth has declined sharply in the last quarter-century. In fact, for the Andean group as a whole, the average TFP growth was 2.5 per cent in the 1950–73 period, falling to 0.2 per cent in 1990–2002 (see bottom of Table 4.7). The average TFP growth rate was a meager 0.8 per cent in 1950–2002. The corresponding contribution of TFP growth to output growth in the same period is around 20 per cent. This is a small contribution if judged by international standards. In Korea, Taiwan, Hong Kong and Singapore TFP growth explains between 44 to 47 per cent of total growth in the period 1960–95 (see Iwata, Khan and Murao, 2003), more than twice the contribution of TFP in the Andean countries.

Table 4.7   Andean region: sources of growth, 1950–2002

	Rate of growth			Contribution of the factor		
	GDP	*L*	*K*	*L*	*K*	TFP
Bolivia						
1950–1973	3.43	0.57	2.43	0.38	0.81	2.24
1973–1980	2.95	2.92	4.62	1.94	1.54	−0.53
1980–1990	0.20	2.81	1.65	1.88	0.55	−2.22
1990–2002	3.49	2.87	3.59	1.92	1.20	0.37
1950–2002	2.76	1.85	2.84	1.23	0.95	0.58
Colombia						
1950–1973	5.13	2.03	3.79	1.22	1.54	2.38
1973–1980	4.98	3.04	5.14	1.89	1.95	1.15
1980–1990	3.42	1.96	4.68	1.11	2.01	0.30
1990–2002	2.51	1.26	3.20	0.67	1.47	0.37
1950–2002	4.18	1.97	4.01	1.16	1.67	1.35
Ecuador						
1950–1973	6.19	1.24	5.51	0.72	2.31	3.15
1973–1980	6.37	2.80	8.07	1.69	3.20	1.48
1980–1990	2.18	4.33	4.89	2.66	1.88	−2.37
1990–2002	2.22	3.12	2.38	2.00	0.86	−0.65
1950–2002	4.52	2.48	5.01	1.52	2.02	0.99
Peru						
1950–1973	5.34	1.74	5.11	1.01	2.14	2.19
1973–1980	3.66	2.75	6.24	1.66	2.49	−0.49
1980–1990	−0.86	2.69	3.03	1.65	1.17	−3.68
1990–2002	3.93	2.82	2.61	1.81	0.93	1.19
1950–2002	3.60	2.31	4.29	1.41	1.72	0.47
Venezuela						
1950–1973	6.48	2.87	6.19	2.03	1.67	2.78
1973–1980	4.16	5.02	7.94	2.97	3.25	−2.07
1980–1990	0.74	1.82	2.85	0.92	1.36	−1.54
1990–2002	1.26	2.94	0.02	1.35	0.01	−0.10
1950–2002	3.86	2.98	4.36	1.79	1.44	0.63
Andean region						
1950–1973	5.32	1.69	4.61	1.07	1.69	2.55
1973–1980	4.42	3.30	6.40	2.03	2.49	−0.09
1980–1990	1.14	2.72	3.42	1.64	1.39	−1.90
1990–2002	2.68	2.60	2.36	1.55	0.89	0.24
1950–2002	3.78	2.32	4.10	1.42	1.56	0.80

Notes:
Capital is machinery and equipment, non-residential structures (*K*).
Labor is hours worked (*L*).
Andean region is arithmetic average for the five countries.

Source: Authors' elaboration.

Table 4.8   *Andean region: sources of growth including natural resources*
          and adjustments for human capital and quality of physical
          capital, 1950–2002

	Rate of growth				Contribution of the factor			
	GDP	N	L	K	N	L	K	TFP
Bolivia								
1950–1973	3.43	0.63	2.05	2.43	0.06	0.49	0.95	1.93
1973–1980	3.30	0.69	4.31	4.56	0.07	1.84	1.67	−0.28
1980–1990	0.06	0.38	4.34	1.80	0.04	1.86	0.70	−2.54
1990–2002	3.58	0.41	4.38	3.46	0.04	1.88	1.31	0.34
1950–2002	2.76	0.58	3.33	2.84	0.06	1.26	1.09	0.36
Colombia								
1950–1973	5.13	0.80	3.42	3.79	0.08	1.24	1.65	2.17
1973–1980	5.20	0.03	4.23	5.14	0.00	1.83	2.04	1.33
1980–1990	3.48	−0.10	3.59	4.73	−0.01	1.09	2.13	0.27
1990–2002	2.65	−0.18	2.45	3.24	−0.02	0.75	1.71	0.21
1950–2002	4.18	0.31	3.35	4.01	0.03	1.18	1.81	1.16
Ecuador								
1950–1973	6.19	−0.08	2.17	5.51	−0.01	0.74	2.47	2.98
1973–1980	8.74	0.84	3.76	7.57	0.08	1.61	3.27	3.78
1980–1990	2.43	1.34	5.23	5.19	0.13	2.42	2.00	−2.13
1990–2002	2.28	0.27	4.07	2.46	0.03	2.01	1.02	−0.77
1950–2002	4.52	0.40	3.38	5.01	0.04	1.46	2.14	0.89
Peru								
1950–1973	5.34	0.65	1.87	5.11	0.07	0.92	2.21	2.14
1973–1980	3.87	0.26	6.10	6.29	0.03	1.81	2.49	−0.46
1980–1990	−0.37	0.19	4.77	3.11	0.02	1.70	1.25	−3.35
1990–2002	3.21	0.15	3.96	2.58	0.01	1.74	0.96	0.49
1950–2002	3.60	0.39	3.53	4.29	0.04	1.39	1.77	0.40
Venezuela								
1950–1973	6.48	0.59	4.56	6.19	0.06	2.00	1.72	2.70
1973–1980	4.42	0.21	7.57	7.53	0.02	2.95	3.23	−1.78
1980–1990	0.49	1.12	4.28	3.13	0.11	1.20	1.66	−2.48
1990–2002	1.66	−0.09	4.14	0.05	−0.01	1.31	0.29	0.08
1950–2002	3.86	0.47	4.76	4.36	0.05	1.79	1.59	0.44
Andean region								
1950–1973	5.32	0.52	2.81	4.61	0.05	1.08	1.80	2.38
1973–1980	5.11	0.40	5.19	6.22	0.04	2.01	2.54	0.52
1980–1990	1.22	0.58	4.44	3.60	0.06	1.65	1.55	−2.04
1990–2002	2.68	0.11	3.80	2.36	0.01	1.54	1.06	0.07
1950–2002	3.78	0.43	3.67	4.10	0.04	1.42	1.68	0.65

Notes:
N is arable land, permanent crop land, permanent pasture and forest land.
L is hours worked adjusted for level of education.
K is machinery, equipment and non-residential structures adjusted for quality of capital.
Andean region is the arithmetic unweighted average for the five countries.

Source: Authors' elaboration.

Within the Andean group we detect considerable differences in TFP growth but around a low mean value. Colombia registered the highest TFP growth in the period 1950–2002 (1.35 per cent) and the lowest is obtained in Peru, although TFP growth accelerated in Peru in the 1990s.

In Table 4.8 we include the land and the measurement of quality effects, education in the case of labor and embodied technical progress in the case of capital, in our estimate of total factor productivity. As was to be expected, the resulting measure shows highly negative values for long periods of time, especially since 1973, in most Andean countries.

4.4 EMPIRICAL ANALYSIS OF GROWTH DETERMINANTS FOR THE ANDEAN COUNTRIES

The previous section of the chapter provided estimates of the relative contribution of factor accumulation and total factor productivity growth to GDP growth in the Andean region.[7] In this section we will look, empirically, at the determinants of the process of economic growth in these countries using semi-reduced forms. For this purpose we shall estimate growth equations for (1) a panel that combines a cross section of five Andean countries for the period 1927–2000 and (2) for each of the five Andean countries in the period 1950–2000.

The variables can be grouped in five blocks: (1) economic initial conditions and demographic control variables, (2) investment rates, (3) variables reflecting economic efficiency and competitiveness, (4) variables measuring macroeconomic instability and (5) governance and institutional variables.

Initial Conditions

An important property of the neoclassical growth models of Ramsey (1928), Solow (1956), Cass (1965) and Koopmans (1965) is the convergence property. This property indicates that a country with a small level of initial GDP per capita, relative to steady-state, is expected to grow faster than a rich country. Nevertheless if the countries differ in several aspects like economic, institutional, political and social conditions, then the convergence concept can be applied just conditionally. The convergence property derives from assuming decreasing returns to capital. In general, the low to intermediate levels of GDP per capita of the Andean countries would lead us to expect higher growth than richer economies. This has not been observed in practice, however, as we saw in the previous section. However, the idea is to test for conditional not absolute convergence.

Investment Ratio

The investment ratio is included to reflect the effect of accumulation of capital on output growth. The investment ratio is expected to have a positive effect on GDP growth in the transition between steady states. As this transition may take decades, this is still a relevant relationship.[8]

Economic Efficiency and Competitiveness

We include variables reflecting the degree of economic efficiency and competitiveness in static and dynamic resource allocation. Here we include the degree of external openness of the economy and the ratio of government consumption to GDP. The more open the economy, the more competitive influences from the rest of the world. Dynamic effect of international trade have been pointed out by several authors. Romer (1986 and 1990) indicates that a greater diffusion of knowledge caused by international trade can accelerate the rate of productivity growth and GDP growth. On the other hand, Grossman and Helpman (1991) and Romer (1990) find that greater international trade elevates productivity and therefore growth by means of greater availability in specialized inputs. The effect of government consumption (as a share of GDP) on the rate of growth of GDP depends largely on the level of the ratio. Economies with a large (or increasing) ratio of government consumption are expected to displace private investment with depressing effects on the rate of GDP growth.

Macroeconomic Instability

There is ample evidence that macroeconomic instability, measured by the rate of inflation (or its standard deviation) or the volatility of the real exchange rate hampers economic growth. The notion is that macro volatility makes it more difficult to disentangle changes in absolute prices from changes in relative prices and real profitability. The later variables guide investment decisions and innovation activities. Pindyck and Solimano (1993) investigated the effects of high and volatile inflation on private capital formation finding negative effects of inflation level and variability on capital formation for medium to high levels of the inflation rate. Servén and Solimano (1993) also found a negative effect of the variance of the real exchange rate on private investment. Other studies (see the paper collection of Loayza and Soto, 2002, and Andrés and Hernando, 1997) stress the effects of macro instability on GDP growth acting through productivity growth. Some economies of the Andean countries have suffered episodes of severe macro instability in recent decades. Bolivia, for example, had hyperinflation in 1985. Peru suffered very high inflation and recurrent exchange rate crises in the late 1980s and early 1990s. Ecuador experienced an escalating inflation and currency crisis in 1998–99, along with massive output decline. Venezuela experienced relatively high inflation and heavy output decline in the early 2000s, although inflation declined and output recovered afterwards.

Governance and Institutional Variables

Several Andean countries have a high turnover of political authorities and high frequencies of presidential crises, besides above average changes in their constitutions (see Solimano, 2005). Governance conditions, including both political instability, political regimes and quality of institutions can affect economic growth through different channels. Political instability, to the extent that is perceived as changing economic rules and property rights, can deter investment and innovation activity. Low quality institutions also increase the costs of doing business and penalize capital formation and growth. Also we postulate that democracy tends to protect more property rights than authoritarian regimes.[9] We use two variables to denote governance conditions (in a broad sense including political instability and political regimes) in our empirical growth equations: (1) a political instability index that measures the frequency of presidential crises measured as the number of years that are needed for a president to complete his or her (constitutional) presidential term. This index has a range that goes from 0 to 4. A value of the index of 0 indicates the absence of presidential crises (presidents complete their full period). At the other extreme an index of 4 indicates that a president is removed from office when he has completed less than 25 per cent of his presidential period;[10] (2) a binary index of political regimes that takes the value of 1 for democracy and 0 for an authoritarian regime. We define democracy as the case in which the president of the republic is elected in general elections.[11] Conversely, countries in which presidents or chiefs of state assume power by coup d'état or by other extra-constitutional means are not democracies and therefore are classified as authoritarian regimes.

Results

The results obtained with respect to the estimation of the growth equations which have as explanatory variables those discussed above, are presented in Table 4.9 for the panel regressions. The method of estimation is generalized least squares (GLS) which uses lagged values of the explanatory variables as instruments to control for endogeneity. To control for country specific characteristics (institutions, technology, social structure) we work with first difference and to eliminate the time effects, all variables will be taken as

Table 4.9 *Economic growth in the Andean region*

	1927–2000					1950–2000						
	[1]	[2]	[3]	[4]	[5]	[6]	[7]	[8]	[9]	[10]	[11]	[12]
Lagged ratio invesment/ GDP (−2)[b]	0.47 [0.65]	0.08 [0.12]	0.53 [0.77]	0.18 [0.28]	0.09 [0.14]	0.67 [2.44]**	0.5 [1.36]	0.44 [1.67]*	0.60 [2.31]*	0.57 [1.71]*	0.46 [1.87]*	0.54 [2.01]**
Population growth rate[a]	−0.84 [−2.18]**	−0.77 [−2.07]**	−0.83 [−2.23]**	−0.76 [−2.13]**	−0.79 [−2.24]**	−3.99 [−5.52]**	−3.59 [−4.43]**	−3.66 [−5.23]**	−3.95 [−5.53]**	−3.82 [−5.21]**	−3.9 [−5.73]**	−3.80 [−5.36]**
Lagged terms of trade change (−1)[a]	0.02 [2.03]**	0.02 [2.10]**	0.02 [2.17]**	0.02 [2.26]**	0.02 [2.47]**	0.03 [10.99]**	0.03 [9.81]**	0.03 [10.93]**	0.03 [11.83]**	0.03 [11.42]**	0.03 [11.99]**	0.03 [12.58]**
Export plus import/ GDP[a]	0.25 [3.52]**	0.25 [3.67]**	0.26 [3.42]**	0.24 [3.51]**	0.24 [3.46]**	0.45 [11.28]**	0.43 [9.99]**	0.41 [10.52]**	0.44 [11.72]**	0.43 [11.09]**	0.42 [11.37]**	0.42 [11.10]**
Inflation[c]	−0.92 [−1.63]	−0.87 [−1.55]	−0.91 [−1.59]	−0.89 [−1.58]	−0.79 [−1.53]	−0.43 [−0.77]	−0.43 [−0.76]	−0.47 [−0.89]	−0.4 [−0.73]	−0.41 [−0.72]	−0.46 [−0.83]	−0.480 [−0.88]
Ratio government consumption/GDP[b]						−1.67 [−2.14]**	−1.86 [−2.37]**	−1.32 [−1.47]	−1.47 [−1.76]*	−1.63 [−2.16]**	−1.09 [−1.25]	−1.06 [−1.22]
Democracy	−0.65 [−1.38]		−0.64 [−1.41]			−0.61 [−2.03]**			−0.24 [−1.13]			
Lagged democracy (−1)		−0.39 [−0.71]		−0.33 [−0.64]			−0.03 [−0.12]			0.06 [0.18]		
Lagged democracy (−2)					0.67 [1.63]*			0.55 [2.65]**			0.48 [2.76]**	0.41 [1.62]
Index of political crises[a]	0.07 [0.41]	0.07 [0.41]				0.42 [2.84]**	0.31 [2.46]**	0.34 [2.59]**				

Variable												
Lagged index of political crises (−1)[a]	−0.03 [−0.21]	0.03 [0.17]	−0.04 [−0.26]							−0.07 [−1.33]	−0.06 [−0.82]	−0.07 [−1.64]*
Lagged index of political crises (−2)[a]												0.03 [0.34]
Lagged initial GDP (−2)[b]	−2.29 [−3.60]**	−2.36 [−3.51]**	−2.3 [−3.56]**	−2.34 [−3.41]**	−2.42 [−3.52]**	−4.15 [−12.03]**	−4.26 [−9.88]**	−4.4 [−10.89]**	−3.94 [−12.38]**	−4.04 [−10.05]**	−4.14 [−11.63]**	−4.12 [−11.33]**
R−squared	0.45	0.46	0.46	0.46	0.47	0.83	0.81	0.82	0.83	0.83	0.83	0.83
Number of observations	97	97	97	97	97	80	80	80	80	80	80	80

Notes:

Dependent variable: GDP per capita growth rate; regression panel, 1927–2000 (average 3 years).

a. In the regression, this variable is included as first difference.

b. In the regression, this variable is included as first difference of log (variable).

c. In the regression, this variable is included as first difference of log (1+variable).

Method of estimation: GLS with cross-section weights and White Heteroskedasticity. Consistent standard errors and covariances.

Values between parentheses correspond to *t*-student.

*   Significant at 95%.

**   Significant at 90%.

Source: Authors' elaboration.

deviations from the mean of the variables of the model. The first five columns show the estimation for the period 1927–2000 and the following columns show the period 1950–2000. In both, the values in parentheses below the coefficient are the *t*-student test.

Panel Regressions

As the theory predicts, a negative and significant relation is found between the initial level of per capita GDP and its growth rate in the panel regressions for both sample periods. This supports the hypothesis of conditional convergence. The rate of population growth has a negative and significant effect on GDP per capita growth.[12] The investment ratio (lagged) is significant in various specifications (not in all) for the 1950–2002 period. The degree of external openness (lagged) and changes in terms of trade are also significant variables affecting GDP growth. The index of political crisis (lagged[13]) has a negative impact on the rate of GDP growth per capita and is significant at the 90 per cent level (1950–2002 sample). This corroborates our prior belief that political instability has a negative effect on growth. Interestingly the post-1950 period is one of a high frequency of political crises in several Andean countries (see Solimano, 2005). We test, in a simple way, the relation between lagged democracy and economic growth finding a positive and significant relationship between the two variables, particularly in the period 1950–2002.[14] The ratio of government consumption to GDP in the Andean countries has a systematically negative effect on GDP per capita growth in the period 1950–2002. The inflation rate has, in all specifications, a negative sign but the variable is statistically insignificant according to the estimates.

Time-Series Country Estimates

The main results of the time series estimates of growth equations at individual country level for the Andean region in the period 1950–2002 are the following (see Table 4.10):

- Terms of trade changes affect growth. This effect is strongest in Venezuela which can be explained by the importance of the oil sector in this economy.
- The degree of external openness has, in general, a positive effect on GDP per capita growth. This variable is statistically significant in Ecuador and Peru.
- The inflation rate has a negative and significant effect on GDP per capita growth in Bolivia (90 per cent) and in Peru (95 per cent). These

Table 4.10   Economic growth by country, Andean region

	Bolivia [1]	Colombia [2]	Ecuador [3]	Peru [4]	Venezuela [5]
Lagged ratio invesment/ GDP (–2)a	0.06 [2.36]**	–0.03 [–1.11]	0.03 [0.77]	–0.11 [–2.62]**	–0.05 [–1.60]*
Population growth rate	–0.02 [–1.54]	–0.03 [–1.65]*	–0.02 [–0.93]	–0.001 [–0.03]	–0.002 [–0.31]
Lagged terms of trade change (–1)	0.001 [1.54]	0.001 [0.58]	–0.001 [–0.47]	0.001 [1.58]	0.001 [2.31]**
Export plus import/ GDP	0.002 [0.14]	–0.001 [–1.03]	0.005 [3.71]**	0.004 [1.84]*	0.001 [0.79]
Inflationb	–0.01 [–1.72]	–0.03 [–0.56]	0.05 [0.81]	–0.02 [–2.97]**	–0.04 [–0.81]
Ratio government consumption/GDPa	–0.02 [–1.57]	–0.03 [–0.83]	0.14 [3.01]**	0.15 [1.87]	–0.06 [–1.01]
Lagged democracy (–1)		–0.01 [–0.74]		0.01 [0.68]	0.005 [0.86]
Lagged democracy (–2)	0.02 [1.25]		0.01 [0.31]		
Lagged index of political crises (–1)	–0.01 [–1.43]				–0.02 [–1.92]*
Lagged index of political crises (–2)		0.005 [0.78]	–0.01 [–2.30]**	–0.01 [–0.39]	
Lagged initial GDP (–1)a	–0.09 [–2.15]**	–0.02 [–0.51]	–0.21 [–4.51]**	–0.22 [–2.50]*	–0.04 [–0.53]
R–Squared	0.52	0.23	0.58	0.47	0.45
(D–W)	1.94	1.88	2.11	1.94	1.85
Number of Observations	51	51	51	51	51

Notes:
Dependent variable: GDP per capita growth rate; regression panel, 1950–2000.
a.   In the regression, this variable is included as log(variable).
b.   In the regression, this variable is included as log(1+variable).
Method of estimation: OLS.
Values between parentheses correspond to *t*-student.
 *   Significant at 95%.
 **   Significant at 90%.

Source: Authors' elaboration.

results are in line with the inflationary history of both countries in recent decades.

- The ratio of government consumption on GDP has a negative effect on GDP growth that is highly significant in Ecuador. The sign of the coefficient is also negative in Bolivia, Colombia, and Venezuela.
- The index of political crisis (with lags) has a negative effect on growth that is significant in Ecuador and Venezuela.
- We failed to find a significant relationship between democracy and growth at the individual country level.
- Initial GDP has in general a negative and significant negative effect on GDP growth rates supporting the conditional convergence hypothesis.

4.5   FINAL REMARKS

In the first half of the twentieth century the Andean region, on average, grew faster than Latin America. However, after 1973 the Andean group experienced a slowdown in economic growth that has been particularly severe in Ecuador and Venezuela, both oil exporting countries. This under-lines the importance of how the cycles of resource booms are managed to ensure long-run growth. As a consequence of their meager growth perform-ance in the last quarter of the twentieth century, all Andean countries reduced their relative importance to the GDP of the United States (a meas-ure of performance relative to the technological leader). The most dramatic decline in relative economic importance in this period was observed in Venezuela followed by Peru and Ecuador. The smallest relative decline took place in Colombia.

The growth decomposition exercise carried out in this chapter shows low values for total factor productivity for the period 1950–2002 ranging from around 0.5 per cent per year in Bolivia, Venezuela and Peru to 1.3 in Colom-bia. These TFP growth rates are far below what is observed for more dynamic emerging economies, particularly in East Asia.

The econometric analysis shows that variables such as the degree of exter-nal openness, positive terms of trade shocks and the investment ratio have a positive effect on GDP growth per capita in the Andean Group. In contrast, inflation, political instability and the ratio of government consumption to GDP have negative effects on GDP growth. The effects of democracy on growth are captured in the panel regressions but not in the time series esti-mates at country level. Further analysis of the quality of democracy and how it affects economic growth is needed. The econometric evidence of both panel and time series for individual countries supports the hypothesis of conditional convergence, although absolute convergence has been absent in the Andean countries in the last three decades of the twentieth century. This underscores the need to understand better the economic and governance factors behind this divergent growth record of the Andean region.

APPENDIX 4.A

Construction of Variables

Capital   The estimates of the capital stock were generated using the perpetual inventory method. The capital stock considered in this study includes non-residential structures, machinery and equipment. Source: Hofman (2000).

Government consumption   Government consumption consists of expenditure, including imputed expenditure, incurred by general government on both individual consumption goods and services and collective consumption services. Source: Heston and Summers (2002), Penn World Table.

Gross domestic product   Gross domestic product is measured in million 1990 international Geary-Khamis dollars. Source: Maddison (2003).

Index of political crises   This index has a rank from 0 to 4. A value of 1 for the index indicates that the President completes at least 75 per cent of his presidential term; a value of 2, the President fulfills between 50 per cent and 75 per cent of his presidential period; a value of 3, the President completes between 25 per cent and 50 per cent of his presidential period; and a value of 4, is the case in which the President fails to complete 25 per cent of its presidential period. Source: authors' elaboration.

Index of political regime   Dummy variable with 1 = democracy and 0 = authoritarian. Source: authors' elaboration.

Inflation   The inflation is the rate of change in the consumer price index. Source: ECLAC statistical yearbook in different editions.

External openness   External openess is measured like percentage of exports plus imports on the gross domestic product. Source: ECLAC statistical yearbook in different editions and ECLAC (1976).

Labor   Labor input is measured as total hours worked equal to the number of annual hours per person employed times the employment rate. Source: Hofman (2000).

Land   The estimates of land were generated using respective weights of 1 for arable and permanent cropland, 0.3 for permanent pasture and 0.1 for forestland. Source: FAO.

Population   Thousands of population at mid-year. Source: Maddison (2003).

Terms of trade   The terms of trade are calculated on the basis of the unitary value of goods exports divided by the unitary value of goods imports. Source: ECLAC statistical yearbook in different editions and ECLAC (1976).

NOTES

*   We thank Rodrigo Cárcamo for comments on a previous version of this chapter. The usual disclaimer applies.
1.   References for Colombia are Ocampo (2005) and for Ecuador, Beckerman and Solimano (2002). A comparative analysis of governance conditions in the Andean region appears in Solimano (2005).
2.   Venezuela's GDP grew from the early 1920s to 1930 at the unprecedented average annual rate of 13 per cent.
3.   This is a comparative benchmark corresponding to the rate of growth per capita of the United States in the twentieth century: see Kehoe and Prescott (2002).
4.   See Hofman (2000) for a more elaborate treatment, with respect to data sources and estimation procedures, of human capital.
5.   See Maddison (1972 and 1987), Denison (1967) and Psacharopoulos (1984) for the rationale of the education adjustment.
6.   See Hofman (2000) for a more detailed treatment of capital stock estimation and its limitations.
7.   Growth accounting can only explain part of the process of economic growth, it does not take into consideration other factors such as economic policy, the national and international environments and non-economic factors such as natural disasters and war. These belong to the realm of what is now generally termed the ultimate causes for growth, in contrast to the proximate causes of growth analyzed earlier.
8.   In the Solow model, the rate of growth of GDP in steady state is independent of the investment ratio and depends only on the exogenous rate of technical progress and the rate of population growth. Still the transitional dynamics of growth may span over decades so it is empirically relevant.
9.   Barro (2000) discusses the various effects on how democracy can affect growth. An earlier analysis of the subject is Przeworski and Limogni (1993).
10. A value of 1 for the index indicates that the president completes at least 75 per cent of his presidential term; a value of 2, that the President fulfills between 50 and 75 per cent of his presidential period; a value of 3, the President completes between 25 per cent and 50 per cent of his presidential period; and a value of 4, is the case in which the president fails to complete 25 per cent of his presidential period.
11. An important and complex issue is the quality of democracy but it will not be considered here.
12. Accelerated population growth may have a negative effect on GDP per capita growth if it leads to greater dependency ratios from active population to younger (and older) cohorts.
13. There exists a strong theoretical argument that the index of political crisis and the democracy variable should be expected to be endogenous. We propose to solve these problems by using their lagged values.

14. It is worth noting that in the second half of the twentieth century, democracy was more stable (with a lower frequency of presidential crises) in Colombia and Venezuela than in Ecuador, Peru and Bolivia.

REFERENCES

Andrés, I. and J. Hernando (1997), 'Does inflation harm growth? Evidence for the OECD', National Bureau for Economic Research working paper 6062, June.

Barro, R. (2000), *Determinants of Economic Growth. A Cross-country Empirical Study*, Cambridge, MA: MIT Press.

Beckerman, P. and A. Solimano (eds) (2002), *Crisis and Dollarization in Ecuador. Stability, Growth and Social Equity*, Washington, DC: World Bank.

Cass, D. (1965), 'Optimun growth in an aggregative model of capital accumulation', *Review of Economic Studies*, **32**.

Denison, E.F. (1967), *Why Growth Rates Differ*, Washington, DC: Brookings Institution.

Economic Commission for Latin America and the Caribbean (ECLAC), *Statistical Yearbook for Latin America and the Caribbean*, various issues, Santiago, Chile.

ECLAC (1976), 'America Latina: Relación de Precios del Intercambio', Cuadernos Estadisticos de la CEPAL, Santiago: United Nations.

FAO, *Production Yearbook*, various issues, Rome, Italy.

Goldsmith, R.W. (1952), *The Growth of Reproducible Wealth in the United States of America from 1805 to 1950: Income and Wealth*, series II, London: International Association for Research in Income and Wealth (Bowes and Bowes).

Grossman, G. and E. Helpman (1991), *Innovation and Growth in the Global Economy*, Cambridge, MA: MIT Press.

Heston, Alan and Robert Summers (1992), 'The Penn World Table (Mark 5): an exapanded set of international comparisons, 1950–1988', *Quarterly Journal of Economics*, **106**, 327–1988.

Hofman, A. (2000), *The Economic Development of Latin America in the Twentieth Century*, Cheltenham, UK and Northampton, MA, USA: Edward Elgar.

Iwata, S., M. Kahn and H. Murao (2003), 'Sources of growth in East Asia: a nonparametric approach', *International Monetary Fund Staff Papers*, **50** (2).

Kehoe, T. and E. Prescott (2002), 'Great depressions of the twentieth century', *Review of Economic Dynamics*, **5** (1), 1–18.

Koopmans, T. (1965). 'On the concept of optimal economic growth', in *The Econometric Approach to Development Planning*, Amsterdam: North Holland.

Loayza, Norman and Raimundo Soto (2002), 'The sources of economic growth: an overview', in N. Loayza and R. Soto (eds), *Economic Growth: Sources, Trends and Cycles*, Santiago: Banco Central de Chile.

Maddison, A. (1972), 'Explaining economic growth', *Banca Nazionale Del Lavoro Quarterly Review*, **25** (September), 211–62.

Maddison, A. (1987), 'Growth and slowdown in advanced capitalist economies: techniques of quantitative assessment', *Journal of Economic Literature*, **25** (2), June.

Maddison, A. (2003), *The World Economy: Historical Statistics*, Paris: OECD Development Centre Studies.

Ocampo, J.A. (2005), 'The economy, conflict and governance in Colombia', in A. Salimano (ed.) *Political Crises, Social Conflict and Economic Development. The*

Political Economy of the Andean Region, Cheltenham, UK and Northampton, MA: Edward Elgar.

Pindyck, R. and A. Solimano (1993), *Economic Instability and Aggregate Investment*, National Bureau for Economic Research Macroeconomics, Cambridge, MA: MIT Press.

Przeworski, A. and F. Limogni (1993), 'Political regimes and economic growth', *Journal of Economic Perspectives*, **7**, 51–69.

Psacharopoulos, G. (1984), 'The contribution of education to economic growth: international comparisons', in John W. Kendrick (ed.), *International Comparisons of Productivity and Causes of Slowdown*, Cambridge, MA: Ballinger.

Ramsey, F. (1928), 'A mathematical theory of saving', *Economic Journal*, **38**.

Romer, P. (1986), 'Increasing returns and long run growth', *Journal of Political Economy*, **94**, 1002–37.

Romer, P. (1990), 'Endogenous technological change', *Journal of Political Economy*, **98**, 71–102.

Servén, L. and A. Solimano (eds) (1993), *Striving for Growth after Adjustment: the Role of Capital Formation*, Washington, DC: World Bank.

Solimano, A. (2003), 'Governance crises and the Andean region: a political economy analysis', *Serie Macroeconomía del Desarrollo*, **23**, ECLAC.

Solimano, A. (ed.) (2005), *Political Crises, Social Conflict and Economic Development: The Political Economy of the Andean Region*, Cheltenham, UK and Northampton, MA, USA: Edward Elgar.

Solow, R. (1956), 'A contribution to the theory of economic growth', *Quarterly Journal of Economics*, **70**, 65–94.

5. Economic growth in Central America

Manuel R. Agosin and Roberto Machado

5.1 INTRODUCTION

Since Robert Barro (1991) gave rise to an abundance of empirical literature on economic growth, many subsequent applied studies have included in their explanations of growth variables related to, inter alia, the accumulation of physical and human capital, macroeconomic stability, level of openness of the economy, availability of external financing, conditions of world trade and the level of institutional development. Despite this voluminous literature, there are no specific studies on Central American countries.[1] This study aims to facilitate understanding of the factors behind economic growth in these countries since 1960, paying special attention to the 1990s. The study is based on stylized facts of growth in Central America, and a theory that is extremely simple but one that is believed to capture the special characteristics of these countries.

The determining factors of economic growth were studied in the following seven countries: Costa Rica, the Dominican Republic, El Salvador, Guatemala, Honduras, Nicaragua and Panama. Belize is also included in the descriptive analysis. Not only do these countries share a geographical location (except the Dominican Republic) and a common history, they also have very similar production structures and resources: historically, they are all exporters of tropical crops (coffee, bananas and sugar) and, over the last decade, have all increasingly specialized in tourism and in processing manufacturing products (mainly clothing) for the United States market.[2] With the exception of Costa Rica and Panama, all the countries have experienced considerable migration over the past two decades and are now receiving significant volumes of family remittances that represent between 8 per cent and probably around 20 per cent of GDP.

The last few decades have been economically, socially and politically turbulent for most of the countries under discussion. Most have suffered prolonged periods of political instability, institutional unrest and even civil wars. They were also seriously affected by dramatic external disturbances such as the oil shocks of 1973 and 1979 and the foreign debt crisis that broke out in 1982. All of this makes econometric work particularly difficult, given the various peaks and breaks in statistical series. The usual way of dealing with such breaks is to include several dummy variables. In practice, this isolates observations where there are structural changes, thereby losing information that could be valuable for policy recommendations and implications based on econometric estimations.

The following section includes a brief overview of empirical literature on economic growth, with the emphasis on the influence of the accumulation of not only productive factors but also 'deep' growth factors, such as the endowment of natural resources, integration in the world economy, and institutions. Section 5.3 comprises a discussion of growth in recent decades compared with other developing countries. Section 5.4 provides a decomposition of growth according to productivity factors and increases in productivity. Section 5.5 presents the results of econometric estimates for a data panel of the seven countries during the period 1971–2000. Section 5.6 gives estimated functions to explain investment variations in machinery and equipment, the level of human capital and institutional development, all of which are part of this theory of growth in Central America. The main conclusions of the chapter are presented in the final section.

5.2   ACCUMULATION OF FACTORS AND DEEP DETERMINING FACTORS OF ECONOMIC GROWTH

Conventional literature points to two main sources of economic growth: productive factors (labor and physical and human capital) and the increased productivity of those factors. This perspective has given rise to a considerable number of empirical studies on 'growth accounting' that attempt to determine the relative contribution of each factor to the growth rate of per capita GDP. The basic formula is:

$$\hat{y} = \alpha\hat{k} + (1-\alpha)\hat{h} + \lambda, \tag{5.1}$$

in which y is GDP per worker, k is physical capital per worker, h is human capital per worker, λ is the growth rate of total factor productivity (TFP), and α is capital-output elasticity. A circumflex accent above a variable indicates a percentage growth rate.

Equation (5.1) shows that growth of per capita GDP is explained by the accumulation of physical and human capital per worker and by improvements in TFP. The value of λ is simply the residual of the regression of (5.1), or can be calculated by replacing the values for growth rate of output, physical and human capital once a value has been assigned to α, which can be interpreted as the participation of capital in GDP in a competition model. The human capital variable is based on several indicators such as the gross enrollment ratio at the various levels of education and the average number of years of schooling of the workforce.

However, breaking down growth into accumulated factors and the residual (TFP) does not provide a deeper understanding of what underlies the process insofar as growth, the accumulation of physical/human capital and increases in TFP are all endogenous, and relations of causality therefore operate in several directions.

Indeed, in the same way that greater accumulation of physical and human capital stimulate growth, so growth has a positive effect on the accumulation of factors as it increases resources available for investment. Also, investment in physical capital may be encouraged by increased training of the workforce, and the accumulation of human capital could be positively affected by investment in physical capital, in that it creates a demand for qualified workers and is conducive to 'learning by doing'.

Acknowledgement of these limitations has resulted in attempts to seek more fundamental sources of economic growth that do not have the problem of growth, accumulation of factors and improvements in TFP being jointly endogenous. In particular, endowment in natural resources, integration into the world economy (international trade, availability of external finance and foreign investment) and institutional development have been identified as 'deep' sources of economic growth. However, as pointed out by Rodrik (2001), only the first of the three is genuinely endogenous, whereas the other two are partially endogenous to growth but also exhibit many exogenous characteristics such as their high sensitivity to public policies. The concept of social capital has also been incorporated as another source of economic growth. This refers to a society's prevailing civil norms, the trust between inhabitants, the capacity to generate social consensus and the level of cooperation between various individuals and groups.

Endowment in natural resources is a key aspect of growth because it has a decisive influence on the allocation of productive factors and determines the comparative advantages of a country and its level of international integration. History also has much influence on institutional development, given that the latter depends largely on countries' colonial past and the type of institutions established there. Endowment in natural resources and history are therefore the only factors that are genuinely exogenous to growth.

Taking advantage of comparative advantages, exploiting economies of scale and the competition of foreign producers usually stimulates the development of an economy's tradable goods sector. In the same way, openness to international trade enables developing countries to import capital goods (which are hardly ever produced domestically) and incorporate technical progress since a significant part of the technology used by developing countries comes with imported machinery and equipment. The availability of external financing complements national savings for funding investment into production. Foreign direct investment not only increases production capacity but also often introduces improved technology and has positive effects on the rest of the economy. This means that adequate integration into the world economy is decisive for achieving consistently high rates of growth.

However, it is also possible for an economy's trade to depend on its growth rate, either because it produces more than it needs to satisfy internal demand, or because high levels of income facilitate imports (including those of capital goods). Also, a rapidly growing economy may have better access to external financing. In spite of this, integration in the world economy would only be partially endogenous to economic growth, given that such integration is highly dependent on the trade regime, regulations of the financial system, exchange rate policy and the level of openness of the capital account.

Lastly, institutions are crucial for economic growth because the existence and efficiency of markets and public and private organizations depend on them. In fact, investment in physical and human capital and the rate of technical progress are mainly dependent on institutions (Burki and Perry, 1998).[3] Institutional aspects such as rule of law, bureaucratic efficiency and power of the judiciary are determining factors when local or foreign enterprises are deciding where to invest. These factors also affect the rest of the world's willingness to provide financing and the willingness of foreign producers to trade with their local counterparts. Institutions therefore influence growth, accumulation of factors and TFP as much as they affect a country's integration in the world economy.

However, institutional development can also be the result rather than the cause of economic growth. Indeed, the experience of developed countries shows that institutions became strengthened following a period of growth. Similarly, a population with very high levels of education would strengthen institutional development due to the availability of more qualified workers and greater respect for the law. Nevertheless, as is the case for integration in the world economy, institutional development is highly dependent on public policies. Institutions are therefore only partly endogenous to growth. In addition, countries' increasing integration into the world economy results in their institutions adapting to international standards from the World Trade Organization and various multilateral and regional agencies. Institutions and integration into the world economy therefore both influence each other.

All of the above is summarized in Figure 5.1 (similar to that of Rodrik, 2001), where arrows represent causality and factors endogenous to growth (in rectangles) can be distinguished from semi-endogenous and exogenous fac-

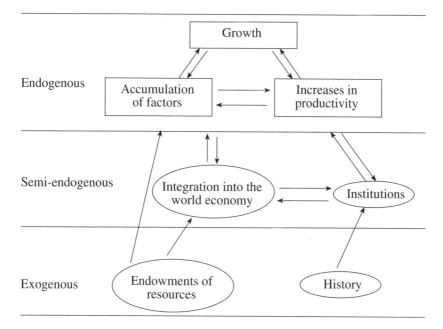

Source: Authors' elaboration based on a similar diagram in Rodrik (2001).

Figure 5.1   Determining factors of economic growth

tors (ovals). In this model, economic policy has an effect on semi-endogenous factors and development policy should therefore be aimed at changing those very factors.

5.3   ECONOMIC GROWTH DURING THE LAST FEW DECADES

Growth in Central America[4] over the last few decades has been characteristically slower than that of leading world economies. Even in comparison with other countries in Latin America, the performance of Central America has been less than satisfactory. Figure 5.2 shows per capita GDP in Central America (measured in current international dollars) as a proportion of per capita GDP in the United States.[5] The countries in Central America can be divided into two groups. The best performers, with the exception of Panama, are the middle-income countries (Belize, Costa Rica and the Dominican Republic) and have remained at a more or less constant difference with the United States since 1975. The difference between the United States and the lower-income countries

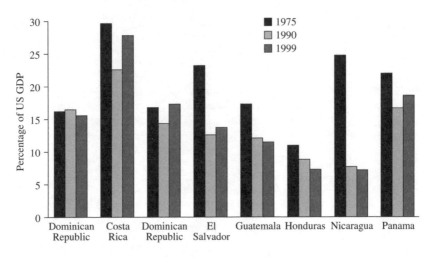

Source: World Bank, *World Development Indicators* (2002).

Figure 5.2   *Central America: per capita GDP in international dollars for each year, as a proportion of the per capita GDP of the United States, 1975–99*

(El Salvador, Guatemala, Honduras and Nicaragua) and Panama has tended to increase during the same period. Nicaragua has the most significant lag in relative terms: in 1975, its per capita GDP was a quarter of the level of the United States, whereas today it represents less than a tenth.[6]

In other words, Central American countries have not been able to take advantage of being behind, that is the ability to absorb technology developed by leading economies, accumulate capital more quickly than them and rapidly approach their levels of income. In Central America, there is no absolute convergence with leading economies in the countries with the best performance and there is absolute divergence is in those lagging farthest behind.

It is illustrative to compare Central American countries with other small, emerging economies such as Chile, Hong Kong, Ireland, Mauritius and Singapore.

Chile and Mauritius are small, open economies that have been traditionally dependent on natural resources. Both of them, like Central American countries, based their initial industrialization strategy on import substitution, which was nevertheless abandoned during the 1970s. The successes of Mauritius in the 1990s were closely linked to exports of clothing produced in free-trade zones, as is the case of some Central American countries (Romer, 1993; Dabee, 2001). Chile has based its production diversification on exports of goods associated with its comparative natural advantages but with greater sophistication. This strategy has also been adopted by some Central American countries (Agosin, 1999).

Unlike those mentioned above, the economies of Hong Kong, Ireland and Singapore have few natural resources and export manufacturing and services. However, they are similar to Central American countries in their small population and openness to foreign trade. Costa Rica has consciously attempted to emulate some of their modernization strategies based on exports and foreign investment.

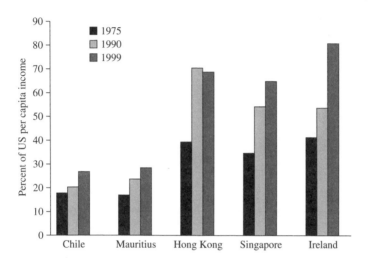

Source: World Bank, World Development Indicators (2002).

Figure 5.3   *Reference countries: Per capita GDP in international dollars for each year, as a proportion of the per capita GDP of the United States, 1975–99*

As can be seen in Figure 5.3, the economic performance of these countries has been superior to that of Central American countries. All of them have been approaching levels of income in the United States, and Ireland, Mauritius and Singapore can now be considered developed countries. In 1975, per capita income in Chile and Mauritius was lower than several Central American countries, and now is closer to the level in the United States than that in Central America. In the past 25 years, Hong Kong and Singapore have practically doubled their per capita income in comparison with the United States (from 37 per cent to 67 per cent). During the same period, per capita income in Ireland has dramatically closed the gap with the United States (from 40 per cent to 80 per cent).

Table 5.1   Growth of real per capita GDP, 1961–2000 (percentage)

	1961–1970	1971–1980	1981–1990	1991–2000	1991–1995	1996–2000
Belize	2.3	5.3	2.4	1.4	1.5	1.2
Costa Rica	2.0	2.8	–0.3	3.2	3.4	3.1
Dominican Republic	2.9	4.3	0.4	4.1	2.2	6.0
El Salvador	2.2	0.0	–1.4	2.4	4.0	0.9
Guatemala	2.6	2.9	–1.6	1.4	1.6	1.1
Honduras	1.6	2.1	–0.7	0.3	0.6	0.1
Nicaragua	3.5	–2.2	–4.1	0.5	1.4	2.4
Panama	4.8	1.5	–0.5	2.7	3.6	1.8
Average[b]	2.7	1.9	–1.0	2.3	2.3	2.3
Reference countries						
Latin American and the Caribbean[b]	2.4	3.3	–0.9	1.6	1.9	1.2
Chile	1.8	1.2	2.1	4.9	6.9	2.9
Mauritius[c]	0.6	4.2	5.1	3.8	3.7	3.9
Singapore[c]	7.3	7.4	4.8	4.4	6.0	2.4

Notes:
a.   In 1995 prices.
b.   Weighted average, in 1995 dollars.
c.   For Mauritius and Singapore, growth rates during the 1990s refer to the period 1991–1999.

Sources: Authors' estimates on the basis of official sources and the World Bank, *World Development Indicators*.

During the decades preceding the armed conflicts that devastated (or indirectly affected) many of the region's countries (Nicaragua, Guatemala, El Salvador and Honduras), the average growth of Central American economies was quite acceptable (see Table 5.1). During the 1960s, the average growth rate of GDP was 6 per cent per year, which resulted in an annual growth rate of per capita GDP of 2.7 per cent. These figures compare favorably with other developing regions. During the 1970s, the average annual growth rate of GDP was 5.9 per cent and that of per capita GDP was 3.2 per cent, except in El Salvador and Nicaragua, which were already experiencing serious political upheavals.

The 1980s were characterized by the breakdown caused by armed conflict and external crises. The result of such adverse factors was that per capita GDP decreased by an average of 1 per cent in the eight countries under consideration. During the 1990s, circumstances conducive to growth included the following: (1) return to peace in countries affected by civil war; (2) recovery of foreign direct investment and access to the international capital market following a decade marked by the debt crisis; (3) implementation of reforms aimed at strengthening the market economy and opening the economy to foreign trade and investment; and (4) strengthening of the Central American Common Market (CACM). Growth accelerated significantly during the 1990s (total GDP at 4.7 per cent per year and per capita GDP at 2.3 per cent), but did not equal the buoyancy of the 1960s or 1970s.

The growth rates of the eight countries varied significantly between the first and second halves of the 1990s. Some experienced reduced growth rates during the second half of the decade (El Salvador, Costa Rica, Honduras, Guatemala and Panama) whereas the other three (Belize, the Dominican Republic and Panama) experienced higher growth rates in the second half than in the first. The growth rate of the Dominican Republic during the second half of the 1990s was one of the highest in the world. In Nicaragua, the first five years were characterized by major reforms that had positive results in terms of growth: reestablishment of democracy and a market economy, improved macroeconomic stability and a dramatic reduction of military expenditure (from 28 per cent of GDP in 1990 to 1.5 per cent in 1996). In El Salvador, on the other hand, the end of the civil war gave rise to a rapid economic recovery in the first half of the decade, but that buoyancy subsequently trailed off significantly.

External disturbances associated with the global economic slowdown since 2000 have left most of the region's countries in a very vulnerable situation, and per capita GDP in almost all of them is falling once again.

5.4   GROWTH ACCOUNTING

In order to determine what proportion of growth rates were related to the accumulation of physical capital and how much could be attributed to quantitative and qualitative increases in the workforce, a decomposition of growth was carried out for those countries with the necessary statistics (Belize was not included in the exercise due to a lack of information). Although this was already stated earlier, it should be pointed out that this decomposition does not imply causal connexion but indicates where to concentrate on seeking out the ultimate causes of economic growth.

The decomposition exercise used a Cobb–Douglas production function with constant returns to scale, capital participation in output equal to one-third and a 5 per cent depreciation of capital stock (in construction, machinery and equipment). Sensitivity analyses were also carried out with a higher

Table 5.2 Annual growth rates of GDP and contribution to growth of capital, labor and productivity, 1991–99 (percentage)

	GDP (1)	K (2)	K* (3)	K** (3a)	L (4)	H (5)	L* (6)=(4)+(5)	TFP (7)=(1)-(2)-(4)	TFP* (8)=(1)-(3)-(6)	TFP** (9)
Costa Rica	4.5	1.7	1.8	–	1.7	0.4	2.1	1.1	0.6	–
Dom. Republic	5.8	2.2	2.3	–	1.8	0.4	2.2	1.7	1.2	–
El Salvador	4.9	1.3	1.4	–	2.4	0.7	3.1	1.2	0.4	–
Guatemala	4.1	1.2	1.3	–	2.2	0.3	2.6	0.7	0.2	–
Honduras	3.0	1.8	2.0	1.2	2.5	0.5	3.0	-1.3	-1.9	-1.2
Nicaragua	3.2	0.5	0.6	0.2	2.6	0.7	3.4	0.1	-0.8	-0.4
Panama	4.7	2.0	2.2	–	1.8	0.4	2.1	0.9	0.4	–
Average	4.3	1.5	1.7	1.5	2.2	0.5	2.6	0.6	0.0	0.2

Note: The first column refers to growth of GDP and the following columns refer to the contributions of capital, labor and total factor productivity.

Source: Authors' calculations based on national accounts. The original data is in national currencies at constant prices

participation of capital and different depreciation rates. These showed that the initial results were reliable. Given that the proportion of gross investment in (generally imported) machinery has an element of increased productivity, the capital stock was adjusted accordingly. Labor input was also corrected because of the productivity increase based on education.[7]

Table 5.2 shows that a third of the annual growth rate during 1991–99 (1.5 percentage points to 4.3) was due to an increase in the rate of accumulation of physical capital (column 2) and half (2.2 percentage points) was due to an increase in the workforce (column 4).[8] The remaining proportion of 0.6 percentage points (column 7) is attributable to the increase in total factor productivity (TFP). This represents growth due to increases in efficiency using basic productive inputs.

The variables that appear in Table 5.2 are as follows:

K = capital stock;

K^* = capital, corrected for the quality of gross investment in machinery and equipment;

K^{**} = K^* corrected for the effects of Hurricane Mitch in Honduras and Nicaragua;

L = labor force;

L^* = labor force corrected for productivity = LH;

H = index of productivity of workforce coming from schooling. It was assumed that $H = \exp(\phi^* s)$ where s is the number of years schooling in the workforce and ϕ is the return on an additional year of education (using a value of 0.10);

TFP = total factor productivity;

TFP^* = TFP adjusted for quality ('residual of residuals');

TFP^{**} = TFP adjusted for quality and the effects of Hurricane Mitch in Honduras and Nicaragua.

As far as individual countries are concerned, there are a variety of factors to explain growth. In Costa Rica, the Dominican Republic and El Salvador, the annual increase in TFP was between 1.1 per cent and 1.7 per cent. In Guatemala and Panama, TFP increased at an annual rate somewhat below 1 per cent. Nicaragua experienced no increases in productivity and, in Honduras, TFP decreased by an annual rate of 1.3 per cent. This was probably a result of an underestimation of the growth rate of GDP, rather than a secular fall in productivity.

According to Denison (1967), TFP is a measure of our ignorance. In other words, the economy as a whole could have been more productive because of various factors included in TFP. There are many factors for adjusting capital and labor input and this study concentrates on two: an increase in labor productivity due to education and an increase in the productivity of capital from imported capital goods. The analysis is restricted to these two sources of improved quality of inputs because they are considered very important for the region's countries and because there was no statistical data on other factors.

These estimates are included in the columns marked with an asterisk in Table 5.2. For the seven countries as a whole, the contribution of labor goes from 2.2 per cent to 2.6 per cent (column 6). The contribution of capital also increases (column 3) but to a lesser extent (1.5 per cent to 1.7 per cent). The reason for this is that the rate of investment in all countries was relatively low and only a modest proportion was invested in machinery and equipment.

In the case of the workforce, the difference between the unadjusted contribution and the contribution adjusted for productivity is the largest in those countries that made more efforts to improve schooling of the population. This is why the contribution of schooling to growth (column 5) is striking in El Salvador and Nicaragua (0.7 per cent) and much more modest in more advanced countries (Costa Rica, the Dominican Republic and Panama) where education contributed to a 0.4 per cent increase in the rate of growth. In other words, some of the poorest countries made significant efforts to improve schooling during the 1990s and were gradually catching up with the more prosperous countries in the region. The exception was Guatemala, where the increase in schooling was insufficient and only contributed to growth by 0.3 per cent per year.

As might be expected, the adjustments carried out for capital and labor input reduce the contribution of TFP growth (column 8). For the seven countries, the simple average contribution of TFP is now close to zero instead of the 0.6 per cent without adjustments (column 7). The figures vary from 1.2 per cent for the Dominican Republic to –0.8 per cent for Nicaragua and –1.9 per cent for Honduras.

There is evidence that points to the growth rate of Honduras during the 1990s having been underestimated. Indeed, whereas the national accounts show a growth rate of per capita GDP of 0.3 per cent, household surveys show an annual growth rate of average household income of 1.8 per cent (UNDP, 2000, pp 55–6). If the underestimate were corrected, the annual growth rate of GDP in Honduras would increase from 3 per cent to 4.5 per cent. This would considerably mitigate the annual fall of TFP, which would only be –0.4 per cent after such a correction. A similar adjustment should be carried out for Nicaragua, but the necessary information is not available.

Another possibility is that the capital contribution has been overestimated for both countries because of the effects of Hurricane Mitch, which destroyed a significant proportion of productive capital in 1998. On the assumption that the hurricane destroyed 20 per cent of the productive capacity of Honduras and 10 per cent of Nicaragua's, the contribution to growth of quality-adjusted capital goes down from 2 per cent to 1.2 per cent in Honduras and from 0.6 per cent to 0.2 per cent in Nicaragua (column 3a). On the basis of these assumptions, the contribution of TFP (adjusted for quality of factors) would have been –1.2 per cent in Honduras and –0.4 per cent in Nicaragua (column 9).

The differences in TFP's contribution to growth between countries are not extreme. The only countries where the contribution is significant and positive are the Dominican Republic and Costa Rica. This is due to the fact both countries undertook major changes in their production structures from the beginning of the 1990s. The changes implemented have given rise to new export sectors, which could be receiving the positive contribution of TFP. In the other countries, the figures are close to zero and are within the error margin for the underlying figures and the calculation methods used.

In summary, the low growth rates in Central America can be explained by the unsatisfactory processes for accumulating physical and human capital. Low rates of investment result not only in a minimal accumulation of capital but also low rates of passive innovation based on imported capital goods. As for human capital, considerable progress was made during the 1990s. However, levels of schooling remain low and increases during the 1990s were not what would have been needed to close the gap between Central American countries and developed countries.

What would have happened to growth with higher rates of investment and greater efforts to increase schooling (with quality being equal)? Table 5.3 shows the results for three simulation exercises. The first simulation calculates the growth rates that would have been achieved between 1991 and 1999 if the rates of gross fixed capital formation had been at least 25 per cent of GDP in all countries. The second simulation shows what growth rates would have been if the increase in years of schooling were doubled. The third simulation is a combination of the first two.

With gross investment rates in fixed capital of at least 25 per cent, the (unweighted) average growth rate of the seven countries would have been 5.1 per cent instead of 4.3 per cent. The effects would clearly be felt more keenly in countries with lower rates of investment (El Salvador, Guatemala, Honduras and Nicaragua). If the increase in years of schooling had doubled during the 1990s, the average annual growth rate would have accelerated by half a percentage point (to 4.8 per cent). The most significant effects would be seen in countries that made the most efforts in education during that decade (El Salvador and Nicaragua). Indeed, with double the rate of schooling, El Salvador would have practically caught up with Costa Rica in terms of average years of schooling in those aged above 15 in 1999 (6.3 years compared with

Table 5.3   Alternative scenarios for growth in Central America, 1991–99 (percentage)

Countries	Observed growth (annual)	Rates of investment greater or equal to 25%[a]	Increased schooling[b]	Increased investment and schooling
Costa Rica	4.5	4.9	4.9	5.3
Dominican Republic	5.8	6.2	6.2	6.2
El Salvador	4.9	5.7	5.7	6.5
Guatemala	4.1	5.4	4.5	5.8
Honduras	3.0	3.9	3.5	4.4
Nicaragua	3.2	4.4	4.0	5.2
Panama	4.7	5.1	5.1	5.5
Simple average	4.3	5.1	4.8	5.6

Notes:
a. Gross fixed investment. Given the low rates of investment in Guatemala, Honduras and Nicaragua, these were linearly adjusted so as to reach 25 per cent of GDP in 1999.
b. Assuming that the increase in years of schooling doubles in the period 1991–99.

Source: Authors' calculations, based on figures from national accounts and Barro and Lee (2001).

6.6 years). If countries had simultaneously increased investment as in the first exercise and doubled the increase in schooling as in the second, the growth rate would have been a fairly solid 5.6 per cent.

5.5   DETERMINING FACTORS BEHIND ECONOMIC GROWTH IN THE PERIOD 1971–2000

In this section we estimate econometrically the model outlined in Section 5.2 above using annual data from the seven countries. The theory for explaining growth rates in Central America may be summarized in the following simultaneous equations:

$$CREC = c(MYE, HUMK, TOTCH, INTS) \tag{5.2}$$

$$MYE = m(LAW, TRADE, CADEF, M2) \tag{5.3}$$

$$HUMK = h(PIBPC, LAW, TRANSF) \tag{5.4}$$

$$LAW = l(CREC, HUMK) \qquad (5.5)$$

where:

CREC	= rate of growth of GDP
MYE	= investment in machinery and equipment as a percentage of GDP
HUMK	= human capital (years of schooling of the workforce)
TOTCH	= percentage change in the terms of trade
INTS	= interest on external debt as a percentage of exports
LAW	= level of development of institutions (rule of law)
TRADE	= openness (exports plus imports as a percentage of GDP)
CADEF	= Net inflows of foreign capital (current account deficit as a percentage of GDP)
M2	= financial deepening (M2 as a percentage of GDP)
PIBPC	= per capita GDP
TRANSF	= transfers from abroad (remittances plus donations) as a percentage of GDP

Equation (5.2) states that annual growth depends on variables such as investment in machinery and equipment and levels of human capital, as well as on others resulting from external shocks (variations in the terms of trade and payment of interest on external debt). Equation (5.3) is the investment function, in that institutional development attracts higher rates of investment. Also, openness, capital inflows and financial deepening are associated with increased investment in machinery and equipment. Equation (5.4) associates human capital with levels of per capita income, institutional development and transfers from abroad. Lastly, equation (5.5) shows institutional development as being dependent on growth and the stock of human capital.

This section includes estimates based on this model with a panel of the seven countries during the period 1971–2000 using methods of fixed effects and random effects. In studies on long-term growth, it is not recommended to use annual growth rates as they have much 'noise' that is associated with short-term fluctuations from output changes below the production frontier and/or transitory disturbances rather than with expansions in potential output. This study therefore uses moving averages of the growth rate of real per capita GDP. This means that, for any given year, the dependent variable is the average of the growth rate for that particular year, the rate for the previous year and the rate for the subsequent year. This reduces the variance by 50 per cent compared with the observed annual growth rate.

Table 5.4 shows the results of the estimated model. The explanatory variables are investment in machinery and equipment lagged as a percentage of GDP in constant prices (*MYER*), interest on the external debt as a

Vanishing growth in Latin America

Table 5.4   Explaining the growth rate of GDP (CREC) *with panel data (1971–2000)*

| Variable | Fixed effects | | |
	Coefficient	Statistical *t*	P > |*t*|
MYER	0.210119	3.45	0.001
INTS	−0.022837	−3.01	0.003
TOTCH	0.038461	2.66	0.008
DUMES	−0.095809	−6.73	0.000

R-squared = 0.2757

F (4.199) = 18.93   (Prob > F = 0.000)

F-test all individual effects $\mu_i = 0$
F (6.199) = 9.38   (Prob > F = 0.000)

| Variable | Random effects | | |
	Coefficient	Statistical *z*	P > |*z*|
MYER	0.179598	3.00	0.003
INTS	−0.025037	−3.41	0.001
TOTCH	0.038611	2.65	0.008
DUMES	−0.094817	−6.67	0.000

R-squared = 0.2158

Wald test
Chi-squared (5) = 73.88   (Prob > Chi-squared = 0.000)

Hausman specification test
Chi-squared (4) = 11.66   (Prob > Chi-squared = 0.0200)

Note: The dependent variable is the moving average of the growth rate of real per capita GDP and the growth rate observed in the previous year and in the subsequent year. DUMES = dummy variable that takes the value of one for El Salvador in the period 1979–82 and zero elsewhere.

Source: Authors' estimations.

percentage of exports of goods and services in dollars at current prices (*INTS*), percentage change in the terms of trade index (*TOTCH*) and a dummy variable with a value of one for El Salvador in the period 1979–82 and zero elsewhere (*DUMES*).[9] For investment in machinery and equipment, the value used had a lag of one period in order to avoid the problem of endogenous regressors associated with the likely interrelationship between rates of growth and investment.

Despite the conviction that there is a connection between the accumulation of human capital and economic growth, it was extremely difficult to find appropriate proxy variables for investment in human capital. Owing to the absence of comparable data between countries, the measure used was the average number of years of schooling in the population aged 15 and 65 (from the Barro and Lee database, 2001). The drawback is that the information is only available for five-year periods. In any event, this variable was not statistically significant in explaining growth.

Investment in machinery and equipment would determine the long-term growth rate. The growth rate could decrease as a result of interest on external debt and increase as a result of positive changes in the terms of trade. The equation may be interpreted as a production function where the main input is capital in machinery and equipment. The rate of growth in the long term would be subject to temporary shocks from the international economy that, in the model, are represented by interest on debt and changes in the terms of trade.

Table 5.4 shows that, in the estimation of fixed effects, the four explanatory variables are statistically significant at the usual confidence levels and the estimated coefficients have the expected signs. The high estimated parameter of the *MYER* ratio should be pointed out: an increase in investment in machinery and equipment (lagged) of one percentage point of GDP is associated with an increase in the rate of growth of per capita GDP of 0.21 percentage points. However, given its standard deviation of 0.06, the value of 0.27 estimated by De Long and Summers (1991) for a cross-section sample of 61 countries for the period 1960–85 is within the range of two standard deviations around the value estimated herein so that the difference is not statistically significant.

The results therefore show that if Central American countries had invested four more GDP percentage points in machinery and equipment than the average investment between 1971 and 2000, real per capita GDP would now be almost 30 per cent higher. This means that, in 2000, the per capita GDP of Costa Rica (measured in current dollars of equal purchasing power) would have been almost the same as that of Argentina, while per capita GDP in Panama and the Dominican Republic would have been higher than that of Brazil.

Analysis of the results of the estimated random effects shows that the sign, magnitude and statistical significance of the coefficients are similar to the estimation of fixed effects. However, R-square is somewhat lower at around 0.22. The Hausman test rejects the null hypothesis that there is no systematic difference between coefficients estimated using the two methods of random and fixed effects, hence the preference for the latter.

In order to analyse the reliability of these results, estimates for the same sample (1971–2000) were made but with data for five-year periods.[10] Reducing the sample size from 121 observations with annual frequency to 42 with five-year observations results in an increase in standard deviations from the estimated parameters, which in turn gives rise to a reduction in the values of the t and z statistics. This means that the estimated coefficients for *INTS* and *TOTCH* are not statistically significant for the estimation of fixed effects. The same applies to the estimated parameter of the latter variable in the estimation of random effects.

The estimated parameters show the expected signs with both methods. Both methods also result in increases in the estimated value of the *MYER* coefficient compared with the estimate from the sample with annual frequency. This, combined with the statistical significance of the estimated parameters, shows the particular importance of investment in machinery and equipment in explaining growth in the seven countries under consideration.

The goodness of fit, for its part, improves by over 50 per cent in the estimation of fixed effects compared with the annual estimates. The resulting R-square of 0.4 is more in line with regressions of growth documented in the literature. Lastly, the Hausman test once again points to a preference for the estimation of fixed effects over random effects.

It should be pointed out that part of the econometric modelling process with the five-year observations was to investigate the hypothesis of conditional convergence including initial real per capita GDP. However, the estimated coefficient (although it was negative) did not appear statistically significant at the usual levels of confidence and its inclusion brought down the statistical significance of all estimated parameters including *MYER*. Many empirical studies of growth work with cross-section samples or panels with few time observations and include a large number of highly heterogeneous countries, combining developed and developing countries (Barro, 1991; Baumol, 1986; De Gregorio, 1992; De Gregorio and Lee, 1999). In sharp contrast, the sample used in this study only has seven countries with much in common, 30 time observations for each with annual data and six in the sample with five-yearly data. This appears sufficient to render the conditional convergence hypothesis somewhat irrelevant in comparison with other studies.

Variables concerning endowment in natural resources have also been excluded for the same reasons. The same applies to historical factors, given that the countries under consideration have a similar colonial past.

In summary, the modest growth of Central American countries during the period 1971–2000 is mainly due to insufficient investment in machinery and equipment.

5.6 INSTITUTIONS, ACCUMULATION OF FACTORS AND GROWTH

This section investigates the relationship between institutional development, accumulation of factors and growth. The institutional variables are from various indices of the International Country Risk Guide based on expert surveys of aspects such as the rule of law, government corruption and the quality of bureaucracy. The indices go from 1 to 6, with higher values indicating better institutions. Out of the three variables, the one that had the strongest explanatory effect according to the specifications and estimation methods used was the rule of law (*LAW*). This is consistent with the importance given by Central American entrepreneurs to crime as an obstacle to business expansion (IDB, 2001a). Including this variable, however, required reducing the sample, as there are no data prior to 1984.

Table 5.5 presents the estimated function of investment in machinery and equipment. The regressors are the index of rule of law lagged one period (*LAWR*), the degree of openness of the economy (*TRADE*), inflows of external capital (*CADEF*) and the level of financial deepening (*M2*). The study postulates that there is a positive relationship between institutional development and investment in machinery and equipment. This is basically because respect for the law and other indicators of progress in governance have positive effects on the investment climate and promote private investment. Openness to trade and capital inflows are both important because imports are the main component of investment in machinery and equipment and must be financed either by exports or net inflows of external capital. Lastly, the savings-investment process can be reasonably expected to be boosted by financial deepening.

The results indicate that the estimated coefficients of the four explanatory variables have the expected signs and are statistically significant. The Hausman test suggests a preference for the estimation of random effects. The major difference between the R-square of the estimation of fixed effects (0.58) and that of random effects (0.014) is due to the low level of the R-square of the between groups estimation, which is only 0.006. In any event, the goodness of fit in the estimation of fixed effects is quite high and the estimated parameters are consistent.

These results would tend to confirm that institutional development affects growth through investment.[11] The importance in the literature of the effects of

Table 5.5   *Explaining investment in machinery and equipment (MYE)*
              (1984–2000)

	Fixed effects		
Variable	Coefficient	Statistical t	$P > |t|$
LAWR	0.004181	2.91	0.004
TRADE	0.033503	4.24	0.000
CADEF	0.070990	3.20	0.002
M2	0.053641	5.19	0.000

R-squared = 0.5832

F (4.108) = 37.77   (Prob > Chi-squared = 0.000)

F-test all individual effects $\mu_i = 0$
F (6.108) = 168.98   (Prob > F = 0.000)

	Random effects		
Variable	Coefficient	Statistical z	$P > |z|$
LAWR	0.004303	3.01	0.003
TRADE	0.033347	4.25	0.000
CADEF	0.068057	3.10	0.002
M2	0.053214	5.18	0.000

R-squared = 0.0144

Wald test
Chi-squared (4) = 151.72   (Prob > Chi-squared = 0.000)

Hausman specification test
Chi-squared (2) = 1.37   (Prob > Chi-squared = 0.850)

Note: *TRADE* is the sum of exports and imports of goods and services as a percentage of GDP, *CADEF* is the current-account deficit as a percentage of GDP and *M2* is expressed as a percentage of GDP. *TRADE* and *CADEF* are expressed in United States dollars at current prices, whereas *M2* is expressed in each country's local currency at current prices.

Source: Authors' estimations.

trade openness on growth would be indirectly confirmed: *TRADE* stimulates growth through investment in machinery and equipment. However, the impact appears small given that an increase of 10 percentage points in this variable would increase investment in machinery and equipment by 0.33 percentage points of GDP. The estimated coefficient in Table 5.2 (0.21) would result in an increase of only 0.07 percentage points in the growth rate of per capita GDP.

The indirect impact of capital inflows on growth would also be small: an increase in external savings of 3 per cent of output would increase *MYE* by only 0.2 percentage points of GDP. This suggests that most of external savings financed consumption and investment in construction (including residential) rather than investment in machinery and equipment. As a result, external saving has displaced rather than complemented domestic saving, possibly because the current-account deficit may be reflecting the fiscal deficit rather than excessive investment over savings on the part of the private sector. Again using the estimated parameter from Table 5.2, this would involve an increase in the rate of per capita growth of only 0.04 percentage points.

Lastly, the degree of financial deepening would also affect growth through investment in machinery and equipment. However, the impact would also be minor as a 10 percentage points increase in *M2* would increase *MYE* by half a percentage point of GDP, which would then increase the growth rate of per capita GDP by only 0.1 percentage points.

As a result, the indirect impact of the various variables included in the machinery and equipment investment function on per capita growth would be relatively small. In general, results are consistent with the relevant theoretical and empirical literature. However, the results do not serve to corroborate the theory that accumulation of human capital stimulates growth through investment. Similarly, including a lagged growth rate in various model formulations resulted in an estimated coefficient that, although positive, was not statistically significant.

It should be pointed out that the rate of inflation was not a statistically significant variable for explaining investment in machinery and equipment. This could be due to the fact that the effects of inflation would be reflected in the *M2* variable, given that when inflation rises, demand for money contracts along with the level of financial deepening and the subsequent negative impact on *MYE*.

The study also explored the possibility that institutional development had an impact on growth through its effect on the stock of human capital. Table 5.6 presents an equation that explains the stock of human capital (number of years of education of those aged 15–65) as a function of the level of lagged per capita GDP (*PIBPCR*), the rule of law index lagged period (*LAWR*) and transfers as a percentage of GDP (*TRANSF*). The three estimated coefficients are positive and statistically significant, although *TRANSF* only at the 90 per

Table 5.6   Explaining human capital (HUMK) *(1984–2000)*

Variable	Fixed effects		
	Coefficient	Statistical t	$P > |t|$
PIBPCR	0.000575	2.34	0.021
LAWR	0.186574	2.35	0.021
TRANSF	2.147502	1.75	0.083

R-squared = 0.1993

F (3.109) = 9.04   (Prob > F = 0.000)

F-test all individual effects $\mu_i = 0$
F (3.109) = 9.04   (Prob > F = 0.000)

Variable	Random effects		
	Coefficient	Statistical z	$P > |z|$
PIBPCR	0.000657	2.89	0.004
LAWR	0.178768	2.29	0.022
TRANSF	2.162336	1.78	0.075

R-squared = 0.4656

Wald Test
Chi-squared (3) = 30.56   (Prob > Chi-squared = 0.000)

Hausman specification test
Chi-squared (3) = 0.79   (Prob > Chi-squared = 0.852)

Note: PIBPCR is expressed in United States dollars at 1995 prices.

Source: Authors' estimations.

cent level. The Hausman test favors estimation using the random effects method, and the R-square of 0.47 represents a good fit.

These results confirm the hypothesis that institutional development also stimulates growth through its effects on the stock of human capital. In this way, institutional development appears as crucial for stimulating investment

Table 5.7   *Explaining institutional development (*LAW*) (1984–2000)*

	Fixed effects		
Variable	Coefficient	Statistical t	$P > |t|$
CRECR	2.943426	1.88	0.063
HUMKR	1.065201	8.47	0.000

R-squared = 0.4884

F (2.110) = 52.50   (Prob > Chi-squared = 0.000)

F-test all individual effects $\mu_i = 0$
F (6.110) = 41.40   (Prob > F = 0.000)

	Random effects		
Variable	Coefficient	Statistical z	$P > |z|$
CRECR	3.974723	2.47	0.013
HUMKR	0.854396	7.38	0.000

R-squared = 0.1372

Wald test
Chi-squared (2) = 85.43   (Prob > Chi-squared = 0.000)

Hausman specification test
Chi-squared (2) = 18.45   (Prob > Chi-squared = 0.000)

Note: The dependent variable is *LAW*.

Source: Authors' estimations.

in physical and human capital. This also suggests that transfers from abroad contribute to the formation of human capital because a proportion of the remittances and donations from abroad are spent in education. Lastly, the level of (lagged) per capita GDP – probably the best measure of a country's economic development – would also have a positive effect on *HUMK*.

Of course, institutional development is not exogenous and must be modeled as in Table 5.7, which shows the results of the regression of *LAW* as a function of the lagged growth rate of per capita GDP (*CRECR*) and of the lagged stock of human capital (*HUMKR*). It can be seen that both variables have the expected sign and are statistically significant, although *CRECR* only at the 90 per cent level in the estimation of fixed effects. The Hausman test indicates the preference for fixed effects, where the goodness of fit is an acceptable 49 per cent.

These results suggest that growth and the stock of human capital both have positive effects on institutional development, thereby confirming the mutual causal link between *LAW* and *HUMK*. In particular, growth has a considerable impact on the institutional variable, given that a 1 per cent increase in the (lagged) rate of growth would generate an increase of 0.3 (on a scale of 1 to 6) in the *LAW* index.

In summary, investment in machinery and equipment is determined by institutional development, the openness of the economy, the level of financial deepening and the inflow of external capital. The stock of human capital, for its part, depends on institutional development, transfers from abroad and the level of per capita GDP. Institutional development is in turn influenced by both the growth rate and the stock of human capital. This proves the hypothesis of mutual influence between institutional development and the level of human capital. Lastly, human capital affects growth through institutional development.

5.7   CONCLUSIONS

During the last few decades, and particularly since 1980, economic growth in Central American countries has been unsatisfactory. In the period 1975–99, no convergence was observed between the levels of per capita income in these countries and that of the United States. In the best cases, some countries more or less maintained their relative lag (Belize, Costa Rica and the Dominican Republic), whereas others fell significantly behind, that is absolute divergence (El Salvador, Guatemala, Honduras, Nicaragua, Panama). This contrasts with the experience of other small, open developing countries that narrowed the gap between their per capita GDP and that of the United States during the same period (Chile, Hong Kong, Ireland, Mauritius and Singapore).

A breakdown of the sources of economic growth reveals that half of the average annual growth rate of Central American countries during the 1990s (4.3 per cent) can be explained by increases in the workforce, while little more than a third can be explained by the accumulation of physical capital. Total factor productivity (TFP) only contributed 14 per cent towards the growth rate (0.6 percentage points). However, there are marked differences between countries: TFP made a considerable contribution to growth in Costa

Rica, the Dominican Republic and El Salvador, whereas Nicaragua and Honduras lagged behind in this respect. In Honduras, the absolute reduction of productivity inferred from the analysis could be due to a significant underestimation of GDP and growth rate and an overestimation of the increase in capital stock (much of which was destroyed by Hurricane Mitch in October 1998).

When productive factors are adjusted for quality (like years of schooling for the workforce and technological progress for physical capital), the contribution of TFP to growth is seen to be nil, while capital and labor account for 40 per cent and 60 per cent respectively of the annual growth rate.

Sensitivity analysis indicates that a higher rate of investment and more emphasis on workers' education would have resulted in considerably higher growth in Central America during the 1990s. With an investment rate of at least 25 per cent of GDP, the annual growth rate would have been 5.1 per cent (0.8 percentage points higher than the observed rate). Guatemala and Nicaragua are the countries that would have benefited the most from such a change. Also, if the increase in the number of years of schooling of the workforce had been double what it was during the 1990s, the annual growth rate would have been 4.8 per cent (half a percentage point more than the observed rate). El Salvador and Nicaragua are the countries that would have benefited the most from this change.

The econometric exercise carried out for 1971–2000 consists of a model where the growth rate of per capita GDP in Central America is basically determined by investment in machinery and equipment. Insufficient investment in machinery and equipment during that period seems to have been the main factor behind the modest growth of those countries. External disturbances, such as changes in the terms of trade or the international interest rate, have been significant determining factors in terms of short-term growth.

Various indices intended to measure the quality of institutional variables were experimented with in order to study the latter's effect on growth during the period 1984–2000. The results show that institutional development (extent of the rule of law) has a significant impact on growth through its effect on investment in machinery and equipment. The limited confidence of national and foreign investors in the rule of law is definitely having an adverse effect on investment in these countries.

In addition to being affected by institutional development, investment in machinery and equipment is also influenced by the level of openness of the economy, inflows of external capital and the level of financial deepening. Clearly, imports are a vital part of investment in machinery and equipment, which is in turn financed by exports or external capital. Financial deepening is important because, in Central America and in all economies, private investment is strongly conditioned by access to financing.[12]

The results show that human capital and institutional development affect each other. The effect on growth of investment in human capital will be seen directly or indirectly through its impact on institutional development. Although the direct effect is presumably on a noticeable scale, it was not possible to detect it with the proxies used in this study and the information available.

In addition to being affected by institutional development, the stock of human capital is also positively affected by the inflow of transfers from abroad (basically emigrant remittances and international development donations). Lastly, institutional development depends as much on the stock of human capital as on the rate of growth of output. This last factor in particular appears to have an important impact.

All of the above is summarized in Figure 5.4, where arrows represent causality and factors that are endogenous and semi-endogenous to growth (in rectangles) can be distinguished from exogenous factors (ovals).

These results suggest that, in order to stimulate growth, the authorities of Central American countries need to adopt a multi-pronged approach. First, it is urgent to strengthen and improve institutions. Investment would benefit and TFP would probably benefit too. This would generate a virtuous circle

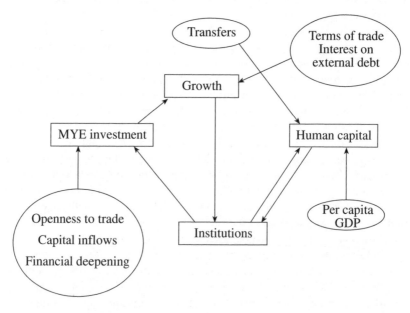

Source: Authors' elaboration.

Figure 5.4   Determining factors of economic growth in Central America

between institutional development, the accumulation of physical and human capital, and growth.

Second, financial deepening needs to be promoted. Investment appears to be restricted by the availability of financial resources. Institutional development would also contribute towards deepening financial markets, improving creditor protection and generating appropriate mechanisms for prudential supervision and regulation of the financial system.

Third, the authorities need to make a significant effort to stimulate exports. According to the model presented herein, exports are the mechanism through which technology importing countries can grow because they finance capital goods imports that embody technical progress in the advanced countries. Furthermore, if exports diversify in small economies such as those in Central America, they provide a boost to growth that is not restricted by demand.

Above and beyond the explanations provided by the model, the uncertainty about why investment rates are so low in Central America must also be acknowledged. The factors identified fail to explain a large proportion of the variations in investment in machinery and equipment. Apart from that, the estimations obtained indicate that the explanatory variables (openness, financial deepening and foreign capital inflows) would yield modest results in terms of growth. This is definitely an area that needs further research.

It is also important to work on a satisfactory measurement for the stock of human capital. Available human capital may be a limiting factor on investment in sectors where these economies could be internationally competitive. It was not possible to investigate this and other interesting hypotheses with the measurements available.

A final comment: attracting foreign direct investment is a complement to stimulating exports. Indeed, Central American countries were very successful at attracting foreign direct investment during the 1990s thanks to free trade zones (*maquila*). This has enabled them to boost exports and diversify their basket of exports with manufactured goods, including in high-tech sectors (as is the case in Costa Rica). However, these new exports sectors still function as enclaves and have little relation to the rest of the economy. It is essential to strengthen production linkages with local enterprises so that the latter may provide inputs to the foreign enterprises. This would transmit the buoyancy of the free-trade-zone enterprises to the rest of the economy and would encourage the transfer of technology.[13]

APPENDIX 5.A

Correcting Inputs by Quality in Growth Accounting

The decomposition-of-growth analysis uses the conceptual framework of Solow (1956), correcting labor and capital for quality. The point of departure is a standard Cobb–Douglas production function with constant returns to scale:

$$Y_t = A_t K_t^{\alpha} L_t^{(1-\alpha)}, \tag{5.A.1}$$

where Y is total income, K is capital stock, L is labor force and A is an exogenous technological coefficient that moves at a constant rate. First, it is considered that labor productivity increases as the economy accumulates human capital. Second, any investment involves passive technical progress insofar as capital goods (mostly imported) have better technology.

If these characteristics are added to the basic model, (5.A.1) is transformed as follows:

$$Y_t = A_t (K_t^{*})^{\alpha} [L_t H_t]^{1-\alpha}, \tag{5.A.2}$$

where H is an index of the quality of the workforce (schooling) and K^* is capital adjusted for quality.

The H variable is years of schooling and productivity of (or return on) education. Following the Mincer tradition, H can therefore be estimated using the following equation:

$$H_t = \exp(\phi s_t), \tag{5.A.3}$$

where s is the number of years of schooling in the workforce and ϕ is the return on an additional year of education. In the calculations to estimate the contribution of education, ϕ is assumed to be equal to 10 per cent.

It is somewhat more complex to find a formula for capital adjusted by quality. Capital can be broken down into machinery and equipment, and construction:

$$K_t^{*} = (1-\delta_c)K_{t-1}^{c} + I_t^{c} + (1-\delta_m)K_m^{t-1} + (I_t^{m})^{*}, \tag{5.A.4}$$

where δ_c is the rate of depreciation of the stock of construction and δ_m is the rate of depreciation of machinery and equipment assets; I^c and $(I^m)^*$ are investment in construction and machinery and equipment, respectively with the latter being corrected for quality. Investment in machinery corrected for quality may be expressed as follows:

$$(I_t^m)^* = (1+\theta)^t I_t^m, \tag{5.A.5}$$

where θ is the annual rate of technical progress incorporated into capital goods, which is assumed to be constant and equal to 1.5 per cent, the rate at which the relative prices of capital goods fell in the United States in the 1990s.

By replacing (5.A.5) in (5.A.4), the capital stock of any given year ($t = n$) can be expressed in terms of stocks of an initial year ($t = 0$,) investment in the period and the rate of technical progress:

$$
\begin{aligned}
K_n^* = (1-\delta_c)^n K_0^c + \sum_{t=1}^{n}(1-\delta_c)^{n-t} I_t^c + (1-\delta_m)^n K_0^m \\
+ \sum_{t=1}^{n}(1-\delta_m)^{n-t}(1+\theta)^t I_t^m
\end{aligned}
\tag{5.A.6}
$$

Although the growth rates of investment in construction and machinery and equipment are constant during the period, the summations in (5.A.6) are geometric progressions than can be resolved the obtain the final capital stock (K_0^*) as a function of the stocks of the initial year (K_0^c, K_0^m), investment during the period 1 (I_1^c, I_1^m), the rates of increase of investment from period 1 to the final year (ρ_c, ρ_m), the rate of technological progress incorporated into investment in machinery and equipment (θ), and the rates of depreciation (δ_c, δ_m):

$$
\begin{aligned}
K_n^* = (1-\delta_c)^n K_0^c + \left[\frac{(1+\rho_c)^n - (1-\delta_c)^n}{\rho_c + \delta_c} \right] I_1^c + \\
(1-\delta_m)^n K_0^m + \left[\frac{(1+\rho_m)^n(1+\theta)^{n+1} - (1-\delta_m)^n(1+\theta)}{\rho_m + \theta + \rho_m\theta + \delta_m} \right] I_1^m,
\end{aligned}
\tag{5.A.7}
$$

where ρ_c is the growth rate of investment in construction and ρ_m is the growth rate of investment in machinery and equipment.

Initial capital in machinery and equipment and construction can be calculated as follows. In the stationary state (see Solow, 1956), the growth rate of capital is identical to the growth rate of total output:

$$K_0^i = I_1^i / (g + \delta_i); \text{ for } i = c, m \tag{5.A.8}$$

where g = trend growth rate of GDP.[14]

APPENDIX 5.B

Definition of Variables and Sources Used in the Database

The variables used and their definitions are as follows:

CREC: Growth rate of per capita GDP in United States dollars at 1995 prices. Source: WB.

MYE: (Gross fixed capital formation in machinery and equipment as a percentage of GDP at constant prices in local currency of each country. Source: ECLAC.

HUMK: Average years of schooling among those aged 15 to 65. Source: Barro and Lee.

PIBPC: Per capita GDP in United States dollars at 1995 prices. Source: WB.

LAW: Index of rule of law. Source: ICRG.

M2: *M2* as a percentage of GDP at current prices in local currency of each country. Source: WB.

TOTCH: Percentage change in the terms of trade index, base 1995 = 100. Source: ECLAC.

CADEF: Current account deficit in United States dollars at current prices as a percentage of GDP. Source: WB.

TRANSF: Current transfers in United States dollars at current prices as a percentage of GDP. Source: WB.

TRADE: Exports plus imports of goods and services as a percentage of GDP at constant prices in local currency of each country. Source: WB.

INTS: Payments of interest on external debt as a percentage of exports of goods and services in United States dollars at current prices. Source: ECLAC.

The five sources used were World Bank *World Development Indicators*, 2002 (WB); ECLAC, *Statistical Yearbook for Latin America and the Caribbean*, various issues (ECLAC); *International Country Risk Guide*, electronic service 2002 (ICRG); and Barro and Lee, unpublished database, 2001).

NOTES

1. The study by Esquivel (2001) is an attempt to explain growth in Central America with parameters obtained from a cross-section regression for developing countries in general, but it is not an econometric study of Central America as such.
2. Panama is atypical. Given its production factors, it could be expected to have experienced a pattern of growth similar to that of other countries in the region. However, the country has specialized in international banking services and the Panama Canal, with light manufacturing accounting for a very small proportion of exports.

3. Most analyses of institutional development as a source of economic growth have tended to concentrate basically on those institutions that protect property rights and enforce contracts. However, institutions affect growth in many other ways, such as social safety nets, market regulation and the supervision of certain economic agents. Social safety nets also encourage the formation of social and human capital.
4. Central American Isthmus plus the Dominican Republic.
5. This procedure consists of estimating the GDP of each country in United States dollars at United States prices.
6. This result does not change significantly, even when corrected on the basis of a possible overestimation of GDP in Honduras and Nicaragua. If that adjustment is applied, in 1999 Honduras could have had a GDP in dollars of purchasing power parity equivalent of a tenth that of the United States (somewhat below the 12 per cent in 1975). Making that adjustment for Nicaragua in 1999 would result in a per capita GDP 14 per cent that of the United States (considerably lower than the 25 per cent from 1975).
7. During the 1990s, the relative prices of capital goods in the United States fell to an average rate of 1.5 per cent per year. This is a good estimate of the annual rate of increase in the productivity of such goods, and this rate was used as an adjustment factor for machinery and equipment. The adjusted workforce was calculated by multiplying the number of workers by a factor that reflects the increases in productivity resulting from the years of schooling among those over the age of 15.
8. Growth rates calculated for the 1990s are slightly different to the estimates in the previous section because here they correspond to 1991–99 (as opposed to 1991–2000) and because the estimates were made in national currencies, whereas those in Section 5.3 were based on United States dollars.
9. Between 1979 and 1982, the growth rate for El Salvador was dramatically affected by the armed conflict.
10. Given the lack of statistical information for previous years, the value of each country's *MYER* variable for 1971–75 is the value observed in 1970.
11. Knack and Keefer (1995) find evidence for institutional development stimulating investment and directly affecting growth through TFP.
12. This is a finding in almost all empirical studies on investment, both in developed and developing countries (see Fazzari et al., 1998, and Galindo and Schiantarelli, 2003).
13. Another aspect that urgently needs to be rectified is the incentive system for attracting foreign enterprises, given that it basically consists of income tax exemptions. This creates serious problems, as it gives rise to a situation where the most dynamic and profitable enterprises do not pay tax. In addition, these types of incentives contravene the standards of the World Trade Organization and will have to be eliminated by the end of 2008 at the latest.
14. The trend growth rate of GDP can be estimated from the following regression: $PIB_t = a + g \cdot t$. As investment in period 1 may have been unusually low or high, it is usually estimated using a similar procedure. In the regression $\ln I_t = c + \rho \cdot t$, the estimated value of the parameter c is the logarithm of investment in period 1.

REFERENCES

Agosin, M.R. (1999), 'Trade and growth in Chile', *CEPAL Review*, **68**, August.

Barro, R. (1991), 'Economic growth in a cross section of countries', *Quarterly Journal of Economics*, **106**, May.

Barro, R. and J. Lee (2001), 'International data on educational attainment: updates and implications'. Harvard University, Cambridge, MA, unpublished database.

Baumol, W. (1986), 'Productivity growth, convergence, and welfare', *American Economic Review*, **76**, December.

Burki, S. and G. Perry (1998), *Beyond the Washington Consensus: Institutions Matter*, World Bank Latin American and Caribbean Studies, Washington, DC: World Bank.

Dabee, B. (2001), 'The role of traditional exports in Mauritius', in G. Helleiner (ed.), *Non-Traditional Export Promotion in Africa: Experience and Issues*, Basingstoke and London: Palgrave.

De Gregorio, J. (1992), 'El crecimiento económico en la América Latina', *El Trimestre Económico*, October–December.

De Gregorio, J. and J. Lee (1999), 'Economic growth in Latin America: sources and prospects', *Global Development Network*, World Bank, December.

De Long, B. and L. Summers (1991), 'Equipment investment and economic growth', *Quarterly Journal of Economics*, **106**, May.

Denison, E.F. (1967), *Why Growth Rates Differ*, Washington, DC: Brookings Institution.

Esquivel, G. (2001), 'Economic growth in Central America: a long-term perspective', in F. Larraín (ed.), *Economic Development in Central America. Vol. I: Growth and Internationalization*, Cambridge, MA: Harvard University Press.

Fazzari, D., G. Hubbard and B. Petersen (1998), 'Financing constraints and corporate investment', *Brookings Papers in Economic Activity*, **1**, 141–95.

Galindo, A. and F. Schiantarelli (eds) (2003), *Credit Constraints and Investment in Latin America*, Washington, DC: Inter-American Development Bank, Latin American Research Network.

IDB (2001a), 'Competitiviness: the business of growth', in *Informe de Progreso Económico y Social en América Latina y el Caribe*, Washington, DC.

IDB (2001b), 'Is growth enough?', *Latin American Economic Policies*, **14**, Washington, DC.

Knack, R. and P. Keefer (1995), 'Institutions and economic performance: cross country tests using alternative institutional measures', *Economics and Politics*, **7**, November.

Rodrik, D. (2001), 'Development strategies for the next century', presentation at the ECLAC seminar Development Theory at the Threshold of the Twenty-First Century, Santiago, August.

Romer, P. (1993), 'Two strategies of economic development: using ideas and producing ideas', *Proceedings of the World Bank Annual Conference on Development Economics 1992*, Washington, DC: World Bank.

Solow, R.M. (1956), 'A contribution to the theory of economic growth', *Quarterly Journal of Economics*, **70**.

United Nations Development Program (UNDP) (2000), *Human Development Report Honduras 2000*, Teguagalpa: United Nations.

World Bank (2002), *World Development Indicators*, Washington, DC: World Bank United Nations Development Program (UNDP) (2000), *Human Development Report Honduras 2000*, Tegucigalpa: United Nations.

6. Changing growth constraints in northern Latin America

Jaime Ros*

6.1 INTRODUCTION

The 1990s brought promising signs for the economies of Mexico and Central America, a region that had been plagued by political instability and economic setbacks in the 1980s. Macroeconomic stabilization was achieved, the end of civil strife in several countries translated into a positive shock for the region and economic growth resumed at a faster rate than in the rest of Latin America, at least in the countries with highest per capita incomes in the region. The recovery has fallen, however, short of the mark. Economic growth since 1990 has tended to be slower than it had been in the 1960s and 1970s, especially in the case of Mexico with the largest economy in the region. Long-standing growth constraints are far from being eliminated in a region where (with the exception of Mexico) all the relevant factors conspire against growth: small economies, lagging competitiveness, dependence on a few commodity exports that have highly volatile prices and a highly concentrated pattern of income distribution compounded by ethnic inequalities, not to mention high exposure to natural disasters. At the same time, new problems that have emerged with the structural transformation of the past two decades also contribute to prevent a more vigorous pace of economic growth.

This chapter examines the stylized facts, current constraints and the prospects of the growth process in Mexico and Central America. Despite the evident heterogeneity of the region with respect to the size of its economies and levels of economic development, these countries do have certain traits in common. All of them suffered particularly severe hardships when the debt crisis was exacerbated by the deterioration of their terms of trade in the 1980s. Some of these countries posted the highest economic growth rates in Latin America since 1990. Much like what has occurred in the Dominican Republic, and unlike the situation in Panama and South America, the recovery has been underpinned by an increasing specialization in the export of manufactures. It has also been driven by an export boom made possible by preferential trade agreements with the United States that have no parallel in

133

the rest of Latin America. This boom is largely being driven by exporting firms having few local linkages and, with some exceptions, little technological content.

The first section of the chapter discusses the factors that underpinned the recovery since 1990. The second section examines growth constraints: long-standing problems, problems that have been alleviated and new problems that have emerged out of the structural transformation of the region's economies over the past two decades. The third section analyses then the outlook for growth: What is the region's growth potential, and what needs to be done to realize it? The last section will draw some final conclusions.

6.2   THE BASIS OF THE RECOVERY OF GROWTH SINCE 1990

The central fact addressed in this section is the recovery of economic growth since 1990. This period contrasted with the times of crisis and instability that preceded it, particularly in the aftermath of the external debt crisis of the early 1980s. In this section, the stylised facts that characterized the decade are discussed, taking into consideration the pillars on which the upturn in growth rested.

The simple average of real per capita GDP growth rates of the economies of the region was 1.3 per cent from 1990 to 2003, well above the average for the 1980s (−1.4 per cent) but below the average of the 1960–80 period (2.0 per cent) (see Table 6.1). Four pillars underpinned this recovery: a favorable international environment that included, above all, the normalization of access to international capital markets; macroeconomic stabilization; the end of political instability; and the transition to a new model of development based on exports of manufactures.

The end of the debt crisis was a key aspect of the international context in which the recovery took place. As a result of external factors (the Brady plan and the reduction of interest rates in the United States in the early 1990s) and internal factors (the structural reform process undertaken in the mid-1980s, particularly the liberalization of the balance of payments and, to a greater or lesser extent, of the financial system, as well as the privatization of State-owned enterprises) the severe rationing of external credit that occurred during the debt crisis came to an end in the late 1980s. The restoration of normal access to international capital markets for the region and the subsequent boom in external capital between 1990 and 1993 created the conditions needed to spur economic recovery, as net transfers of external resources experienced a turnaround and thus eased the balance-of-payments constraints on growth (see Table 6.1 on the turnaround in the trade balance, measured as a percentage of GDP, between 1982–88 and 1989–2002). Such transfers came in the form of massive portfolio investments in Mexico in the early part of the decade, as well as foreign direct investment associated with privatizations and the creation of export processing zones (INTEL in Costa Rica and garment assembly factories in the rest of Central America). The intense, prolonged economic recovery of the United States, which acted as a driving force in the expansion of the region's exports, was also part of the favorable international context.

In the 1980s, balance-of-payments constraints (associated with the interruption of external lending and adverse terms-of-trade shocks) had led to successive devaluations, and public finances had deteriorated as a result of the recession. Moreover, armed conflicts forced governments in the region to resort to the inflation tax in order to cover the shortfall in financing caused by these developments. In a region traditionally characterized by low inflation, these circumstances triggered inflationary spikes, although – with the exception of Nicaragua and, to a lesser degree, Mexico – they were less marked than in the rest of Latin America. The restoration of access to international capital markets, together with the adoption of stabilization programmes, ushered in a new period of stability. Inflation dropped throughout the 1990s,[1] reaching single-digit rates by the early years of the present decade in every country except Costa Rica (see Table 6.1).

The region's political stability was undermined in the 1980s by the aggravation of long-standing conflicts (Guatemala) and the eruption of new armed conflicts (El Salvador and Nicaragua), whose negative effects spilled over into other countries (particularly Honduras). The economic difficulties of the period were exacerbated by the impacts of these conflicts, which included the displacement of war refugees (9 per cent and 14 per cent of the populations of El Salvador and Nicaragua, respectively – see Tavares, 2001), the closing of schools in conflict-ridden areas, the deterioration of public finances due to the war effort, the destruction of infrastructure and an overall climate of uncertainty and instability that weighed heavily on production levels and investments. The most directly affected countries (El Salvador, Guatemala and Nicaragua) were precisely the ones that saw their per capita income levels plummet in the 1980s (see Table 6.1). The 1990s saw a reversal of these trends, with the end of the armed conflict in Nicaragua in 1990 and the peace accords in El Salvador (1992) and Guatemala (1996). In addition to other benefits, the end of these conflicts made it possible to cut military spending and implement a radical fiscal adjustment. Nicaragua was the most remarkable case with a turnaround of its public finances from a deficit of 19.3 per cent of GDP in 1990 to one of just 0.5 per cent in 1995 (see Table 6.2). This set the stage for (and was partially due to) the end of the hyperinflation of the late 1980s.

Table 6.1 *Growth and macroeconomic variables*

	Per capita GDP[a]	Economic growth[b]			Trade deficit (% of GDP)		Inflation[c]			Export coefficient[d]		Manufactures (as % of total exports)[e]	
	2003	1960–1980	1980–1990	1990–2003	1982–1988	1989–2002	1980s	1990s	2001	1990	2000	1990	2000
Costa Rica	8 252	2.4	−0.5	2.6	0.5	2.1	25.6	15.6	11.3	30.4	51.6	31.1	60.5
Mexico	7 945	3.5	−0.3	1.2	−3.9	1.9	65.1	19.4	6.4	14.9	36.2	57.6	78.2
El Salvador	4 343	1.0	−1.5	2.0	6.0	14.2	19.0	8.5	3.8	16.8	35.5	29.1	80.9
Guatemala	3 584	2.8	−1.6	1.0	2.8	7.2	13.9	10.1	7.3	17.4	25.8	24.3	50.0
Honduras	2 311	1.8	−0.7	0.3	3.5	8.6	7.8	17.3	9.7	48.4	39.6	17.7	72.0
Nicaragua	2 194	0.3	−4.0	0.8	9.5[f]	35.0[g]	618.8	35.1*	7.4	27.0	39.0	3.0	44.4
Latin America and the Caribbean	6 380	2.9	−0.9	1.0									

Notes and sources:
a. United States dollars (purchasing power parity 1995). Source: *World Bank, World Development Indicators* (online)
b. Per capita GDP annual growth rate. Source: *World Bank, World Development Indicators* (online)
c. Annual change in consumer prices. Source: ECLAC, *Statistical Yearbook, 2002;* UNDP (2002).
d. Percentage of GDP, at 1995 prices. Source: ECLAC, *Statistical Yearbook, 2002.*
e. Excludes natural-resource-based manufactures. Source: Moreno Brid (2003).
f. 1988–2002.
g. 1999.
* Shorter period than indicated.

Table 6.2   *Fiscal deficit (percentages of GDP)*

	1990	1995	2000
Mexico	0.2[a]	0.8	1.5
Costa Rica	4.4	3.5	3.0
El Salvador	1.2	0.5	2.3
Guatemala	2.1	0.5	1.8
Honduras	7.2	4.2	6.0
Nicaragua	19.3	0.5	7.7

Note: a. 1991.

Sources: ECLAC (2002); Moreno Brid (2003).

Growth in the 1990s went hand in hand with a transition from the traditional economic model – based on agricultural commodity exports (and oil, in the case of Mexico) and associated with a heavy dependence on a small number of products having highly volatile prices – to a model in which growth is driven by labor-intensive and intermediate technology content manufactures (with, in the case of Costa Rica and Mexico, a significant share of manufactures with high-technology content) (see Table 6.3).[2] Exports of manufactures increased as a percentage of total exports from 27.1 per cent in 1990 to 64.3 per cent in 2000 (simple averages), signaling a radical change in the composition of the region's major exports compared to just 10 years earlier. Thus, by 2000, the percentage of exports of manufactures already far

Table 6.3   *Structure of exports of manufactures, 1999–2001 (percentages)*

	Low technology	Intermediate technology	High technology	Total[a]
Mexico	18.9	46.5	34.6	100
Costa Rica	23.1	18.8	58.1	100
Nicaragua	46.7	48.0	5.3	100
Guatemala	47.6	39.6	12.8	100
Honduras	54.5	40.3	5.2	100
El Salvador	60.5	26.8	12.7	100

Note: a. Totals do not include natural-resource-based manufactures.

Source: ECLAC, *Latin America and the Caribbean in the World Economy*, 2001–02.

exceeded the average for Latin America. This model, stimulated by the opening of trade and the negotiation of preferential subregional trade agreements
(NAFTA and the Caribbean Basin Initiative, in particular), in addition to the
rapid expansion of the United States economy in the 1990s, has exhibited
strong export growth. Exports/GDP ratios rose sharply during the decade
(with the exception of Honduras) and more than doubled in Mexico and El
Salvador (see Table 6.1). The process was accompanied by a further concentration of exports by country of destination, with the United States playing an
increasingly important role as an importer of products from the region.

In addition to the progressive specialization in exporting labor-intensive
manufactures, the region has become a major exporter of labor services, with
worker remittances from abroad being one of the main sources of foreign
exchange income recorded in the current account of the balance of payments
(see CEPAL 2002). In some countries (Mexico and Costa Rica), tourism has
also gained in importance within this pattern of trade-specialization.

The weight of each of these factors has varied from country to country. The
peace process directly affected El Salvador, Guatemala and Nicaragua. The
economic recovery was interrupted by natural disasters in Honduras and
Nicaragua (Hurricane Mitch in 1998) and El Salvador (the earthquakes of
2001). Macroeconomic stability was not entirely lost in Honduras, while
instability was particularly pronounced in Nicaragua and, to a somewhat
lesser extent, in Mexico. Exports gathered considerable momentum in Mexico
and El Salvador but have been less buoyant in Honduras, where the export
coefficient has in fact dropped. The transition towards a new development
style has been the most vigorous in Mexico, Costa Rica and El Salvador and
less so in Guatemala and Nicaragua.

6.3   OLD AND NEW CONSTRAINTS ON GROWTH

The constraints on growth differ today from those of the past. Old problems
have disappeared as political instability has been overcome and macroeconomic stability attained. Meanwhile, other problems persist, such as lagging
competitiveness and inequality in income distribution. The high volatility of
external capital in the 1990s has continued to adversely affect Mexico, but is
having less of an impact on the Central American countries owing to the
shallowness of their financial markets and the lesser degree to which capital
movements have been liberalized. Still other problems – such as dependence
on commodity exports and the sluggishness of external markets – have been
mitigated. Meanwhile, new obstacles to growth have arisen, such as the lack
of local integration of new export sectors and their low potential for productivity growth.

Lagging Competitiveness

The analysis of the constraints on growth associated with lagging competitiveness in the region, relies on data compiled to construct the World Economic Forum (WEF) global competitiveness indices (WEF 2002). These indices have been criticized (see Lall, 2001, in particular) for, among other factors, the lack of objective criteria for aggregating their components, the selection of competitiveness factors and the causal relationships between the selected variables and per capita income. Bearing these reservations in mind, Table 6.4 gives the ranking of each country relative to Latin America as a whole in each area of competitiveness.

The simple averages of the competitiveness factors shows that, with the exception of Costa Rica and Mexico, the region is lagging considerably behind the rest of Latin America. In which areas are these economies lagging the furthest behind? In the following order, the major lags (or areas of least relative progress) experienced by each country are: Costa Rica: exchange rate competitiveness, macroeconomic environment, business climate; Mexico: exchange rate competitiveness, institutional development, business climate; El Salvador: business administration, exchange rate competitiveness, business climate; Guatemala: business administration, business climate, institutional development; Nicaragua: business administration, macroeconomic environment, business climate; Honduras: business administration, business climate, institutional development.

The quality of business administration appears to be the area in which the region as a whole is lagging the furthest behind, since it is the most underdeveloped area in every country except Costa Rica and Mexico. These last two countries are lagging behind the most in the area of exchange rate competitiveness (particularly Mexico), whereas they rank above Latin America as a whole in the area of business administration. Business climate and institutional development are two other major problem areas, while the macroeconomic environment is an important issue in Costa Rica and Nicaragua.

Inequality in Income Distribution

All the countries of the region except Costa Rica exhibit highly unequal income distributions within a region, Latin America, which has the highest levels of inequality in the world. As shown in Table 6.5, most of the countries in the region (Mexico, Guatemala, Honduras and Nicaragua) fall into either the third or fourth quartiles of inequality in income distribution among 20 Latin American and Caribbean countries. All of them (except, once again Costa Rica) have Gini coefficients that – at over 0.50 – are among the world's highest.

Table 6.4 Competitiveness: relative ranking compared to Latin America as a whole, 2001

	Costa Rica	Mexico	Latin America	El Salvador	Guatemala	Nicaragua	Honduras
Exchange rate competitiveness	100	88	100	79	93	124	84
Macroeconomic environment	108	114	100	106	102	68	83
Technological development	126	119	100	98	85	81	83
Business administration	137	115	100	78	72	65	63
Business climate	108	106	100	88	78	76	67
Institutional development	116	102	100	96	82	85	77
Simple average	116	107	100	91	85	83	76

Note: the rankings are calculated as $[1 + (Ii - IAL)/IAL]$ 100, where *IAL* is the average for Latin America and *Ii* that of the individual country.

Source: Author's calculations based on World Economic Forum 2002.

Table 6.5   Income distribution in Latin America and the Caribbean (Gini coefficient, c. 1999)

Jamaica	0.38	Chile	0.55
Trinidad and Tobago	0.40	Colombia	0.55
Uruguay	0.44	Panama	0.56
Dominican Republic	0.47	Ecuador	0.56
Costa Rica	0.49	Mexico	0.57
Venezuela	0.49	Honduras	0.57
Peru	0.50	Guatemala	0.58
El Salvador	0.52	Nicaragua	0.59
Argentina	0.53	Bolivia	0.60
Paraguay	0.54	Brazil	0.64
Memorandum			
Sweden	0.25	India	0.38
Germany	0.30	United States	0.41
Republic of Korea	0.32	South Africa	0.59

Source: UNDP (2002).

This level of inequality is an obstacle to a growth process oriented towards reducing poverty. Countries with highly unequal income distribution patterns need to grow more rapidly to lower the poverty rate as much as other countries with less inequality. Moreover, the recent literature on growth determinants has identified two types of mechanisms through which greater inequality adversely affects growth. First, the economic mechanisms have to do with the negative effects of inequality on the size of markets for industries with increasing returns to scale (see the structuralist literature of the 1960s and the more recent formalization by Murphy et al. 1989) and on aggregate demand and the utilization of productive capacity (which, in turn, dampens investment; see Dutt, 1984), the links between distribution and investment in education[3] and the reduction in population growth and fertility rates associated with less inequality (Perotti, 1996).[4]

In addition, there are sociopolitical mechanisms at work, such as the fiscal effects (for example, taxes on capital) of the redistributive pressures generated by income concentration (Alesina and Rodrik, 1994), the effects of inequality on political instability and social unrest (Alesina and Perotti, 1994) and the effects of highly concentrated income patterns on polarization, which then undermines consensus-building on economic policy (Keefer and Knack, 1997) and hampers the management of external shocks in the absence of a

Table 6.6   Inequality and incidence of growth collapses in developed and developing countries

Level of inequality	Number of countries	Number of collapses	Incidence of collapses (%)
High[a]	21	11	52
Medium[b]	20	11	55
Low[c]	21	0	0
Total	62	22	35

Notes:
a.   Gini coefficient > 0.45.
b.   Gini coefficient 0.45 and 0.36.
c.   Gini coefficient < 0.36.

Source: Ros (2003).

consensus on how the cost of the adjustment should be distributed (Rodrik, 1998).

Table 6.6 illustrates how inequality (measured by the Gini coefficient) influences the incidence of growth collapses, defined as the experiences of economies whose real per capita income levels of the late 1990s were on a par with the levels they had reached between the 1960s and 1980s. As shown in the table, none of the low-inequality countries experienced such episodes, while over 50 per cent of the medium- and high-inequality countries did. The group that did have such setbacks includes four Central American countries (Nicaragua, El Salvador, Guatemala and Honduras), in addition to many African countries and others in Latin America and the Caribbean.

Dependence on Commodity Exports

In recent years, the literature on growth determinants has rediscovered the impact of an economy's dependence on commodity exports as a limiting factor in the development process. In fact, dependence on commodity exports is one of the most robust variables (with a negative sign) in econometric analyses of growth. In a study analyzing the determinants of growth in Central America, Esquivel (2001, Table 4–5) found that a strong reliance on commodity exports was the single most important reason Central America grew more slowly than Latin America 1960 and 96. This growth determinant accounts for 107 per cent and 84 per cent of the difference in growth rates between Central America and two sets of Latin American countries (grouped by the size of their economies).

The mechanisms through which this dependence can adversely affect growth can be summed up as follows:[5] (1) commodity export booms can lead to the onset of 'Dutch disease,' that is to say, they can have destructive effects on non-resource-intensive tradable goods sectors that persist after the boom has subsided (see Corden and Neary, 1982; Sachs and Warner, 1997, 2001; Rodríguez and Sachs, 1999); (2) international trade in resource-intensive goods can cause income distribution to worsen and prompt society to associate trade with the interests of the wealthy; (3) commodity prices are more volatile than prices of manufactured goods, and conditions may therefore be conducive to growth collapses in the absence of export diversification; (4) the terms of trade for primary products tend to deteriorate over the long run (that is, the celebrated Prebisch–Singer thesis, which is applicable today and relevant for the past two decades); and (5) rents from natural resources distract the state and society from focusing on the development of human resources and the creation of wealth and set the stage for rent-seeking behavior on the part of interest groups (Tornell and Lane, 1999).[6]

Table 6.7 shows the incidence of growth collapses, as defined earlier, in various economies that have been grouped by size and resource abundance. As suggested by the recent literature on commodity export dependence and growth, collapses are more common in resource-abundant economies than in resource-poor ones (30 per cent versus 17 per cent in large economies and 70 per cent versus 55 per cent in small economies). The impact of the economy's

Table 6.7   *Incidence of growth collapses in developing countries*

Type of economy	Number of countries	Number of collapses	Incidence of collapses (%)
Large	16	4	25
Poor[a]	6	1	17
Rich[b]	10	3	30
Small	54	36	67
Poor[a]	11	6	55
Rich[b]	43	30	70
Total	70	40	57

Notes:
a.   Resource-poor countries, defined by Auty (1997).
b.   Resource-rich countries, defined by Auty (1997).

Source: Ros (2003).

size on growth should also be noted, as small economies are more prone to growth collapses, irrespective of their resource-abundance. The impact of economic size probably reflects small economies' vulnerability to external shocks generated by a high degree of openness and dependence on foreign trade.

Export diversification in the 1990s lessened the impact of external shocks on international commodity markets (such as those that occurred in the 1990s in the cases of coffee and bananas). However, various countries in the region continue to rely on a few commodity exports and therefore remain vulnerable to such external shocks. This dependence is not clearly observable in Table 6.1, which provides a somewhat misleading picture of the share of manufactures in total exports. This is because a large share of these manufactures are produced by the *maquila* sector, which adds relatively little value to them, since such a large percentage of the inputs are imported. In order to provide a more accurate picture of the structure of exports, the estimates given in Table 6.8 base the share of *maquila* exports on the value added within this industry. As the table shows, with the exception of Mexico and El Salvador, the countries' shares of commodity exports continue to be quite significant (at least greater than 35 per cent).[7]

Table 6.8   Structure of exports, 2002

	% Primary	% Manufactures[a]	% *Maquila*[b]	% Other	Total
Guatemala[c]	59.6	10.9	22.7	6.7	100
Costa Rica	40.4	37.7	16.5	5.4	100
Honduras	35.6	n.d.	29.6	34.8	100
Mexico	16.1	60.5	23.1	0.1	100
El Salvador	9.0	33.7	29.0	28.3	100
Nicaragua	49.8[d]	n.a.	n.a.	n.a.	100

Notes:
a. Does not include *maquila* exports.
b. Value-added.
c. Does not include exports to Central America.
d. Figures for *maquila* exports have not been adjusted.

Source: ECLAC (2002).

Dynamism of External Markets

Do sluggish external markets for the region's products impede export growth? Table 6.9 gives the breakdown of the total exports of the countries in the

Table 6.9   *Market dynamism: main categories of exports to the United States, 1990–2000 (as percentage of the value of exports)*

	Dynamic markets			Non-dynamic markets		
	1990	2000	Average	1990	2000	Average
Costa Rica	52.4	79.1	65.8	47.6	20.9	34.3
El Salvador	33.8	86.5	60.2	66.2	13.5	39.9
Honduras	26.9	82.4	54.7	73.1	17.6	45.4
Mexico	35.2	51.7	43.5	64.8	48.3	56.6
Guatemala	21.3	54.0	37.7	78.7	46.0	62.4
Nicaragua	3.4	55.1	29.3	96.6	44.9	70.8

Source: Author's calculations based on the ECLAC Module for the Analysis of Growth of International Commerce (MAGIC) computer program.

region[8] (in 1990, 2000 and the average for 1990–2000) into those corresponding to sectors whose shares of total United States imports were growing (dynamic) and sectors whose shares were declining (non-dynamic) during the period 1990–2000. A first aspect to be noted here is the lack of dynamism of the external markets in the early 1990s. In all the countries of the region except Costa Rica, non-dynamic sectors accounted for over 50 per cent of total exports in 1990, and the figure was over 78 per cent in the cases of Guatemala and Nicaragua. The second observation to be made from the table concerns the radical transformation that occurred during the decade in the countries' types of international trade linkages. In 2000, the percentage of exports accounted for by non-dynamic sectors had dropped to below 50 per cent in every country, with the declines in El Salvador and Honduras being particularly noteworthy.

This transformation is due to the emergence of new manufacturing export sectors – particularly the *maquila* garment industry and, in the case of Costa Rica and Mexico, the electronic goods assembly sector – which have radically changed the structure of exports in the region. The limitations of this process, however, should be borne in mind. As shown in Table 6.10, with the exception of Costa Rica and Mexico, sectors with highly dynamic international markets account for less than 50 per cent (and in most cases much less) of the exports produced by leading manufacturing export sectors. In other words, although more dynamic than in the past, the external markets of most countries in the region continue to be rather sluggish.

Table 6.10 *Highly dynamic export sectors among leading manufacturing export sectors, 2000ᵃ (percentages)*

Costa Rica	78.8
Mexico	50.1
Honduras	47.2
Nicaragua	36.5
El Salvador	33.9
Guatemala	14.5

Note:
a. Sectors with high dynamism in international markets are defined as those whose products increased their share of United States imports by over 0.1 per cent between 1990 and 2000. The leading manufacturing export sectors are the five major categories of exports of manufactured products (four-digit level), with the exception of Mexico, where the 10 leading categories were considered in view of the greater diversification of that country's export base.

Source: author's calculations based on the ECLAC Module for the Analysis of Growth of International Commerce (MAGIC).

The Lack of Local Integration and the Productivity Growth Potential of the New Export Sectors

The new export sectors feature a low development of local linkages, including those of a fiscal nature. These sectors performed well in the 1990s, but their lack of local linkages, particularly in the case of *maquila* industries, is well known. Table 6.11 illustrates this point by showing the high import content of *maquila* exports. Furthermore, as shown in the table, there is no indication that the large percentage of the value of exports represented by imports is declining significantly as time goes on. The concomitant of this high import content is the fact that in most cases local inputs account for barely 5 per cent of the *maquila* sector's total inputs, which translates into the low level of value-added in total *maquila* exports. This lack of local integration is not limited to *maquila* industries. The rapid penetration of imports resulting from trade liberalization has led to a 'disintegration of linkages' in the manufacturing sector as a whole.

This lack of integration of the export sector tends to curb the growth of overall output, since the sector's capacity to generate externalities for other sectors of the economy is so limited. A recent study (see Ocampo, 2004) attests to the weakness of the export/output link in Latin America; in other words, exports must now grow faster than before if they are to generate the same rate of GDP growth. Together with the disintegration of pre-existing linkages created during the import-substitution period, this is due to the

Table 6.11   Import coefficient and value-added in the maquiladora *industry*

	Import coefficient		Value-added contribution	
	1990	2001	1990	2001
Mexico	75.5	68.2	24.5	31.8
Costa Rica	63.4	84.8	36.6	15.2
El Salvador	72.8	70.8	27.2	29.2
Guatemala	86.3	74.9	13.7	25.1
Honduras	86.2	74.0	13.8	26.0
Nicaragua	68.9[a]	77.4	31.1[a]	22.6
Simple average	75.5	75.0	24.5	25.0

Note:
a.   1995.

Source: ECLAC, *Latin America and The Caribbean in the World Economy*, 2001–02.

reduction in the local linkages associated with the expansion of new export sectors.

Another limitation of the pattern of trade specialization followed by the region is the low potential for productivity growth in new export sectors. The other side of the coin of the *maquila* sector's high labor absorption capacity is its low and stagnant labor productivity. As mentioned in an UNCTAD report (2002), statistics indicating that a significant share of these countries' exports are made up of mid- and high-technology manufactures are misleading. Much of the technological content of these manufactures is in fact embedded in the components produced by technologically advanced countries, while developing countries are involved in the assembly of these components, characterized by its low technological content, the use of unskilled labor and little value-added. (UNCTAD, 2002, p. 53).

These characteristics are reflected in the low productivity growth rates of the manufacturing sector as a whole, as labor is redirected towards, and is expanding rapidly in, low-productivity industries having a very low productivity/output elasticity. As shown in Table 6.12, this is especially the case of Guatemala, Honduras and Nicaragua.[9] With little or no productivity growth, the *maquila* sector can expand only on the basis of low wages. Given the tendency for wages to rise in tandem with productivity gains in other sectors, *maquila* plants' ability to maintain their internal competitiveness rests on having an undervalued currency. For example, in the case of Mexico, as the real exchange rate has appreciated in recent times and wages, measured in

Table 6.12   Output, employment and productivity growth in the
manufacturing sector (average annual growth rates, 1990–
2000)

	Output	Employment	Productivity	Elasticity[a]
Costa Rica[b]	4.9	0.6	4.3	0.9
Mexico[c]	4.4	2.2	2.1	0.5
El Salvador[d]	5.5	4.3	1.2	0.2
Nicaragua[c]	1.9	2.1	−0.2	−0.1
Honduras[c]	4.0	4.2	−0.2	−0.1
Guatemala[c]	2.7	5.8	−2.9	−1.1

Notes:
a.   Productivity/output elasticity.
b.   1990–97.
c.   1990–2000.
d.   1991–98.

Source: ECLAC database; Jenkins et al. (2001).

dollars, have consequently increased, profit margins in the *maquila* sector
have narrowed. This development, together with the recession in the United
States, has reined in the expansion of the production capacity and output of
the *maquila* industry, with a corresponding drop in employment starting in
the third quarter of 2000 (see Frenkel and Ros, 2003).

6.4   GROWTH PROSPECTS

Given recent trends and the possibility that some of the growth constraints
may ease, what is the outlook for growth in the region over the long term? In
order to answer this question, the first step is to estimate the economic growth
potential of countries in the region based on the assumption of a full employment of factors.[10] The methodology used here is a modified version of the one
proposed by Taylor and Rada (2003). The next step will be to estimate the
level of investment required to achieve the potential growth rate. Then, given
the required investment rate, the analysis evaluates the levels of domestic
saving and export growth needed to achieve the full-employment path.

Growth Potential: the Full Employment Path

A   A 'catching up' model
We begin with the following identity:

$$y^* = l^* + \rho, \qquad\qquad (6.1)$$

where: y^* = potential GDP growth rate;
    l^* = labor force growth rate;
    ρ = potential labor productivity growth rate.

As do Taylor and Rada (2003), we consider the following factors to be determinants of potential labor productivity growth. These factors reflect both the heterodox and orthodox traditions in the analysis of the growth potential.

1. The effect of increasing returns to scale in industrial sectors of the economy that operate through Verdoorn's elasticity (γ). Thus, we will assume that the labor productivity growth rate responds to GDP growth with a Verdoorn elasticity.
2. The effect of human capital accumulation (h), where it is assumed that a more rapid increase in education (rather than a higher level education) will lead to a higher productivity growth rate. It seems more realistic to assume that it is the increase in numbers educated, rather than the level of education, that influences the productivity growth rate, since, as noted by Taylor and Rada, developed countries are not growing faster now than they were several decades ago despite considerably higher levels of education.
3. The effect of technological backwardness (Γ). This term reflects the productivity growth associated with the gap between the income level of a given country and the prevailing level in rich countries. This can be rationalized à la Gershenkron (1962), who emphasized the 'advantages of backwardness', or can be seen as the result of a convergence process in a neoclassical growth model.
4. The effect of industrialization and other factors (Z). This term captures the effect of several factors. Expansion of the industrial sector typically raises productivity in other sectors of the economy (Kaldor, 1966, Cripps and Tarling, 1973; for a sample of Latin American countries, De Gregorio (1991) shows that a positive relationship exists between the economy's growth rate and the increase in industry's contribution to GDP). From a more orthodox standpoint, greater trade openness can stimulate productivity growth in tradable goods sectors and in the overall economy (De

Gregorio, 1991). Another possibility would be an acceleration in productivity growth brought about by industrial policy.

The above discussion leads to the following formulation:

$$\rho = \rho_0 + \gamma y + \eta h + Z + \Gamma, \tag{6.2}$$

where ρ_0 is an autonomous rate of productivity growth. Equations (6.1) and (6.2) imply:

$$y^* = \frac{1}{(1-\gamma)}(l^* + \rho_0 + \eta h + Z) + \frac{1}{(1-\gamma)}\Gamma$$

or:

$$y^* = A + B\Gamma \tag{6.3}$$

where:

$$A = \left[\frac{1}{(1-\gamma)}\right](l^* + \rho_0 + \eta h + Z)$$

$$B = \frac{1}{(1-\gamma)}$$

Term Γ is, as previously mentioned, an inverse function of the gap, $\lambda = (Y/P)/(Y/P)r$, between per capita income (Y/P) and the per capita income of developed countries, $(Y/P)r$:

$$\Gamma = D - E\lambda; \ D = E\lambda_0; \ \lambda_0 = \text{intial value of } \lambda.$$

B   Assumptions and results

The main assumptions made in the growth simulations can be summarized as follows:

Population and labor force growth   The simulations are based on ECLAC projections. In the case of the labor force, the projection for the working age population was used, thus assuming that the upward trend in the women's participation rate will be offset by a reduction in the rate among school-aged youth. Both population and labor force growth rates show a downward trend during the period of analysis in every country. The highest growth rates and the largest differentials between the growth rate of the labor force and that of population are found among the lowest-income countries (Guatemala, Honduras and Nicaragua), where the resulting demographic bonus has, as we shall see, a significant impact on the potential growth of per capita income.

Returns to scale   For the lowest-income countries – Guatemala, Honduras and Nicaragua – we have assumed that the combination of a low productivity growth potential, low wages and a rapidly growing labor force will cause economic growth to be highly labor-intensive, with a very low Verdoorn elasticity (0.15).[11] This coefficient is somewhat higher than the slightly negative values recorded in those countries in the 1990s (see Table 6.12). For the higher-income countries (Mexico and Costa Rica), which have a larger percentage of exports with mid- to high-technology content, the Verdoorn coefficient starts off at 0.3 and then gradually rises to 0.4 in 2010–15, a value close to that characterizing developed countries (0.5). El Salvador, with a low income level but moderate growth in the labor force, is an intermediate case with a Verdoorn coefficient that rises from 0.2 to 0.3, similar to what it was in the 1990s.

Human capital accumulation   This indicator is measured by the growth of the educational level index used in the *Human Development Report* (a weighted average of the literacy rate and enrolment in the three levels of education). We have assumed that by 2015 the educational index for Costa Rica and Mexico will have reached the level achieved by high-income OECD countries in 2000 (which implies annual growth rates of 0.8 per cent and 1 per cent, respectively). In El Salvador, which had the fastest rising educational index for the period 1995–2000, the index grows at an annual rate of 2 per cent until it reaches Costa Rica's 2000 level by 2008, and from then on grows at the same rate as Costa Rica. Guatemala, Honduras and Nicaragua, which currently have the lowest indicators, achieve Costa Rica's 2000 level by the end of the period of analysis. This implies relatively high annual growth rates (on the order of 2.2 per cent in Guatemala, 1.4 per cent in Honduras and 1.9 per cent in Nicaragua). For the parameter η, which shows how productivity growth responds to human capital growth, we have used Maddison's estimate (1995) and assume $\eta = 1$ for all countries.[12]

Industrialization effect   We have assumed that productivity growth in all countries is 1 per cent higher as a result of the effects of industrialization or of trade and industrial policies aimed at boosting productivity growth.

Effect of technological catching up   As the technological gap narrows, growth tends to slow down. This effect is captured by the equation: $\Gamma = D - E\lambda$

where a positive value for parameter *E* means that productivity growth slows as the ratio (λ) between a given country's per capita income and the per capita income of developed countries (high-income OECD countries) approaches unity. As Taylor and Rada did for Latin America, this value is assumed to be 0.06 (that is, half the value corresponding to post-war Japan). The value of the constant, *D*, in the equation is such that the value of the effect of technological backwardness is initially zero. The growth of per capita income in developed countries is assumed to be 1.7 per cent (the value recorded for 1990–2000).

Table 6.13   *Projections of the potential growth of GDP (y*) and per capita GDP (g*) and the income gap relative to OECD countries (λ)*

	2000–2015		λ as a %		g	
	y^*	g^*	λ2000	λ2015	1960–80	1990–2003
Mexico	4.9	3.6	32.0	44.0	3.5	1.2
Costa Rica	5.1	3.3	31.0	42.0	2.4	2.6
El Salvador	5.6	4.0	16.0	23.0	1.0	2.0
Guatemala	7.3	4.7	14.0	21.0	2.8	1.0
Honduras	6.4	4.1	9.0	13.0	1.8	0.3
Nicaragua	7.0	4.6	8.0	12.0	0.3	0.8

Source: For historical rates, World Bank, World Development Indicators (online)

The simulations are summarized in Table 6.13. For comparison, the table also presents per capita GDP growth rates (*g*) for 1960–80 and 1990–2003. Two observations are called for here. First, with the exception of Mexico during the period 1960–80, potential growth rates are much higher (two percentage points or more in most cases) than in the past, whether compared to the rates recorded in 1960–80 or in the 1990s (not to mention those recorded during the 'lost decade' of the 1980s). This is especially the case of the lowest-income countries (Guatemala, Honduras and Nicaragua). This is due to the effects of industrialization and public policies, which tend to raise potential productivity growth by 1 per cent per annum above what it would otherwise be, and, in particular, to the considerable educational effort that has been assumed, since human capital accumulation in these three countries is higher than in the country that made the most educational progress during the period 1995–2000 (El Salvador).

Second, if potential or natural growth rates were achieved, convergence towards the more developed countries' income levels would take place. This

Table 6.14 Relative income levels

	2000	2015
Mexico	100	100
Costa Rica	97	95
El Salvador	50	52
Guatemala	44	48
Honduras	28	30
Nicaragua	25	27

Source: Author's calculations.

would be associated with a regional homogenization process, although this would undoubtedly take place within the context of a persistent heterogeneity. As shown in Table 6.14, the relative gap that separates the higher-income countries (Mexico and Costa Rica) from the others would tend to narrow, with El Salvador and Guatemala eventually having the equivalent of 50 per cent or more of Mexico's per capita income level, and Honduras and Nicaragua reaching a level close to one third of Mexico's. Although moderate, this trend would represent a reversal of the historical trend towards a divergence in these countries' income levels, which was particularly evident in the period 1960–80.

Investments

Equation (6.3) defines the economy's potential growth rate. This is associated with a required rate of capital accumulation (k^*). Since $y = k + \rho k$, where k is the growth rate of capital stock and ρk is the growth rate of average capital productivity, then (6.3) leads to:

$$k^* = A + B\Gamma - \rho k. \tag{6.4}$$

The investment rate required to achieve the growth potential is then:

$$(I/Y)^* = (k^* + \delta)(K/Y), \tag{6.5}$$

where δ is the rate of depreciation of the capital stock and (K/Y) is the capital–potential output ratio.

Equations (6.3), (6.4) and (6.5) give us the full-employment growth rates for GPD and capital, as well as the investment rate required to achieve the potential growth path. Given a flow of external savings, we can also determine the domestic saving and export growth requirements.

Domestic Savings and Export Growth Requirements

By identity we have:

$$I/Y = S_d/Y + (S_f/Y) \sim \tag{6.6}$$

Where (S_d/Y) is the rate of domestic saving and $(S_f/Y) \sim$ the rate of foreign saving. Using equation (6.6), the required domestic savings rate is simply:

$$(S_d/Y)^* = (I/Y)^* - (S_f/Y) \sim$$

In turn, the required export growth rate can be estimated as the product of the income elasticity of imports and the potential growth rate. Thus, if the required rate is reached, the trade deficit, measured as a percentage of exports, remains constant between the initial and final years of the projection.

Assumptions and results

Table 6.15 shows the estimates of the investment rates, $(I/Y)^*$, required to achieve the potential growth rate together with the average investment rate observed during the period 1991–2000. The required gross investment rate $(I/Y)^*$ is the net rate required plus the rate of depreciation (d, as a percentage of GDP), the required net investment rate being the potential growth rate multiplied by the capital–output ratio.[13] For the Central American countries, both the capital–output ratio and the depreciation rate are taken from ECLAC estimates (1995) for the early 1990s. In the case of Mexico, the source is

Table 6.15   Required investment rates

	y^*	K/Y	d	$(I/Y)^*$	I/Y
Mexico	4.9	2.6	12.0	24.7	23.2
Costa Rica	5.1	2.0	14.8	25.0	22.1[a]
El Salvador	5.6	1.5	11.7	20.1	17.3
Guatemala	7.3	1.0	8.0	15.3	15.4
Honduras	6.4	2.0	9.1	21.9	28.2
Nicaragua	7.0	2.4	20.0	36.8	27.6

Note: a.   1994–2000.

Source: Author's calculations.

Hofman (2000), and a depreciation rate of 12 per cent (as a percentage of GDP) has been assumed.

As can be seen from the table, achieving the potential growth rate will require increasing investment above the levels recorded in the 1990s in all countries except Guatemala and Honduras.[14] The additional investment effort will be particularly large in Nicaragua followed by Costa Rica and El Salvador. It is worth noting that even in the presence of an abundant supply of external savings, the investment demand may not be forthcoming at the required rate as a result of the operation of the constraints on growth discussed earlier, which have prevented so far the achievement of the required investment rate.

Moreover, given a flow of external savings, the achievement of the potential growth rate requires a complementary amount of domestic savings. These domestic saving requirements are presented in Table 6.16. The required domestic saving rate, $(S_d/Y)^*$, is estimated as the difference between required investment and the rate of available external saving (S_f/Y) ~, the latter being equal to the rate observed in 1998–2000 (the implicit assumption is that the abundant flows of external capital that characterized the rest of the 1990s, and particularly the period 1990–93, will not be repeated in the future).

Table 6.16   Domestic savings requirements (as a percentage of GDP)

	$(I/Y)^*$	S_f/Y ~	$(S_d/Y)^*$	S_d/Y
Mexico	24.7	3.3	21.4	19.8[a]
Costa Rica	25.0	5.0	20.0	13.2
El Salvador	20.1	2.6	17.5	15.0
Guatemala	15.3	6.3	9.0	8.8
Honduras	21.9	3.9	18.0	25.2[a]
Nicaragua	36.8	32.7[b]	4.1	1.0[b]

Notes:
a.   1998–2001.
b.   2000–02.

Source: Author's calculations

As shown in the table, additional savings requirements are an important factor in every country except Guatemala and Honduras. In Mexico and El Salvador, the additional domestic saving effort required is less than three percentage points of GDP, so that these savings constraints are not insurmountable. Costa Rica and Nicaragua are atypical cases. In Costa Rica, the large difference between the required domestic savings rate and the actual domestic savings rate in recent years is due to the fact that the domestic savings rate has declined considerably in recent years, thus creating a situation of large savings requirements to reach an investment rate not very different from that recorded in the 1990s. In contrast, the gap between the required investment rate and the average rate for the 1990s is much narrower, which is consistent with the fact that Costa Rica's potential growth rate is not too different from the rate recorded in the 1990s. The case of Nicaragua is, in a sense, just the opposite. The difference between the required and observed investment rates in the 1990s is considerable as we have seen but the domestic savings rate has been on the rise (in the midst of an abundant supply of external savings), thereby easing domestic savings requirements. In order for these relatively low requirements to remain so in the future, however, the hefty external capital flows that characterized the 1990s will have to continue in the coming years.

Table 6.17 gives estimates of the required export growth rates, x^*, which are equal to the potential growth rate (y^*) multiplied by the income elasticity of imports (μ). The table also includes the export growth rates recorded in the 1990s for purposes of comparison (1990–2000).

Table 6.17   Required export growth rates^a

	y^*	μ^b	x^*	x1990–2000
Mexico	4.9	2.5	12.3	13.4
Costa Rica	5.1	1.5	7.7	10.7
El Salvador	5.6	2.4	13.4	12.5
Guatemala	7.3	2.1	15.3	8.3
Honduras	6.4	1.1	7.0	1.2
Nicaragua	7.0	1.5	10.5	7.6

Notes:
a.   The required rate is based on the assumption that the terms of trade will remain constant. If, as has happened in the past, the terms of trade were to deteriorate, the required rate would be even higher.
b.   Sources for the income elasticities of imports: Moreno Brid (2002), Galindo (2002).

Source: Author's calculations.

Taking into account the already strong export growth of the 1990s, it will be difficult to achieve the even higher export growth that is required in the region as a whole, except perhaps in the case of Costa Rica and Mexico (where the required rate of export growth is actually lower than the historical value) and, to a point, Honduras (where, despite the country's low historical rates of export growth, the relatively small income elasticity of imports generates the lowest required export growth rate in the region). Even in the case of Mexico and Costa Rica, the export growth rates of the 1990s seem to be unrepeatable as they incorporated the once-and-for-all effect of trade liberalization and, in the case of Mexico, of the North American Free Trade Agreement. However, the income elasticities of imports will also tend to decline in the future since the high values of the 1990s also incorporate a once-and-for-all effect. In the other countries, required export growth rates are significantly higher than historical rates, particularly in the cases of Guatemala and Nicaragua (given their very high potential growth rates).

6.5   CONCLUSIONS

Following the 'lost decade' of the 1980s, growth rates rebounded in Mexico and Central America in the 1990s. Several factors came together to make this recovery possible: the normalization of the region's access to international capital markets, macroeconomic stabilization, the end of political instability and the transition towards a growth model driven by manufacturing exports. Even though the region has been the most dynamic grouping in Latin America, economic growth since 1990 has tended to be slower than it had been in the 1960s and 1970s, especially in the case of Mexico with the largest economy in the region.

There are several factors that hold the region back from achieving higher growth rates. With the exception of Mexico and Costa Rica, the region lags far behind the rest of Latin America in terms of competitiveness broadly defined. Business administration and climate appear to be the major factors explaining the lags in competitiveness in most of the region, with exchange rate appreciation playing a role in Mexico and Costa Rica. Its highly unequal income distribution is an obstacle to growth and hinders efforts to combat poverty. Despite the diversification of exports in the 1990s, the region, with the exception of Mexico and El Salvador, continues to be quite vulnerable to fluctuations in international commodity markets, and although they are more dynamic than in the past, external markets for its main exports are not characterized by high growth rates. Moreover, new export sectors display very little local integration and have a low potential for productivity growth. Both of these weaken their capacity to generate growth in the economy as a whole.

At the same time, the region's potential growth rates – given the rapid growth of its labor force and its productivity growth potential – are much higher than in the past. The magnitude of these rates is such that a considerable increase in investment demand will be needed in the region as a whole and this demands addressing the current constraints on growth. A domestic savings effort will be also be called for, especially in Costa Rica, Nicaragua, Mexico and El Salvador, while export growth rates will have to be raised above their levels in the recent past in all the countries except Costa Rica and Mexico. In order to accomplish this, systematic efforts will have to be made to avert any appreciation of the real exchange rate.

NOTES

*   The author is grateful to Juan Carlos Moreno Brid and Andrés Solimano for valuable comments on an earlier version of this chapter. He is also grateful to Liliana Castilleja for her assistance in processing the foreign trade data and to Rubén Guerrero for his assistance in preparing the growth projections. An earlier version of the chapter was prepared for the ECLAC regional office in Mexico City.

1.   With the exception of Honduras, where inflation accelerated in the early 1990s after the country unpegged its currency from the dollar.

2.   See, however, the discussion in a later section on the limitations of the current model of trade specialization. On the transition towards a new development style in the 1990s and the key role played by exports in the growth of Central America, see Moreno Brid (2003). Ros and Lustig (2001) examine the role of exports in Mexico's economic recovery during the second half of the 1990s.

3.   With imperfect credit markets, less inequality eases the budgetary constraints of the poor and allows higher levels of investment in education (Galor and Zeira, 1993; Birdsall et al. 1995).

4.   It is clear that in the case of these economic mechanisms, income inequality inhibits growth by exacerbating poverty (at a given level of per capita income); poverty is what limits market size and aggregate demand, diminishes investment in education and spurs high population growth rates. This observation highlights the importance of social policy and poverty reduction programs for the economic growth of the region.

5.   See Ros (2000 and 2003).

6.   It is important to note that the literature also presents the 'staple thesis', which, contrary to these hypotheses, emphasizes the positive effects that an abundant supply of natural resources can have on growth (Ros, 2000, reviews the literature).

7.   At least higher than this percentage, since the unclassified products, which surely include some commodities, make a sizable contribution in the case of Honduras.

8.   More precisely, we refer to the export contribution of the 20 main export categories (four digits of the harmonized system), which ranged from 62 per cent (Mexico) to 94 per cent (Nicaragua) of total exports to the United States in 2000.

9.   Although they may in part to due to errors of measurement (including the fact that the output of the *maquila* sector is not fully captured in national accounts: see Zubekas, 2000), these countries' negative productivity growth rates may also be reflecting the effects of redirecting labor towards industries, such as the maquilas, with below-average labor productivity.

10.   This refers to the potential or natural growth rate estimated on the assumption of full employment of the labor force and the potential productivity growth. It should not be confused with the growth rate of potential GDP, which can be limited by the full employment of one of the factors (for example, capital).

11.   Compared to a value of around 0.5 for developed countries. In the case of Honduras, the coefficient increases to 0.2 during the period 2010–15 due to a significantly lower growth in the labor force.

12.   This assumption is optimistic. Ros (2000) estimate yields $\eta = 0.5$ for a sample of developing and developed countries.

13. This assumes that average capital productivity remains constant.
14. The chapter by Agosín and Machado in this book emphasizes the role of investment in the growth process of the region.

REFERENCES

Alesina, A. and R. Perotti (1994), 'The political economy of growth: a critical survey of the recent literature', *World Bank Economic Review*, **8**.

Alesina, A. and D. Rodrik (1994), 'Distributive politics and economic growth', *Quarterly Journal of Economics*, **109**.

Auty, R. (1997), 'Natural resource endowment, the state and development strategy', *Journal of International Development*, **9** (4).

Birdsall, N., D. Ross and R. Sabot (1995), 'Inequality and growth reconsidered: lessons from East Asia', *World Bank Economic Review*, **9**.

CEPAL (2002), 'Estilos de desarrollo y mutaciones del sector laboral en la región norte de América Latina', LC/MEX/L, **539**.

Corden, W.M. and J.P. Neary (1982), 'Booming sector and de-industrialisation in a small open economy', *Economic Journal*, **92**.

Cripps, F. and R. Tarling (1973), *Growth in Advanced Capitalist Economies, 1950–1970*, Cambridge: Cambridge University Press.

De Gregorio, J. (1991), 'Economic growth in Latin America', International Monetary Fund, mimeo.

Dutt, A.K. (1984), 'Stagnation, income distribution and monopoly power', *Cambridge Journal of Economics*, **8**.

Economic Commission for Latin America and the Caribbean (ECLAC) (2002), database from Mexico regional office.

ECLAC (2001–2), *Latin America and the Caribbean in the World Economy, 2001–2002*, International Trade and Integration Division, January.

Esquivel, G. (2001), 'Economic growth in Central America: a long run perspective', in F. Larrain (ed.), *Economic Development in Central America*, Cambridge, MA: Harvard University, John F. Kennedy School of Government.

Frenkel, R. and J. Ros (2003), 'Unemployment, macroeconomic policy and labor market flexibility. Argentina and Mexico in the 1990s', mimeo.

Galindo, L.M. (2002), *Modelos econométricos para los países de Centroamérica*, CEPAL.

Galor, O. and J. Zeira (1993), 'Income distribution and macroeconomics', *Review of Economic Studies*, **60**.

Gershenkron, A. (1962), *Economic Backwardness in Historical Perspective*, Cambridge, MA: Harvard University Press.

Hofman, A. (2000), 'Standardised capital stock estimates in Latin America: a 1950–1994 update', *Cambridge Journal of Economics*, **24** (1).

Jenkins, M., G. Esquivel and F. Larrain (2001), 'Export processing zones in Central America', in F. Larrain (ed.), *Economic Development in Central America*, Cambridge, MA: Harvard University John F. Kennedy School of Government.

Kaldor, N. (1966), *Causes of the Slow Rate of Economic Growth of the United Kingdom*, Cambridge: Cambridge University Press.

Keefer, P. and S. Knack (1997), 'Polarization, property rights, and the links between inequality and growth', manuscript.

Lall, S. (2001), 'Competitiveness indices and developing countries: an economic evaluation of the Global Competitiveness Report', *World Development*, **29** (9).

Maddison, A. (1995), *Monitoring the World Economy 1820–1992*, Paris: Organisation for Economic Co-operation and Development.

Moreno Brid, J.C. (2002), 'Liberalización comercial y la demanda de importaciones en México', *Investigación Económica*, **240**, April–June.

Moreno Brid, J.C. (2003), 'El crecimiento económico de América central en los noventa: un nuevo estilo de desarrollo?', mimeo.

Murphy, K., A. Shleifer and R. Vishny (1989), 'Income distribution, market size, and industrialization', *Journal of Political Economy*, **97**.

Ocampo, J.A. (2004), 'Latin America's growth and equity frustrations during structural reforms', *Journal of Economic Perspectives*, **18** (2) (Spring).

Perotti, R. (1996), 'Growth, income distribution and democracy: what the data say', *Journal of Economic Growth*, **1**.

Rodríguez, F. and J. Sachs (1999), 'Why do resource abundant economies grow more slowly? A new explanation and an application to Venezuela', *Journal of Economic Growth*, **4** (3).

Rodrik, D. (1998), 'Where did all the growth go? External shocks, social conflict, and growth collapses', National Bureau for Economic Research working paper 6350, Cambridge, MA.

Ros, J. (2000), *Development Theory and the Economics of Growth*, Ann Arbor, MI: University of Michigan Press.

Ros, J. (2003), 'Divergencia y retrocesos de crecimiento: teoría y evidencia empírica', mimeo.

Ros, J. and N. Lustig (2001), 'Mexico: trade and financial liberalization with volatile capital inflows. Macroeconomic consequences and social impacts during the 1990s', in L. Taylor (ed.), *External Liberalization, Economic Performance And Social Policy*, Oxford: Oxford University Press.

Sachs, J. and A. Warner (1997), 'Fundamental sources of long-run growth', *American Economic Review*, **87** (2).

Sachs, J. and A. Warner (2001), 'The curse of natural resources', *European Economic Review*, **45** (4–6).

Tavares, J. (2001), 'Crisis and recovery: Central America from the eighties to the nineties', in F. Larrain (ed.), *Economic Development in Central America*, Cambridge MA: Harvard University John F. Kennedy School of Government.

Taylor, L. and C. Rada (2003), 'Can the poor countries catch up? Sources of growth accounting gives weak convergence for the early 21st century', mimeo, June.

Tornell, A. and P. Lane (1999), 'The voracity effect', *American Economic Review*, **89** (1).

UNCTAD (2002), *Trade and Development Report*, United Nations.

United Nations Development Program (UNDP) (2002), *Human Development Report*, United Nations.

World Economic Forum (2002), *Global Competitiveness Report, 2001–2002*.

Zubekas, C. (2000), *The Dynamics of Sectoral Growth in Central America: Recent Trends and Prospects for 2020*, Hamburg: Institut für Iberoamerika-Kunde.

7. Economic growth in Latin America: the role of investment and other growth sources*

Mario A. Gutiérrez

7.1 INTRODUCTION

The modest recovery of Latin America after a period of stabilization and reforms that followed the 1980s debt crisis has added momentum to the interest in the factors that contribute to economic growth in the region and, in particular, about the role played by investment as a source of economic growth. Under a new outward-looking development approach, growth and investment recovered during the 1990s and early 2000s from the slump of the 1980s. The recovery has been modest, however. Growth performance has not yet reached the growth rate levels observed in 1960s and 1970s and growth rates remain well below those observed in other developing countries in Asia, the Middle East and Eastern Europe.

Disagreement persists about the role of investment in the growth process. Some authors have concluded that investment has been the main factor explaining economic growth. In a study of East Asia, Young (1994) concluded that investment was the main source of growth in the experience of the East Asian economies. Other economists have acknowledged the important role played by fixed investment but argued that productivity has been the engine that has marked the difference between fast and slow growth experiences (Blomstrom et al., 1996; Harberger, 1996 and 1998; Klenow and Rodriguez-Clare, 1997b). Elias (1992) produced evidence showing that total factor productivity explained about one-third of GDP growth in Latin America during the period 1940–85. In a more recent study, Solimano and Soto (Chapter 2 in this volume) produced evidence showing that total factor productivity was the most important factor explaining the evolution of GDP growth in Latin America during the 1960–2002 period. Other economists have focused on specific categories of investment. Some have emphasized the role of machinery as a main determinant of a country's economic growth (De Long and Summers, 1991 and 1993). Others have found evidence of a positive correlation between growth and private investment and the potential complementarities between private investment and public investment (Kahn and Kumar, 1997; Kahn and Reinhart, 1990; Servén and Solimano, 1992; and Greene and Villanueva, 1991). The roles played by foreign direct investment (FDI) and infrastructure as factors contributing to growth have been also documented, but the evidence is more controversial. The roles of FDI have been addressed by Lim (2001), Borensztein et al. (1998), and Olofsdotter (1998). The roles of infrastructure have been addressed by Calderón and Servén (2004) and Moguillansky and Bielchowsky (2000) for Latin America.

The role assigned to investment in the process of economic growth is relevant to growth theory and policy making. Should countries focus on increasing investment rates through, for example, massive investment programs in order to accelerate the pace of economic growth? What types of investments have the strongest impacts in raising growth? What is the role played by productivity? What are the roles played by economic policies as factors contributing to investment and growth? Are there reinforcing effects between investment and growth?

This chapter produces evidence about the contribution of investment and other sources to the growth process of Latin America from 1960 to 2002, and provides answers to the questions listed above. In our research we combine growth accounting and regression analysis to reinforce our conclusions, which confirm and qualify some previous findings about the process of economic investment, growth, and productivity in Latin America during in this period.

We have used data for the six largest Latin American countries: Argentina, Brazil, Chile, Colombia, Mexico and Venezuela. These countries produce nearly 90 per cent of Latin America's GDP (World Bank, 2004). The selection of countries and period used for the study was also based on the availability and quality of the data. Reliable national accounts data before 1960 are not available for many Latin American countries and the quality of disaggregated investment data by type of assets and sectors is either non-existent or weak.

We examine the investment–growth process from three perspectives. First, we use alternative growth accounting methodologies to measure the contributions of the sources of growth to GDP growth in 1960–2002 (Section 7.2). Secondly, we estimate the effects of investments in machinery and equipment and construction structures (Section 7.3). Thirdly, we estimate the effects of private and public investment on per capita GDP growth (Section 7.4). Our main findings are summarized in Section 7.5.

In our research we found that investment has played an important role in the six largest Latin American countries but that total factor productivity has made the difference between faster and slower growth experiences (across time and countries). In line with endogenous growth theory, we then explored the main factors that contributed to the productivity differences in the region. We use per capita GDP growth as a proxy for productivity growth and we found that investment and policy related factors together have been main factors explaining per capita GDP growth. We found that investment in the form of machinery and equipment and private investment have been effective in boosting per capita growth, but that some key policy related variables have helped to explain the difference between fast and slow growth countries and episodes during the 1960–2002 period. We also show evidence about a reverse causality between private investment and GDP growth, which helps explain some of the virtuous and vicious cycles in Latin America, especially at times of prolonged recession and expansion. We also examined the stability of the findings and qualified them as needed. We found that the incidence on economic growth have not only varied across the key growth determinant factors but also within the 1960–2002 period. In some sub-periods some key variables have been more relevant than in others. The main long-run trends and conclusions are not severely affected by the structural shifts, however.

7.2 SOURCES OF GROWTH: CAPITAL, LABOR AND TOTAL FACTOR PRODUCTIVITY

In this section we run an exercise of growth accounting to obtain estimates of the contribution of investment to real GDP growth for the six Latin American countries considered in our sample. The growth accounting approach has some advantages compared to the regression approach for measuring the contributions of the three broad categories of sources of growth (capital, labor and total factor productivity) (Barro 1999; Klenow and Rodriguez-Clare 1997a, 1997b; Pack 1994; and Easterly 2001). The growth accounting approach overcomes three main problems present in the regression approach for measuring the growth sources: (1) the changes in capital and labor are usually endogenous to total factor productivity; (2) if the changes in capital and labor are measured with errors, the regression coefficients would be inconsistent estimates of the shares of capital and labor (this problem aggravates when the capital stock is not adjusted by 'utilization' of the capital stock); (3) regression estimates usually assume no variations in factor shares or total factor productivity through time and across countries.

The growth accounting approach has also some disadvantages, however. Its main limitations stem from the use of factor prices to estimate factor contributions to real GDP growth. Deviations between factor prices and marginal products would be included in measured total factor productivity (the residual in the growth accounting). As long as we interpret total factor productivity as a broad measure of 'real cost reductions', however, those deviations could be considered as forming part of the residual interpreted, broadly interpreted as a measure of economy-wide real cost reductions (Harberger, 1996).

A   Methodology: 'Traditional Modified' and 'Extended' Approaches

To obtain the growth accounting estimates for the six Latin American countries we will develop and apply two approaches. We will build a 'traditional modified' approach (TMA) and an 'extended' approach (EA). Under the TMA we generate capital stock series using the series on gross capital formation at constant prices of each country, a usual practice in most growth accounting exercises, but we innovate by decomposing the wage bill between the payments to 'raw labor' and to 'human capital'. We use a proxy for the remuneration of raw labor to deflate the wage bill and obtain the two separate labor components. Through this exercise we want to determine whether the conclusions about the contributions of the three basic sources of growth on economic growth are sensitive to the growth accounting methodology. We show below that enriching the traditional growth accounting framework with some strong deviations did not changed the main conclusions. The modifications and extensions that we introduce to the traditional growth accounting approach also allow us to obtain additional insights into the growth process.

In the EA we decompose the wage bill series between the raw and human capital components, as in the TMA but, in addition, we generate an alternative series of physical capital, deflating the gross capital formation series at current prices by the GDP deflator, and adjust the capital series to reflect the 'utilization' of physical capital. We also use a notion of 'invested' physical capital, in line with capital theory by expressing capital stock series in the same GDP basket units as GDP at constant prices: GDP units of capital are used or invested to generate GDP (both capital and GDP expressed in the same GDP basket units). In both approaches we use annual shares of labor and physical capital for each of the six countries during 1960–2002. Most growth accounting exercises use constant factor shares across time and countries, limitations that contribute to distort the derived total factor productivity series.

We start from the basic national accounts identity where output is distributed between the payments to capital and labor:

$$py = \rho n K + \omega n L. \tag{7.1}$$

Real changes are expressed as:

$$\Delta y = \rho \Delta K + \omega \Delta L + R, \tag{7.2}$$

where:

Δ = change in the variable;
y = real GDP;
p = GDP deflator;
K = real capital stock;
L = employed labor force;
ρn = nominal return of capital;
ωn = nominal wage rate;
ρ = real gross of depreciation return to capital = real net return to capital
  (ρr) + depreciation (δ).
ω = average wage;
R = residual = total factor productivity = real cost reductions.

In growth accounting it is usual to refer to the residual R as total factor productivity or 'real cost reductions' (Harberger, 1998 and 1996). In terms of annual per cent changes we can derive the contributions of each factor to real GDP growth and the contribution of total factor productivity (or real cost reductions to growth): $R^*(R/y)$:

$$\frac{\Delta y}{y} = S_K \frac{\Delta K}{K} + S_L \frac{\Delta L}{L} + R^*, \qquad (7.3)$$

i.e. growth of real GDP = contribution of capital + contribution of labor + contribution of total factor productivity.

where:

$$S_K = \frac{\rho \Delta K}{py} = \text{share of capital in output;}$$

$$S_L = \frac{\omega \Delta L}{py} = \text{share of labor in output.}$$

The interpretation of equation (7.3), as the sources of growth equation (measuring the contributions of physical capital, labor, and total factor productivity to output growth) builds on the assumption that factor payments are good approximations of marginal products. Any deviations between factor payments and marginal products ($MP_K - \rho$) and ($MP_L - \omega$) would be reflected in R and R^*. These deviations stem from all types of distortions that make factor payments deviate from marginal products such as economies of scale and taxes. However, as long as these distortions raise production costs, then, they should be appropriately reflected in R^* if we interpret it as reflecting all type of real cost changes in the economy.

Equation (7.3) can also be derived from a Cobb–Douglas production function $y = AK^{S_K} L^{S_L}$ with: $S_K + S_L = 1$, or any production function homogeneous of degree one. But the specification of a production function is not a prerequisite to the sources of growth equation (7.3).

Equation (7.3) represents the 'traditional' growth accounting equation used in most growth accounting studies. We will now deviate from the traditional approach along two roads. We first proceed to decompose the wage bill between the component representing the payments to 'raw' labor and the component representing the payments to the quality or 'human capital' component. We will then proceed to generate the series of 'invested' physical capital. We follow these roads based on the 'two deflators' approach developed by Harberger (1998), but we also add additional extensions. We derive series of physical capital adjusted for utilization rates. Let us first proceed to divide the wage bill between 'raw' labor and 'human capital'. Let us define:

$$L^* = \frac{\omega L}{\omega^*} = \text{raw labor equivalent units of the wage bill;}$$

$$\omega^* = \text{wage rate of raw labor.}$$

Then, the wage bill can be decomposed as:

$$\omega \Delta L = \omega^* \Delta L + \omega^* (\Delta L^* - \Delta L),$$

i.e., wage bill = payments to raw labor + payments to the human capital component (human capital maintenance + human capital upgrade).[1]

Our TMA growth accounting equation would be:

$$\frac{\Delta y}{y} = SK \frac{\Delta K}{K} + \frac{\omega^* \Delta L}{y} + \frac{\omega^* (\Delta L^* - \Delta L)}{y} + R^*, \qquad (7.4)$$

Growth of real GDP = contribution of physical capital + direct contribution of raw labor + direct contribution of the quality improvement of the labor force (human capital) + contribution of total factor productivity (R^*).

An 'ideal' decomposition of labor payments (into raw labor and the human capital component) should be derived by using as raw labor wage deflator the most representative wage index of unskilled labor. A proxy for this could be wages for textiles workers as mentioned by Harberger (1998), a proxy for the wage bill of low skilled workers. We examined this possibility using the International Labor Office (ILO) statistics but we found serious problems regarding the quality, time consistency and data gaps. We decided to use instead a fictitious low skilled wage category defining its average wage as equal to two-thirds of per capita GDP.[2] The use of annual factor shares is crucial in our work not only to better capture the contributions of capital and labor to the growth but also to obtain series for the raw labor and human capital components of the labor share.[3]

To further generate what we call the EA we further expressed the physical capital series in terms of 'GDP baskets'. The growth accounting interpretation of this alternative K^* series is better associated with capital theory: K^* units of capital are invested to obtain GDP with both expressed in the same units (GDP baskets). In addition, we adjust the physical capital series to reflect the notion of 'utilized' physical capital as a vector of 'rates of utilization', which we approximate by the ratios of actual GDP to 'potential' GDP. We define 'potential' GDP as a centered seven-year moving average of actual GDP.[4]

K^* = physical capital series deflated by the GDP deflator:

$$K_{inv}^* = K^* \left(\frac{y}{y_p} \right).$$

The rate of utilization of capital is defined as $RUK = (y/y_p)$. Our EA growth accounting equation would, therefore, be expressed as:

$$\frac{\Delta y}{y} = SK \frac{\Delta K^*}{K^*} + \frac{\omega^* \Delta L}{y} + \frac{\omega^* (\Delta L^* - \Delta L)}{y} + R^{**}, \tag{7.5}$$

i.e., growth of real GDP = contribution of 'invested' capital + direct contribution of raw labor + direct contribution of the quality improvement of the labor force (human capital) + contribution of adjusted total factor productivity (R^{**}).

The capital stock series are derived in both approaches using a perpetual inventory method and based on the following capital equation:

$$K_{t+1} = K_t(1 - \delta) + I_t(1 - \delta/2). \tag{7.6}$$

I_t = gross fixed capital formation: (1) at constant prices in the TMA, and (2) in GDP baskets in the EA. The initial capital stock (1960) is calculated with the expression:

$$K_0 = \frac{I_0}{k + \delta}$$

This expression assumes that around the initial year (1960 in our case) capital is growing at the same pace as GDP (a steady-state assumption). We take k as average annual real GDP growth during 1955–75. We take δ as 4 per cent (similar value used in growth accounting estimates by Loayza et al., 2002, and Nehru, 1993). We preferred to use declining balance depreciation instead of straight line depreciation as the former assimilates better to the concept of economic depreciation (efficiency and obsolescence make older capital stock increasingly less valuable through time). The value of initial investment I_0 is obtained running a simple regression of gross fixed capital formation against time for the 1955–65 period, taking the intercept as the value estimate for I_0.[5, 6]

In summary, the characteristics of our two growth accounting methodologies would be:

1. *Traditional modified approach (TMA)*: (a) the wage bill is decomposed between the raw labor and quality (or human capital upgrade) components; and (b) the physical capital stock series, generated using the series of gross fixed capital formation at constant prices (in local currency). The TMA is basically the traditional growth accounting modified by splitting the labor contribution between the part due to raw labor and the part due to its quality or human capital component.
2. *Extended approach (EA)*: (a) the wage bill is decomposed between the raw labor and quality (or human capital); (b) the physical capital stock series is generated using the series of gross fixed capital formation at current prices (in local currency), deflated by the GDP deflator, and adjusted to reflect the actual utilization of physical capital.

B   Results

We applied both growth accounting methodologies to a sample of six Latin American countries: Argentina, Brazil, Chile, Colombia, Mexico, and Venezuela. We took the period 1960–2002. Our six countries are the largest countries of the region and produce about 90 per cent of total Latin America's GDP (WDI, 2004, World Bank). The selection of countries and the period was based on the availability and quality of the data. Reliable national accounts data before 1960 are not available for many Latin American countries. The selected countries have longer and better quality national accounting series and more frequent revisions of the national accounting statistics than other smaller countries in the region.

We have distinguished four broad periods in Latin America's growth experience: (1) the 1960s, representing the last 'gold decade' of the import substitution industrialization (ISI) strategy combined with mixed external conditions (falling terms of trade but low real external interest rates); (2) the 1970s, representing the accelerated decay of the ISI model and mixed external conditions (improved terms of trade for oil exporters but falling terms of trade for non-oil exporters, and low real external interest rates);[7] (3) the 1980s, representing the debt crisis and lost 'decade', which marks the accelerated transition from the ISI to a new export-led development strategy, a period of stabilization and reforms combined with deteriorated external conditions (falling terms of trade and higher real external interest rates, compared to the 1970s); and (4) the 1990s and early 2000s, associated with the gradual insertion of Latin America into the new globalization era: growth is recovering, but modestly compared to the 1960s and 1970s, adverse external conditions prevail: falling terms of trade, higher external interest rates in 1999 and 2000, and negative contagion from a series of shocks (Asia 1997, Russia 1998, Brazil 1999, Argentina 2001–2). In the early 2000s the globalization experi-

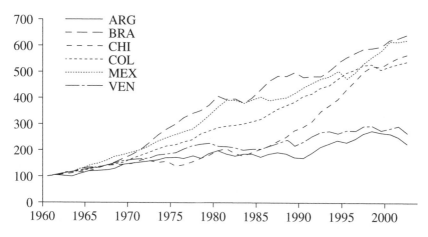

Note: (1960 = 100).

Source: Author's elaboration.

Figure 7.1   Real GDP growth

Table 7.1   Traditional modified growth accounting approach (TMA) (percentage)

Country	1961–65	1966–70	1971–75	1976–80	1981–85	1986–90	1991–95	1996–02	1961–02
Argentina									
GDP growth	3.99	4.02	3.12	2.96	-2.43	-0.33	6.70	-0.28	2.22
Capital contribution	2.19	1.77	2.17	2.22	1.31	0.40	0.80	1.37	1.53
Share of GDP growth	54.93	44.09	69.47	75.21	54.07	119.03	11.94	482.39	68.98
Raw labor contribution	0.39	0.39	0.24	0.24	0.06	0.04	-0.06	0.28	0.20
Share of GDP growth	9.66	9.65	7.79	7.98	2.43	13.43	-0.97	96.85	8.83
Human capital contribution	0.44	0.50	0.30	0.25	0.05	0.04	-0.09	0.25	0.22
Share of GDP growth	10.96	12.56	9.75	8.41	1.94	12.22	-1.33	87.15	9.82
Total factor productivity	0.98	1.35	0.41	0.25	-3.85	-0.82	6.05	-2.18	0.27
Share of GDP growth	24.45	33.70	13.00	8.40	-158.44	-244.69	90.35	-766.39	12.37
Brazil									
GDP growth	4.58	7.80	10.32	6.70	1.20	2.09	3.16	2.03	4.73
Capital contribution	1.02	1.46	3.00	3.22	1.72	1.31	0.72	0.86	1.66
Share of GDP growth	22.21	18.71	29.10	48.07	143.41	62.43	22.68	42.30	35.11
Raw labor contribution	0.52	0.52	0.82	0.88	0.64	0.66	0.61	0.47	0.64
Share of GDP growth	11.44	6.63	7.92	13.06	53.49	31.74	19.23	23.00	13.50
Human capital contribution	1.56	1.38	1.62	1.52	1.04	1.03	0.91	0.66	1.21
Share of GDP growth	33.95	17.67	15.73	22.71	86.37	49.21	28.78	32.32	25.63
Total factor productivity	1.48	4.44	4.87	1.08	-2.20	-0.91	0.93	0.05	1.22
Share of GDP growth	32.41	56.99	47.25	16.16	-183.27	-43.38	29.31	2.39	25.76
Chile									
GDP growth	3.69	4.60	-1.12	7.28	1.14	6.75	8.71	3.84	4.36
Capital contribution	1.31	1.18	0.86	0.29	0.69	1.06	2.16	2.63	1.27
Share of GDP growth	35.49	25.72	76.76	4.00	60.31	15.64	24.80	68.59	29.19
Raw labor contribution	0.30	0.29	0.38	0.39	0.37	0.92	0.65	0.49	0.47
Share of GDP growth	8.11	6.25	33.90	5.33	32.11	13.63	7.49	12.76	10.85
Human capital contribution	0.57	0.57	0.80	0.81	0.72	1.69	1.11	0.79	0.88
Share of GDP growth	15.35	12.42	71.57	11.18	62.54	24.99	12.71	20.55	20.21
Total factor productivity	1.51	2.56	-3.17	5.79	-0.63	3.09	4.79	-0.07	1.73
Share of GDP growth	41.04	55.61	-282.23	79.49	-54.96	45.74	55.01	-1.89	39.75

Colombia

GDP growth	4.65	5.88	5.67	5.38	2.25	4.95	4.14	1.12	4.25
Capital contribution	2.07	1.58	1.98	1.95	2.28	1.86	1.94	1.36	1.88
Share of GDP growth	44.59	26.91	34.94	36.21	101.23	37.52	46.85	121.51	44.11
Raw labor contribution	0.50	0.50	0.64	0.69	0.42	0.58	0.41	0.16	0.49
Share of GDP growth	10.79	8.47	11.22	12.73	18.64	11.76	9.85	14.17	11.42
Human capital contribution	1.13	1.31	1.60	1.46	0.81	0.98	0.62	0.31	1.03
Share of GDP growth	24.31	22.30	28.23	27.09	35.84	19.79	14.94	27.33	24.12
Total factor productivity	0.94	2.49	1.45	1.29	-1.25	1.53	1.17	-0.70	0.87
Share of GDP growth	20.30	42.32	25.62	23.97	-55.71	30.94	28.36	-63.01	20.35

Mexico

GDP growth	7.25	6.26	6.27	7.14	2.03	1.72	1.61	3.96	4.53
Capital contribution	4.05	4.33	3.67	3.09	3.11	1.69	2.57	2.11	3.08
Share of GDP growth	55.91	69.14	58.55	43.27	153.01	98.12	159.59	53.35	67.94
Raw labor contribution	0.47	0.46	0.68	0.71	0.47	0.48	0.50	0.72	0.56
Share of GDP growth	6.54	7.33	10.83	9.91	23.09	27.69	31.26	18.28	12.40
Human capital contribution	0.79	0.86	1.43	1.53	0.78	0.51	0.40	0.65	0.87
Share of GDP growth	10.86	13.82	22.76	21.36	38.43	29.59	24.64	16.46	19.16
Total factor productivity	1.93	0.61	0.49	1.82	-2.33	-0.95	-1.86	0.47	0.02
Share of GDP growth	26.69	9.72	7.85	25.46	-114.54	-55.39	-115.49	11.91	0.51

Venezuela

GDP growth	6.18	4.02	2.97	2.54	-0.91	2.76	3.53	-0.37	2.59
Capital contribution	1.80	2.09	2.12	3.68	1.36	0.76	0.94	0.62	1.67
Share of GDP growth	29.19	51.91	71.53	145.21	149.29	27.52	26.48	166.24	64.54
Raw labor contribution	0.62	0.62	0.89	0.95	0.48	0.48	0.72	0.48	0.66
Share of GDP growth	10.03	15.51	30.14	37.39	53.15	17.48	20.38	128.23	25.34
Human capital contribution	1.91	1.72	2.08	1.79	0.76	0.63	0.81	0.56	1.28
Share of GDP growth	30.90	42.85	69.95	70.45	83.75	22.94	22.80	149.92	49.49
Total factor productivity	1.85	-0.41	-2.13	-3.88	-3.52	0.89	1.07	-2.02	-1.02
Share of GDP growth	29.88	-10.27	-71.62	-153.05	-386.19	32.07	30.34	-544.39	-39.37

Note: Capital stock series generated using the series of gross capital formation at constant prices but unadjusted by rates of 'utilization' of capital. The wage bill is decomposed between the raw labor and quality (or human capital) components. Based on GDP and gross fixed capital formation at constant prices in local currency.

Source: Author's elaboration, based on ECLAC database, World Bank database, UN Statistical Office database.

Table 7.2 Extended growth accounting approach (EA)

Country	1961–65	1966–70	1971–75	1976–80	1981–85	1986–90	1991–95	1996–02	1961–02
Argentina									
GDP growth	3.99	4.02	3.12	2.96	-2.43	-0.33	6.70	-0.28	2.22
Capital contribution	2.47	1.50	2.19	3.47	-0.31	-0.33	1.80	0.41	1.40
Share of GDP growth	61.86	37.34	70.28	117.26	-12.74	-99.91	26.84	142.73	63.09
Raw labor contribution	0.39	0.39	0.24	0.24	0.06	0.04	-0.06	0.28	0.20
Share of GDP growth	9.66	9.64	7.79	7.98	2.43	13.43	-0.97	96.85	8.83
Human capital contribution	0.44	0.50	0.30	0.25	0.05	0.04	-0.09	0.25	0.22
Share of GDP growth	10.96	12.56	9.75	8.41	1.94	12.22	-1.33	87.15	9.82
Total factor productivity	0.70	1.62	0.38	-0.99	-2.23	-0.09	5.06	-1.21	0.41
Share of GDP growth	17.52	40.45	12.19	-33.65	-91.63	-25.74	75.45	-426.73	18.27
Brazil									
GDP growth	4.58	7.80	10.32	6.70	1.20	2.09	3.16	2.03	4.73
Capital contribution	0.93	1.37	3.31	4.03	1.37	1.81	1.40	1.37	1.95
Share of GDP growth	20.29	17.59	32.14	60.10	114.63	86.35	44.30	67.46	41.17
Raw labor contribution	0.52	0.52	0.82	0.88	0.64	0.66	0.61	0.47	0.64
Share of GDP growth	11.44	6.63	7.92	13.06	53.49	31.74	19.23	23.00	13.50
Human capital contribution	1.56	1.38	1.62	1.52	1.04	1.03	0.91	0.66	1.21
Share of GDP growth	33.95	17.67	15.73	22.71	86.37	49.21	28.78	32.32	25.63
Total factor productivity	1.57	4.53	4.56	0.28	-1.85	-1.41	0.24	-0.46	0.93
Share of GDP growth	34.33	58.10	44.22	4.13	-154.49	-67.30	7.69	-22.77	19.70
Chile									
GDP growth	3.69	4.60	-1.12	7.28	1.14	6.75	8.71	3.84	4.36
Capital contribution	1.13	1.75	0.62	2.52	0.08	1.57	2.78	2.82	1.66
Share of GDP growth	30.62	38.01	55.07	34.57	6.77	23.21	31.89	73.54	38.00
Raw labor contribution	0.30	0.29	0.38	0.39	0.37	0.92	0.65	0.49	0.47
Share of GDP growth	8.11	6.25	33.90	5.33	32.11	13.63	7.49	12.76	10.85
Human capital contribution	0.57	0.57	0.80	0.81	0.72	1.69	1.11	0.79	0.88
Share of GDP growth	15.35	12.42	71.57	11.18	62.54	24.99	12.71	20.55	20.21
Total factor productivity	1.69	1.99	-2.92	3.56	-0.02	2.58	4.18	-0.26	1.35
Share of GDP growth	45.91	43.32	-260.53	48.92	-1.42	38.17	47.92	-6.84	30.94

Colombia									
GDP growth	4.65	5.88	5.67	5.38	2.25	4.95	4.14	1.12	4.25
Capital contribution	1.85	1.64	1.61	1.99	1.76	2.30	2.32	1.66	1.89
Share of GDP growth	39.79	27.93	28.44	36.99	78.20	46.60	55.97	148.85	44.48
Raw labor contribution	0.50	0.50	0.64	0.69	0.42	0.58	0.41	0.16	0.49
Share of GDP growth	10.79	8.47	11.22	12.73	18.64	11.76	9.85	14.17	11.42
Human capital contribution	1.13	1.31	1.60	1.46	0.81	0.98	0.62	0.31	1.03
Share of GDP growth	24.31	22.30	28.23	27.09	35.84	19.79	14.94	27.33	24.12
Total factor productivity	1.17	2.43	1.82	1.25	-0.73	1.08	0.80	-1.01	0.85
Share of GDP growth	25.11	41.30	32.11	23.19	-32.69	21.85	19.24	-90.35	19.98
Mexico									
GDP growth	7.25	6.26	6.27	7.14	2.03	1.72	1.61	3.96	4.53
Capital contribution	3.94	4.08	3.56	3.57	3.25	1.86	1.58	3.27	3.14
Share of GDP growth	54.41	65.21	56.76	50.02	160.09	108.19	98.22	82.53	69.31
Raw labor contribution	0.47	0.46	0.68	0.71	0.47	0.48	0.50	0.72	0.56
Share of GDP growth	6.54	7.33	10.83	9.91	23.09	27.69	31.26	18.28	12.40
Human capital contribution	0.79	0.86	1.43	1.53	0.78	0.51	0.40	0.65	0.87
Share of GDP growth	10.86	13.82	22.76	21.36	38.43	29.59	24.64	16.46	19.16
Total factor productivity	2.04	0.85	0.61	1.34	-2.47	-1.13	-0.87	-0.68	-0.04
Share of GDP growth	28.19	13.65	9.65	18.71	-121.61	-65.46	-54.12	-17.27	-0.86
Venezuela									
GDP growth	6.18	4.02	2.97	2.54	-0.91	2.76	3.53	-0.37	2.59
Capital contribution	2.29	2.61	2.14	4.17	0.57	0.84	1.39	0.23	1.78
Share of GDP growth	37.05	65.04	72.05	164.18	62.82	30.47	39.43	62.95	68.78
Raw labor contribution	0.62	0.62	0.89	0.95	0.48	0.48	0.72	0.48	0.66
Share of GDP growth	10.03	15.51	30.14	37.39	53.15	17.48	20.38	128.23	25.34
Human capital contribution	1.91	1.72	2.08	1.79	0.76	0.63	0.81	0.56	1.28
Share of GDP growth	30.90	42.85	69.95	70.45	83.75	22.94	22.80	149.92	49.49
Total factor productivity	1.36	-0.94	-2.14	-4.37	-2.73	0.80	0.61	-1.64	-1.13
Share of GDP growth	22.01	-23.40	-72.14	-172.02	-299.71	29.12	17.39	-441.11	-43.61

Note: Capital stock series adjusted by rates of 'utilization' of capital and using the series of gross capital formation at current prices to generate the capital stock series (deflated by the DDP deflator). The wage bill is decomposed between the raw labor and quality (or human capital) components. Based on GDP at constant prices in local currency and gross fixed capital formation at current prices in local currency.

Source: Author's elaboration, based on ECLAC database, World Bank database, UN Statistical Office database.

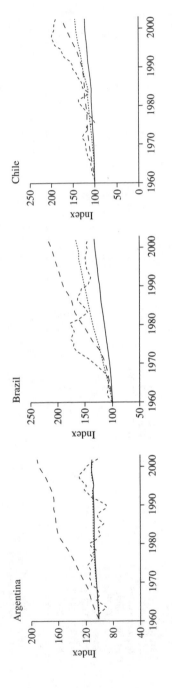

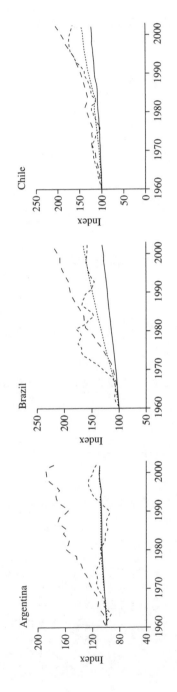

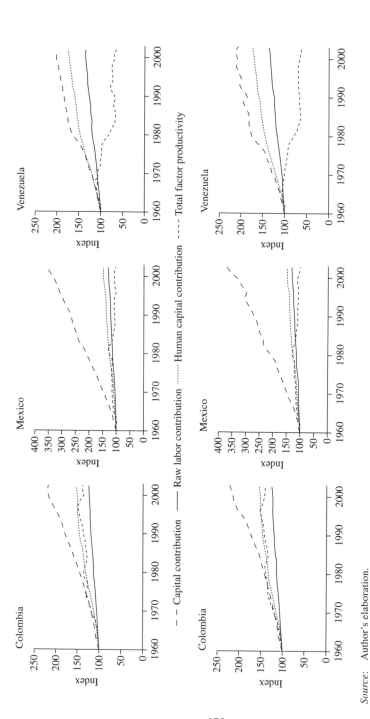

Source: Author's elaboration.

Figure 7.2 Source of growth for Latin American countries: traditional modified growth accounting approach (TMA, top figures) and extended growth accounting approach (EA, bottom figures)

ence has been subjected to growing scrutiny by economists and politicians in Washington and across the region.

For additional analytical insights we further sub-divided the four broad periods into five-year sub-periods, except for the last one (1996–2002) which spans seven years. We divided the six countries into a group of faster growth countries (FGCs) (Brazil, Chile, Colombia and Mexico) and a group of slower growth countries (SLCs) (Argentina and Venezuela). This classification was based on the accumulated growth performance for the whole 1960–2002 period. The FGCs reached levels of real GDP by 2002 more than five times the levels in 1960 while the SGCs reached GDP levels less than three times the real GDP levels in 1960 and also developed a downward GDP trend since the mid-1990s (Figure 7.1).

Tables 7.1 and 7.2 summarize the results from the growth accounting exercises. Table 7.1 shows the result associated with the TMA exercise and Table 7.2 shows the results from applying the EA. Our first observation is about the broad results obtained under each approach. The trends and structures of the growth sources are similar under TMA (Table 7.1) and the EA (Table 7.2), which is comforting in the sense that our main analytical observations and conclusions will not depend on the alternative methodologies used. Some relevant insights emerge from the TMA and EA, however.

Looking at the results from Tables 7.1 and 7.2, we observe that physical capital appears at first sight to be the leading source of growth for all six countries in the whole 1960–2002 period. Its impact, however, in terms of average shares of capital contribution on GDP growth, has varied across time and between countries (see Figure 7.2). Further examinations of the growth process leads to the conclusion that other growth sources, and in particular, total factor productivity, have marked the difference between faster and slower growth episodes.

Observation 1 Physical capital has played an important role in the growth process, but the other growth sources have made the difference between better and worse growth experiences.

Physical capital contributed about 60 to 70 per cent to accumulated GDP growth during 1960–2002 in Argentina, Mexico, and Venezuela (one FGC and two SLCs). Growth performances did not have direct association to the physical capital contributions however. High capital contributions were associated with both high and low growth performances across countries and sub-periods (see Figure 7.2). Despite having similar average shares of physical capital contribution on real GDP growth we observe that Mexico grew at an average rate about double the rates of Argentina and Venezuela on average during the whole 1960–2002 period (4.5 per cent compared to 2.2 per cent and 2.6 per cent, respectively). In the case of the three other FGCs (Brazil, Chile, Colombia), real GDP growth was less dependent on physical capital. The shares of physical capital contributions on GDP growth fluctuated between 30 per cent and 45 per cent for these countries, about half the shares of the more capital-dependent growth countries.

Some key remarks emerged observing the differential performance of the FGCs compared to the SLCs in terms of the shares of the physical capital contributions on real GDP growth during 1960–2002.

Among the FGCs, Brazil was the leader in terms of average real GDP growth considering the whole 1960–2002 period (although after the 1980s its performance fell sharply). Brazil is followed by Mexico, Chile and Colombia in terms of average GDP growth during the whole 1960–2002 period. In the cases of Brazil and Mexico, the shares of physical capital contributions on real GDP growth exhibited a rising trend through the different sub-periods, reaching a peak in 1981–85 for Brazil and 1991–95 for Mexico (and declined thereafter). Real GDP growth reached the lowest average rates in those sub-periods, however. These observations hold under the TMA and the EA. Under the EA, however, Mexico reached the peak in terms of the share of physical capital contribution on GDP growth in 1981–85 (160 per cent), when the average real GDP growth was the third lowest of all sub-periods (2 per cent).

In the cases of Chile and Colombia (the countries with the lowest average shares of physical capital contributions on real GDP growth) the physical capital contributions increased through the 1990s and early 2000s, but as in the other two FGCs there was a positive relationship between growth and capital contribution. Chile reached the highest share of physical capital contribution on growth in 1971–75 (69 per cent) with the TMA and 1996–2002 (74 per cent) with the EA, but Chilean average real GDP growth was negative in 1971–75. During 1996–2002, average real GDP growth was less than half the average rate in the peak years (1991–95) but with a share of capital contribution on real GDP growth of nearly three times higher. Colombia reached the lowest average GDP growth in 1996–2002 when the capital contribution (as a share of GDP growth) was at the peak (122 per cent with TMA and 149 per cent with EA). Meanwhile, in the best growth years (5.9 per cent real GDP growth in 1966–70) the share of capital contribution on growth was the lowest of all sub-periods (about 28 per cent).

In three of the four FGCs (Brazil, Chile and Colombia), in the best growth years, total factor productivity was the leading source of growth, followed by physical capital or human capital, depending on the sub-period. Mexico is the exception of the FGCs showing physical capital contributions as the main force of growth in the best growth years. However, as we indicated above, we

also observe that the years Mexico had the highest physical capital contributions (as shares of GDP growth) are also the years of the lowest average GDP
growth.

In the case of the SGCs the highest shares of contributions on real GDP
growth coincide with the years of negative or low growth while the best
growth years also coincide with the lowest shares of capital contributions on
growth.

Observation 2   Labor has played a mixed role in the growth process, helping to push growth in the fastest growth countries (FGCs) but not in the
slowest growth countries (SGCs). The role of the human capital component
has been more important than the raw labor component.

The role of labor as a source of growth has been mixed but did not mark
the difference between high growth and low growth experiences. The role of
labor has been driven mostly by the human capital component, with raw labor
playing a secondary role. We also observe that the share of the labor contribution on growth has been above the shares of the physical capital contribution
on growth on many occasions across time and between countries.

In the case of Brazil, the role of labor as a source of growth has been larger
than the role of physical capital in all the sub-periods shown in Tables 7.1 and
7.2. Venezuela is at the top of the performers in terms of direct contributions
from raw and human capital, but ranks at the bottom of the growth performers. As for the case of physical capital, the effectiveness of labor in stimulating
growth appears to have depended on additional factors, which are being
measured as total factor productivity (TFP). TFP has made the difference
between high and low GDP growth experiences.

Observation 3   Total Factor Productivity (TFP) was the main source that
marked the difference between better and worse growth experiences.

TFP was clearly the main source of growth in two of the FGC group,
Brazil in the mid-1960s through the mid-1970s and Chile between the second
half of the 1980s and the first half of the 1990s. Colombia also experienced
high contributions from TFP as a share of GDP growth, though they declined
in the second half of the 1980s and again in the second half of the 1990s.
Mexico appears as the exception in the FGC group, with shares of contributions from TFP on growth below the shares of the contributions from physical
capital. For the whole set of six countries we observe that while record high
contributions from physical capital have coexisted with negative or low GDP
growth. In all four of the FGCs the shares of TFP on growth was the highest
in the best and worse growth years, and above the shares of the contributions

from the other growth sources (Tables 7.1 and 7.2, and Figures 7.1 and 7.2 excluding Venezuela).

In the case of the SGCs the leading role of TFP is also evident. TFP has marked the difference between the high and low real GDP growth years. Argentina experienced a modest jump in TFP growth in the early 1990s, which has reversed since 1997 in tandem with a declining trend of GDP growth (GDP growth turned positive again in 2003–04). The case of Venezuela is even worse, the contribution from TFP never took off and it has been declining since the early 1970s. The poor growth performance of Venezuela has been only partly attenuated by the positive direct contributions from human capital.

Additional evidence of the key role played by TFP in the growth process of Latin America is obtained from the exercises summarized in Tables 7.3 (for TMA) and 7.4 (for EA). We selected from the panel of all annual growth rates (across countries and years) the best ten and the worst ten growth rates in each of the following four decades: 1961–70, 1971–80, 1981–90, and 1991–2002. In Tables 7.3 and 7.4 we show the means and medians for the average growth rates, average physical capital contributions, and average TFP contributions. We also show the difference in the means and medians between the ten highest and ten lowest growth events last two rows) and the ratios of the differences in the means and medians between the average the contributions physical capital and real GDP growth and between the contribution from TFP and real GDP growth. These last columns show the relative incidences of physical capital and TFP in marking the difference between the ten highest and the ten lowest growth episodes.

The exercise provides crucial evidence about the leading role of TFP. The results in the last columns of Tables 7.3 and 7.4 show that capital TFP explains between 76 per cent and 95 per cent of the differences in the means in the case of the TMA and between 49 per cent and 70 per cent in the case of the EA. Using the medians, TFP explains between 81 per cent and 100 per cent of the GDP growth differences with the TMA and between 50 per cent and 79 per cent in the case of the EA.

Similar calculations are shown for physical capital in the lowest parts of tables 7.3 and 7.4. The ratios of the differences of medians and means are below 8 per cent and in some cases negative in the case of TMA, and between 28 per cent and 43 per cent in the case of the EA, clearly much below the incidences of the TFPs.

Similar evidence about the primary role played by TFP in explaining fast growth episodes have been provided in recent research on economic growth such as Easterly (2001) and Easterly and Levine (2001) in a global analysis; Easterly and Pack (2001) for Africa; Elias (1990 and 1992) for Latin America; Harberger (1996 and 1998) for East Asia, Latin America, and the United

Table 7.3 *Highs and lows, real GDP growth rates: differential impacts from total factor productivity and capital (TMA)*

	GDP growth				TFP contribution				Ratio of differences			
	1961–70	1971–80	1981–90	1991–02	1961–70	1971–80	1981–90	1991–02	1961–70	1971–80	1981–90	1991–02
10 highest GDP growth rates												
Mean	10.43	10.34	7.87	9.51	5.11	4.81	4.96	6.26				
Median	10.20	9.74	7.91	8.93	4.99	4.09	4.94	5.42				
10 lowest GDP growth rates												
Mean	0.45	-2.44	-6.13	-5.04	-2.95	-4.87	-8.38	-6.18				
Median	0.79	-1.42	-5.32	-4.31	-2.65	-5.37	-8.31	-5.64				
Difference in means	9.97	12.78	14.00	14.55	8.07	9.69	13.33	12.44	0.81	0.76	0.95	0.86
Difference in medians	9.41	11.16	13.23	13.23	7.64	9.45	13.24	11.06	0.81	0.85	1.00	0.84

	GDP growth				Capital contribution				Ratio of differences			
	1961–70	1971–80	1981–90	1991–02	1961–70	1971–80	1981–90	1991–02	1961–70	1971–80	1981–90	1991–02
10 highest GDP growth rates												
Mean	10.43	10.34	7.87	9.51	1.98	2.85	0.99	1.57				
Median	10.20	9.74	7.91	8.93	1.55	2.84	0.82	1.76				
10 lowest GDP growth rates												
Mean	0.45	-2.44	-6.13	-5.04	1.84	2.04	1.61	1.57				
Median	0.79	-1.42	-5.32	-4.31	1.95	1.89	1.36	1.55				
Difference in means	9.97	12.78	14.00	14.55	0.14	0.81	-0.62	0.00	0.01	0.06	-0.04	0.00
Difference in medians	9.41	11.16	13.23	13.23	-0.40	0.95	-0.54	0.21	-0.04	0.08	-0.04	0.02

Source: Author's elaboration.

Table 7.4 Highs and lows, real GDP growth rates: differential impacts from total factor productivity and capital (EA)

	GDP growth				TFP contribution				Ratio of differences			
	1961–70	1971–80	1981–90	1991–02	1961–70	1971–80	1981–90	1991–02	1961–70	1971–80	1981–90	1991–02
10 highest												
GDP growth rates												
Mean	10.43	10.34	7.87	9.51	5.20	4.46	2.94	4.73				
Median	10.20	9.74	7.91	8.93	5.26	4.41	2.41	4.54				
10 lowest												
GDP growth rates												
Mean	0.45	-2.44	-6.13	-5.04	-1.74	-4.71	-4.45	-2.39				
Median	0.79	-1.42	-5.32	-4.31	-1.45	-4.41	-4.26	-3.33				
Difference in means	9.97	12.78	14.00	14.55	6.94	9.16	7.39	7.12	0.70	0.72	0.53	0.49
Difference in medians	9.41	11.16	13.23	13.23	6.71	8.82	6.67	7.87	0.71	0.79	0.50	0.59

	GDP growth				Capital contribution				Ratio of differences			
	1961–70	1971–80	1981–90	1991–02	1961–70	1971–80	1981–90	1991–02	1961–70	1971–80	1981–90	1991–02
10 highest												
GDP growth rates												
Mean	10.43	10.34	7.87	9.51	3.78	4.56	3.01	3.78				
Median	10.20	9.74	7.91	8.93	3.92	4.46	2.90	3.75				
10 lowest												
GDP growth rates												
Mean	0.45	-2.44	-6.13	-5.04	0.54	0.86	-2.31	-2.22				
Median	0.79	-1.42	-5.32	-4.31	1.28	1.11	-2.42	-1.99				
Difference in means	9.97	12.78	14.00	14.55	3.24	3.69	5.33	6.00	0.33	0.29	0.38	0.41
Difference in medians	9.41	11.16	13.23	13.23	2.64	3.35	5.32	5.74	0.28	0.30	0.40	0.43

Source: Author's elaboration.

States and Mexican manufacturing sectors; Klenow and Rodriguez-Clare (1997b) in a global analysis; and Loayza et al. (2004) and Fajnzylber and Lederman (1999) for Latin America. As mentioned before, Solimano and Soto (Chapter 2, this volume) also showed in a sample of 12 Latin American countries for the period 1960–2000 that TFP was the main determinant of GDP growth.[8]

Despite the modifications and extensions we introduced to the traditional growth accounting methodology the main conclusion prevails in favor of the leading role played by TFP and not physical capital in 'explaining' the difference between fast and slow growth experiences in Latin America. Argentina and Venezuela have performed at the bottom of the six largest Latin American economies, taking the whole 1960–2002 period, with modest TFP growth being a main feature of their poor growth performance. At the other extreme, Chile has experienced the fastest GDP growth on average since the 1980s, despite some weakening after the mid-1990s (see Figure 7.2), and mostly driven by total factor productivity growth. It is interesting to observe in the Chilean case that the EA assigns a lower role to TFP compared with physical capital, which in large part reflects the incidence of TFP on the return of physical capital.[9]

In the next section we examine how the composition of investment and other key factors have contributed to economic growth. We use per capita GDP growth as a proxy for aggregate labor productivity growth.

7.3   COMPOSITION OF INVESTMENT BETWEEN MACHINERY AND EQUIPMENT AND CONSTRUCTION

In the previous section we provided evidence showing that physical capital played an important role in the process of economic growth in Latin America during 1960–2002, but that it was not the main factor that explained the difference between fast and slow growth experiences. We showed evidence that total factor productivity was the key force making the difference. In this section we will explore in more detail the additional ingredients that contributed to GDP growth in Latin America during the 1960–2002 period. We use regression analysis and examine the effects on per capita GDP growth of fixed investment by type of assets and policy related variables. We use GDP per capita growth as a proxy for labor productivity growth. This approach has been followed in seminal endogenous growth estimates; see for example Barro and Lee (1994), De Long and Summers (1991 and 1993), Klenow and Rodriguez-Clare (1997b), and Loayza et al. (2004).[10] In this section we examine the composition of fixed investment between machinery and equipment and construction. In the next section we analyze the composition of fixed investment between private and public investment.

Some quantitative studies have emphasized the role of machinery investment in augmenting the role of physical capital and labor in the growth process. Since the industrial revolution machinery investment has played a key role, directly as a production factor, and also as a mean of acquisition and transmission of technological improvements across and within countries. De Long and Summers (1991 and 1993) found evidence of high social returns from investments in machinery, assigning to machinery investment a primary role in boosting productivity growth (proxied by per capita GDP). They showed that high rates of machinery investment accounted for most of Japan's successful growth experience after the Second World War. They concluded that fast-growing countries were those with favorable supply conditions for machinery investments and that developing countries benefited as much as richer economies from the technologies embodied in machinery. Building projects are usually less effective in promoting growth because the technologies embodied in construction have less potential for being transmitted across production process. In addition, the output of the construction sector is mostly non-tradable and technologically less dynamic.

The structure of investment by type of assets matters for economic growth because the different technologies embodied in different types of investment assets have different effects on productivity and growth. Economic policies also play a main role in affecting economy-wide productivity and economic growth as they provide the framework for the allocation and use of production factors and decision making by economic agents. The contributions of physical capital and labor to economic growth depend on the quality of the economic framework. Price stability has become an important factor adding to growth because of irreversible characteristics of investment makes investment decisions highly sensitive to factors affecting inflation prospects and associated uncertainty about the evolution of relative prices (see Pindyck and Solimano, 1993). The size of the government also has been shown to matter for growth because an increase of fiscal vulnerability affects economic prospects and economic stability, and because public spending could be crowding out private saving and investment. Economic instability and uncertainty about economic prospects have been shown to be main factors that have contributed to discourage investment. Schmidt-Hebbel et al. (1996a) concluded in a review of the literature that investment is necessary but not a sufficient condition for growth and that human capital, technological innovation, and appropriate policies are also necessary for sustained high growth. Evidence about the role of education as a factor contributing to growth has also been provided in other seminal studies (for example Barro and Lee, 1994). Education facilitates the adoption of modern technologies embodied in new machinery and equipment and creates positive externalities (Lucas, 1988).

In Tables 7.5 and 7.6 we provide evidence about the impact of total fixed investment, and its composition between machinery and equipment, and buildings on per capita GDP growth. In Section 7.2 we included regression estimates for aggregate fixed investment to enrich the conclusions reached. We tested the impact on per capita GDP growth of fixed investment and its composition by type of assets combined with some key policy variables (including education). We tried with a selected number of variables that are related to economic policy making: (1) inflation (annual percentage change in the consumer price index), a measure of the degree of price stability and also related to consistency of macroeconomic policies; (2) trade openness (percentage share of trade in GDP), related to the degree of trade protection; (3) government consumption (percentage of GDP), related to policies that assign different roles to the size of the government sector in the economy; (4) external debt (percentage of GDP), related to macroeconomic policies that have been conducted with different degrees of exposure to external debt; (5) foreign direct investment (FDI) (percentage of GDP), related to policies that affect the degree of openness to capital and regulations affecting FDI; (6) infrastructure (per capita telephone lines), related to policies that have assigned different priorities to the development of infrastructure; and (7) education (ratio of gross secondary enrollment to the population of the same age group), related to education policies and the priorities assigned to the extension of education. We call these variables policy related variables because they reflect or are the result of economic policies.[11]

We also included initial per capita GDP (values at the initial year of each sub-period) to account for conditional convergence, which has been reported as important in other growth studies (see for example Barro and Lee, 1994; and Loayza et al., 2004 among others). We used panel data for the six Latin American countries for the period 1960–2002 and used, for the estimates shown in Table 7.5, five-year averages to reduce the effect of short-term fluctuations (we obtained 48 observations). We ran panel regressions using OLS with country fixed effects and corrected for heteroskedasticity as needed.[12] We used national accounts data at constant prices in local currency and variables expressed as shares of GDP. Appendix 7.A contains a detailed reference to the sources and description of the variables used.

For the estimates shown in Table 7.6 we used annual data to obtain estimates for the whole period (258 observations), but we broke also the whole period into several sub-periods in order to appreciate the stability of the coefficients derived from the whole period (long-run) estimates. The structural analysis allowed us to appreciate changes in the relevance of the explanatory variables through the different sub-periods considered. In Table 7.6 we include the results from computing structural break tests (Chow test)

Table 7.5   GDP per capita growth determinants: total investment, machinery and equipment, and buildings

	(1)	(2)	(3)	(4)	(5)	(6)	(7)	(8)	(9)	(10)	(11)
Inv. rate (% GDP)	0.0046*** (2.70)										
Mach. & equip. rate (% GDP)		0.0037** (2.43)	0.004*** (3.10)	0.0035*** (2.69)	0.0074*** (3.66)	0.0071*** (3.65)	0.0072*** (3.46)	0.0069*** (3.44)	0.0064*** (3.53)	0.0052*** (2.80)	0.0057*** (3.19)
Constructions rate (% GDP)							0.0022 (1.03)	0.0013 (0.68)	0.0008 (0.40)		
Inflation (annual %)			-0.00003* (-1.83)	-0.00005** (-2.52)					-0.00005** (-2.50)	-0.00004 (-2.38)	-0.00006*** (-3.17)
Openness (exports+ imports) (% GDP)			0.0007 (1.63)							0.0006 (1.20)	
Gov. consumption (% GDP)			-0.0034*** (-3.05)	-0.003** (-2.50)						-0.0022** (-1.75)	-0.0022** (-1.70)
External debt (% GDP)			-0.0005* (-1.83)							-0.0005* (-1.85)	
Foreign direct investment (% GDP)			-0.0037 (-0.95)							-0.0002 (-0.04)	
Infrastr. (ln teleph. lines per capita)			0.0217 (1.43)							0.0146 (1.06)	
Education (ln ratio second. enroll.)			0.0007* (1.72)	0.0008*** (3.01)					0.0004* (1.67)	0.0003 (0.71)	0.0004* (1.76)
Population growth (%)	-0.0129 (-1.18)				-0.0046 (-0.51)		-0.0097 (-0.87)				
Per capita GDP (ln of value at the beginning of each sub-period)	-0.06*** (-3.02)	-0.041*** (-3.86)	-0.1331*** (-4.19)	-0.0671*** (-3.62)	-0.048*** (-2.89)	-0.042*** (-4.29)	-0.058*** (-2.88)	-0.043*** (-4.53)	-0.0606*** (-3.23)	-0.1052*** (-3.83)	-0.0505*** (-2.93)
R-squared	0.41	0.38	0.78	0.57	0.43	0.43	0.45	0.44	0.55	0.76	0.58
F stat	3.32	3.45	5.37	4.98	3.75	4.29	3.51	3.8	4.54	4.78	5.15

Notes:

t-statistics in parentheses; asterisks mean: statistical significance at the 10% level (*), 5% level (**), and 1% level (***).
Fixed effects; Corrected for heteroskedasticity

Source: Author's elaboration.

185

Table 7.6 GDP per capita growth determinants: total fixed investment, machinery and equipment, and buildings

	(1) 1960–2002 5-year averages	(1a) 1960–2002 annual	(1b) 1960–1980 annual	(1c) 1981–1990 annual	(1d) 1991–2002 annual	(1e) 1960–1990 annual	(2) 1960–2002 5-year averages	(2a) 1960–2002 annual
Investment rate (% GDP)	0.0046*** (2.70)	0.0048*** (4.76)	0.0032*** (2.46)	0.0083** (2.37)	0.0052** (2.44)	0.0044*** (3.92)	0.0037** (2.43)	0.0043*** (4.78)
Mach. and equip. rate (% GDP)								
Buildings rate (% GDP)								
Inflation (annual %)								
Openness (exports+imports) (% GDP)								
Gov. consumption (% GDP)								
External debt (% GDP)								
Foreign direct investment (% GDP)								
Infrast. (ln phone lines per capita)								
Education (ln ratio second. enroll.)								
Population growth (%)	−0.0129 (−1.18)	−0.0088 (−1.27)	−0.0379** (−2.12)	−0.0195 (−0.46)	−0.0334 (−0.64)	−0.0078 (−0.81)		
Per capita GDP (ln of value at the beginning of each sub-period)	−0.06*** (−3.02)	−0.0586*** (−3.93)	−0.0609** (−2.17)	−0.392*** (−3.09)	−0.2536*** (−3.74)	−0.0659*** (−3.32)	−0.041*** (−3.86)	−0.0457*** (−5.29)
R-squared	0.41	0.2	0.19	0.32	0.43	0.2	0.38	0.19
F stat	3.32	7.81	3.33	3.07	6.04	5.39	3.45	8.67
Chow tests:								
1960–80/ 1981–90/ 1991–2002	20.97							5.74
1960–80/ 1981–2002	14.09							1.19
1960–90/ 1991–2002	2.32							2.68

	(2b) 1960–1980 annual	(2c) 1981–1990 annual	(2d) 1991–2002 annual	(2e) 1960–1990 annual	(3) 1960–2002 5-year averages	(3a) 1960–2002 annual	(3b) 1960–1980 annual	(3c) 1981–1990 annual
Investment rate (% GDP)	0.0023* (1.85)	0.008** (2.39)	0.0046** (2.37)	0.0041*** (3.94)	0.004*** (3.10)	0.0052*** (5.06)	0.0041*** (2.72)	0.0097*** (3.39)
Mach. and equip. rate (% GDP)								
Buildings rate (% GDP)								
Inflation (annual %)					−0.00003* (−1.83)	−0.00004*** (−4.99)	0.0002*** (−4.98)	−0.00004*** (−3.90)
Openness (exports+imports) (% GDP)					0.0007 (1.63)	0.0003 (0.79)	−0.0009 (−0.76)	0.001 (−0.86)
Gov. consumption (% GDP)					−0.0034*** (−3.05)	−0.0051*** (−3.84)	0.0026 (−0.67)	−0.007** (−1.77)
External debt (% GDP)					−0.0005* (−1.83)	−0.0006*** (−3.28)	−0.0015** (−2.13)	−0.0002 (−0.59)
Foreign direct investment (% GDP)					−0.0037 (−0.95)	−0.0048** (−2.48)	−0.0046 (−0.87)	−0.0081 (−1.24)
Infrast. (ln phone lines per capita)					0.0217 (1.43)	0.0317** (2.54)	0.0572 (1.38)	0.117*** (2.47)
Education (ln ratio second. enroll.)					0.0007* (1.720)	0.0012*** (3.24)	0.0026*** (3.21)	0.0031 (1.43)
Population growth (%)								
Per capita GDP (ln of value at the beginning of each sub-period)	−0.0179 (−0.94)	−0.393*** (−3.09)	−0.2231*** (−5.10)	−0.056*** (−4.00)	−0.1331*** (−4.19)	−0.1823*** (−6.51)	−0.1649** (−2.48)	−0.4913*** (−4.88)
R-squared	0.15	0.32	0.42	0.19	0.78	0.45	0.62	0.61
F stat	2.92	3.52	6.81	6.09	5.37	9.96	5.91	5.13
Chow tests:								
1960–80/ 1981–90/ 1991–2002						6.34		
1960–80/ 1981–2002						4.63		
1960–90/ 1991–2002						2.37		

Table 7.6 continued

	(3d) 1991–2002 annual	(3e) 1960–1990 annual	(4) 1960–2002 5-year average	(4a) 1960–2002 annual	(4b) 1960–1980 annual	(4c) 1981–1990 annual	(4d) 1991–2002 annual	(4e) 1960–1990 annual
Investment rate (% GDP)	0.0065*** (3.29)	0.0054*** (3.88)	0.0035*** (2.69)	0.0046*** (4.90)	0.0017* (1.66)	0.0084*** (3.16)	0.0066*** (3.72)	0.0038*** (3.61)
Mach. and equip. rate (% GDP)								
Buildings rate (% GDP)								
Inflation (annual %)	0.0001 (0.81)	−0.0005*** (−4.38)	−0.00005** (−2.52)	−0.00004*** (−5.72)	−0.00018*** (−4.27)	−0.00004*** (−4.53)	0.0002 (1.61)	−0.0001*** (−5.82)
Openness (exports+imports) (% GDP)	0.0016*** −3.09	−0.0008 (−0.96)						
Gov. consumption (% GDP)	−0.0032 (−1.15)	−0.0085*** (−2.96)	−0.003** (−2.50)	−0.00401*** (−3.84)	−0.0048 (−1.69)	−0.0041 (−1.26)	−0.0007 (−0.41)	−0.0058*** (−2.96)
External debt (% GDP)	−0.0011* (−1.16)	−0.0008*** (−2.79)						
Foreign direct investment (% GDP)	0.0007 (0.22)	−0.0076 (−1.99)						
Infrast. (ln phone lines per capita)	0.7778 (1.51)	0.0443** (2.37)						
Education (ln ratio second. enroll.)	−0.0005 (−1.02)	0.003*** (4.05)	0.0008*** (3.01)	0.0011*** (4.44)	0.0019*** (2.77)	0.0054*** (3.80)	0.0005 (1.61)	0.0013*** (3.57)
Population growth (%)								
Per capita GDP (ln of value at the beginning of each sub-period)	−0.3834*** (−4.70)	−0.2583*** (−5.56)	−0.0671*** (−3.62)	−0.0896*** (−5.11)	−0.06342** (−2.12)	−0.4674*** (−4.57)	−0.2378*** (−4.48)	−0.0994*** (−4.25)
R-squared	0.63	0.5	0.57	0.3	0.31	0.55	0.54	0.3
F stat	5.49	7.98	4.98	9.99	5.01	6.1	5.88	7.47
Chow tests:								
1960–80/ 1981–90/ 1991–2002				7.17				
1960–80/ 1981–2002				2.45				
1960–90/ 1991–2002				1.86				

	(5) 1960–2002 5-year averages	(5a) 1960–2002 annual	(5b) 1960–1980 annual	(5c) 1981–1990 annual	(5d) 1991–2002 annual	(5e) 1960–1990 annual	(6) 1960–2002 5-year averages	(6a) 1960–2002 annual
Mach. and equip. rate (% GDP)	0.0074*** (3.66)	0.009*** (6.86)	0.0072*** (2.82)	0.0186*** (4.20)	0.0089*** (3.15)	0.0078*** (4.37)	0.0071*** (3.65)	0.0088*** (6.78)
Buildings rate (% GDP)								
Inflation (annual %)								
Openness (exports+imports) (% GDP)								
Gov. consumption (% GDP)								
External debt (% GDP)								
Foreign direct investment (% GDP)								
Infrast. (ln phone lines per capita)								
Education (ln ratio second. enroll.)								
Population growth (%)	-0.0046 (-0.51)	-0.0019 (-0.31)	-0.0288 (-1.71)	-0.0355 (-0.84)	-0.0006 (-0.01)	-0.0001 (-0.01)		
Per capita GDP (ln of value at the beginning of each sub-period)	-0.048*** (-2.89)	-0.0546*** (-4.18)	-0.0618** (-2.32)	-0.4529*** (-4.41)	-0.1829*** (-2.76)	-0.0576*** (-3.06)	-0.042*** (-4.29)	-0.0519*** (-6.20)
R-squared	0.43	0.23	0.2	0.42	0.43	0.2	0.43	0.23
F stat	3.75	9.19	3.51	4.78	6.04	5.35	4.29	10.52
Chow tests:								
1960–80/ 1981–90/ 1991–2002		6.12						6.29
1960–80/ 1981–2002		1.95						1.18
1960–90/ 1991–2002		1.30						1.49

Table 7.6 continued

	(6b) 1960–1980 annual	(6c) 1981–1990 annual	(6d) 1991–2002 annual	(6e) 1960–1990 annual	(7) 1960–2002 5-year averages	(7a) 1960–2002 annual	(7b) 1960–1980 annual	(7c) 1981–1990 annual
Mach. and equip. rate (% GDP)	0.0067** (2.62)	0.0175*** (4.06)	0.0089*** (3.10)	0.0078*** (4.46)	0.0072*** (3.46)	0.0087*** (6.69)	0.0064** (2.37)	0.0186*** (4.27)
Buildings rate (% GDP)					0.0022 (1.03)	0.0025* (1.85)	0.0012 (0.47)	0.0002 (0.04)
Inflation (annual %)								
Openness (exports+imports) (% GDP)								
Gov. consumption (% GDP)								
External debt (% GDP)								
Foreign direct investment (% GDP)								
Infrast. (ln phone lines per capita)								
Education (ln ratio second. enroll.)								
Population growth (%)					−0.0097 (−0.87)	−0.0078 (−1.11)	−0.0322* (−1.84)	−0.0356 (−0.83)
Per capita GDP (ln of value at the beginning of each sub-period)	−0.0323 (−1.60)	−0.4527*** (−4.43)	−0.1824*** (−3.71)	−0.0575*** (−4.25)	−0.058*** (−2.88)	−0.0659*** (−4.54)	−0.0645** (−2.33)	−0.4541*** (−3.99)
R-squared	0.18	0.41	0.43	0.2	0.45	0.24	0.2	0.42
F stat	3.44	5.31	7.01	6.15	3.51	8.79	3.12	4.16
Chow tests:								
1960–80/ 1981–90/ 1991–2002						5.61		
1960–80/ 1981–2002						2.36		
1960–90/ 1991–2002						1.96		

	(7d) 1991–2002 annual	(7e) 1960–1990 annual	(8) 1960–2002 5-year averages	(8a) 1960–2002 annual	(8b) 1960–1980 annual	(8c) 1981–1990 annual	(8d) 1991–2002 annual	(8e) 1960–1990 annual
Mach. and equip. rate (% GDP)	0.0085*** (3.31)	0.0067*** (3.69)	0.0069*** (3.44)	0.0084*** (6.60)	0.0072** (2.50)	0.0175*** (4.08)	0.0082*** (3.08)	0.0068*** (3.67)
Buildings rate (% GDP)	0.0066** (2.28)	0.0026 (1.46)	0.0013 (0.68)	0.0019 (1.57)	−0.0007 (−0.30)	0.00001 (0.004)	0.0056** (2.21)	0.0022 (1.38)
Inflation (annual %)								
Openness (exports+imports) (% GDP)								
Gov. consumption (% GDP)								
External debt (% GDP)								
Foreign direct investment (% GDP)								
Infrast. (ln phone lines per capita)								
Education (ln ratio second. enroll.)								
Population growth (%)	−0.0337 (−0.66)	−0.0061 (−0.62)						
Per capita GDP (ln of value at the beginning of each sub-period)	−0.2499*** (−3.24)	−0.0663*** (−3.33)	−0.043*** (−4.53)	−0.0545*** (−6.50)	−0.0328 (−1.62)	−0.4528*** (−3.93)	−0.216*** (−4.28)	−0.0587*** (−4.29)
R-squared	0.48	0.21	0.44	0.24	0.17	0.41	0.48	0.21
F stat	6.49	5.13	3.8	9.71	2.99	4.56	7.21	5.75
Chow tests:								
1960–80/ 1981–90/ 1991–2002				5.74				
1960–80/ 1981–2002				1.03				
1960–90/ 1991–2002				1.75				

Table 7.6   continued

	(9) 1960–2002 5– year averages	(9a) 1960–2002 annual	(9b) 1960–1980 annual	(9c) 1981–1990 annual	(9d) 1991–2002 annual	(9e) 1960–1990 annual	(10) 1960–2002 5-year averages	(10a) 1960–2002 annual
Mach. and equip. rate (% GDP)	0.0064*** (3.53)	0.0078*** (6.51)	0.0035 (1.37)	0.0164*** (4.70)	0.0068*** (3.21)	0.0063*** (3.42)	0.0052*** (2.80)	0.0079*** (5.71)
Buildings rate (% GDP)	0.0008 (0.40)	0.0016 (1.14)	0.0011 (0.51)	0.0009 (0.22)	0.0064** (2.29)	0.0019 (0.97)		
Inflation (annual %)	−0.00005** (2.50)	−0.00004*** (−4.81)	−0.0002*** (−4.42)	−0.00003*** (−6.67)	0.0002* (1.77)	−0.00004*** (−4.40)	−0.00004** (−2.38)	−0.00005*** (−5.31)
Openness (exports+imports) (% GDP)							0.0006 (1.20)	0.00007 (0.15)
Gov. consumption (% GDP)							−0.0022** (−1.75)	−0.0038*** (−2.98)
External debt (% GDP)							−0.0005* (−1.85)	−0.0007*** (−3.18)
Foreign direct investment (% GDP)							−0.0002 (−0.04)	−0.0035 (−1.77)
Infrast. (ln phone lines per capita)							0.0146 (1.06)	0.0291** (2.40)
Education (ln ratio second. enroll)	0.0004* (1.67)	0.0005 (2.34)	0.0011* (1.90)	0.0053*** (3.90)	0.0005 (1.38)		0.0003 (0.71)	0.0008** (2.29)
Population growth (%)						0.0007 (1.57)		
Per capita GDP (ln of value at the beginning of each sub-period)	−0.0606*** (−3.23)	−0.0839*** (−4.61)	−0.0507* (−1.75)	−0.5268 (−5.80)	−0.2392*** (−3.97)	−0.089*** (−3.40)	−0.1052*** (−3.83)	−0.1553*** (−6.46)
R-squared	0.55	0.28	0.29	0.6	0.54	0.27	0.76	0.44
F stat	4.54	8.98	4.51	7.51	5.83	6.3	4.78	9.7
Chow tests:								
1960–80/ 1981–90/ 1991–2002		7.94						6.45
1960–80/ 1981–2002		1.72						3.22
1960–90/ 1991–2002		1.52						1.77

	(10b) 1960–1980 annual	(10c) 1981–1990 annual	(10d) 1991–2002 annual	(10e) 1960–1990 annual	(11) 1960–2002 5-year averages	(11a) 1960–2002 annual	(11b) 1960–1980 annual	(11c) 1981–1990 annual
Mach. and equip. rate (% GDP)	0.01*** (3.73)	0.0218*** (5.36)	0.0066*** (2.58)	0.0086*** (4.29)	0.0057*** (3.19)	0.0074*** (5.97)	0.0046*** (2.21)	0.0168*** (5.09)
Buildings rate (% GDP)								
Inflation (annual %)	-0.0002*** (-4.41)	-0.00004*** (-4.65)	0.0001 (0.99)	-0.00006*** (-4.46)	-0.00006*** (-3.17)	-0.00005*** (-6.25)	-0.0002*** (-3.87)	-0.0004*** (-4.84)
Openness (exports+imports) (% GDP)	-0.0016 (-1.32)	-0.0013 (-1.05)	0.0018*** (2.93)	-0.007 (-0.81)				
Gov. consumption (% GDP)	-0.0032 (-0.83)	-0.0015 (-0.53)	-0.0023 (-0.86)	-0.0073*** (-2.68)	-0.0022* (-1.70)	-0.0029*** (-2.78)	-0.0055* (-1.83)	0.0004 (0.13)
External debt (% GDP)	-0.0013* (-1.86)	0.003 (0.78)	-0.0015** (-2.20)	-0.0008*** (-2.64)				
Foreign direct investment (% GDP)	-0.0064 (-1.09)	-0.0053 (-1.00)	0.0009 (0.26)	0.076** (-2.04)				
Infrast. (In phone lines per capita)	0.0541 (1.36)	0.1618 (2.79)	0.054 (1.07)	0.0383** (2.00)				
Education (In ratio second. enroll.)	0.0027*** (3.43)	0.0011 (0.46)	-0.0007 (1.54)	0.0024*** (3.42)	0.0004* (1.76)	0.0006*** (2.75)	0.0019*** (2.71)	0.0053*** (3.86)
Population growth (%)								
Per capita GDP (In of value at the beginning of each sub-period)	-0.1942*** (-2.84)	-0.5677*** (-6.62)	-0.278*** (-3.89)	-0.2242*** (-5.56)	-0.0505*** (-2.93)	-0.0677*** (-4.38)	-0.0698** (-2.34)	-0.0544*** (6.41)
R-squared	0.63	0.68	0.59	0.49	0.58	0.3	0.32	0.6
F stat	6.37	7.06	4.72	7.76	5.15	9.95	5.15	7.49
Chow tests:								
1960–80/ 1981–90/ 1991–2002						7.16		
1960–80/ 1981–2002						2.15		
1960–90/ 1991–2002						1.36		

Table 7.6 concluded

	(11d) 1991–2002 annual	(11e) 1960–1990 annual
Mach. and equip. rate (% GDP)	0.0075*** (3.14)	0.0067*** (4.05)
Buildings rate (% GDP)		
Inflation (annual %)	−0.0002 (1.57)	−0.00005*** (6.81)
Openness (exports+imports) (% GDP)		
Gov. consumption (% GDP)	−0.0006 (−0.37)	−0.0054*** (−2.78)
External debt (% GDP)		
Foreign direct investment (% GDP)		
Infrast. (In phone lines per capita)		
Education (ln ratio second. enroll.)	0.0001 (0.40)	0.0008** (2.21)
Population growth (%)		
Per capita GDP (ln of value at the beginning of each sub-period)	−0.1694*** (−3.16)	−0.0758*** (−3.57)
R-squared	0.49	0.30
F stat	4.79	7.40
Chow tests:		
1960–80/ 1981–90/ 1991–2002		
1960–80/ 1981–2002		
1960–90/ 1991–2002		

Notes: t-statistics in parentheses; asterisks mean: statistical significance at the 10% level (*), 5% level (**), and 1% level (***). Fixed effects; Corrected for heteroskedasticity

Source: Author's elaboration.

194

for three types of breaks: (1) 1960–80/1981–90/1991–2002; (2) 1960–80/
1981–2002; and (3) 1986–90/1991–2002.

Three main sub-periods fall within the whole 42 years: (1) 1960–80:
representing the gradual exhaustion of the old import substitution industrialization strategy; (2) 1980–90: the debt crisis, economic instability and beginning
of the stabilization and reforms conducted to put in place a new outward
looking and export led development strategy; and (3) 1990–2002: gradual
consolidation of the outward approach. In Table 7.6 we show in the first
columns the same type of equations shown in Table 7.5 (estimated on the base
of five-year averages) and in the second columns the estimates using annual
data. In the rest of the columns we compute the annual equations for the breaks
used to compute the Chow tests (whose results are shown in the last rows under
the annual equation estimates for the whole period of each equations group).
We used annual estimates to compute the structural break tests in order to have
an appropriate number of degrees of freedom to assess the structural changes.

The results of the annual estimates for the whole 1960–2002 period confirm in general the results obtained using five-year averages, which helps to
reinforce the long-run trends (see the first two columns for each set of
equations in Table 7.6). The observations stated below (observations 4–6) are
based on the results shown in Table 7.5. We consider them as benchmark
long-rung estimates and trends. Among the policy related variables, FDI and
infrastructure showed significance in the annual estimates for the whole
period but we did not include them in our general long-run observations as
their significance disappears in the equations using five-year averages, which
we consider to be the benchmark for the long-run observations.[13] However,
due qualifications to each of the long-run observations and trends are drawn
from the results of the structural analysis.

Observation 4   Key factors affecting per capita GDP growth have been: (1)
investment; (2) inflation performance; (3) the size of the government; (4) the
size of the external debt; and (5) education.

Confirming the findings of section 7.2 we found that: (1) investment was
shown to be an important ingredient in the growth processes of Latin America
during 1960–2002; (2) some key policy variables appeared also as main
factors explaining per capita GDP growth during 1960–2002, contributing to
the difference between fast and slow growth experiences; and (3) the incidence of investment and the related policy variables varied through the whole
period but the long-run observations appear to hold.

Columns 1–4 of Table 7.5 show the regression results for total fixed investment. We present the best four regressions after experimenting with several
combinations of dependent variables.[14] From the results the importance of

fixed investment as a determinant of per capita GDP growth seems clear but other key policy related variables were also shown to be relevant in explaining per capita GDP growth. In addition to fixed investment, we found that key determinants of per capita GDP growth in Latin America during 1960–2002 were inflation, the size of government consumption, the size of the external debt in terms of GDP, and education (proxied by the ratio of secondary enrollments). However, we found that in the long run (taking the whole 1960–2002 period), the most significative policy related variables explaining per capita GDP growth were inflation and the size of the government. We tried additional equations (not shown) including foreign direct investment (FDI) and infrastructure (per capita telephone lines) but their coefficients were not significant (even at the 1 per cent level) in our long-run estimates based on five-year averages.

We interpret the findings as indicating that fixed investment was important for growth in Latin America but other key related policy variables, mainly those that induced price stability, low external debt, reduced government size, and education helped make the difference between fast and slow growth experiences. Population growth appears to have a slight negative effect and the results showed consistency with other evidence about conditional convergence (see for example, Barro and Lee, 1994, and Loayza et al., 2004).[15]

To examine in more detail the conclusions obtained from the long-run 1960–2002 estimates, we examined the stability of the respective equations and results using the breaks indicated above. This procedure seemed appropriate given the structural changes and shocks experienced by Latin America through that period. The qualifications are based on the structural evidence summarized in Table 7.6 Equations: 1a–1e; 2a–2e; 3a–3e, and 4a–4e; and from the information shown in Figure 7.3 and Appendix Table 7.B.1.

Our conclusions are as follows:

1.   The impact of total fixed investment appeared significant in all of the sub-periods considered but the coefficients are higher in the 1980s and in the 1990s. The growth slump of the 1980s was to a great extent reflected also an investment slump.[16] The growth recovery during 1990–2002, though modest, appeared to have been supported by a recovery of investment and a boost from investments in machinery and equipment (see below), which were stimulated by the trade reforms and privatization processes. The recovery in the 1990s was not uniform across countries, however, as can be observed in Figure 7.3 and Appendix Table 7.B.1. In the cases of Chile, Brazil and Mexico the recovery of investment rates and GDP growth was stronger as compared to Argentina, Colombia and Venezuela.

2.   The stability of the equations containing investment on per capita GDP growth is confirmed in half of the 12 Chow Test F-values shown for the

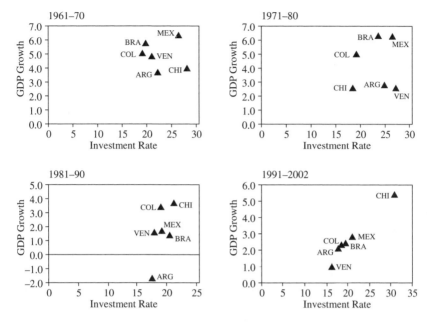

Source: Author's elaboration.

Figure 7.3   GDP growth and total investment rates (constant prices; WDI)

group of equations 1–4. When adding policy related variables the stability of the estimates is confirmed also for half of the six Chow test F-values (with a 5 per cent rejection area). Fixed investment was shown to be significant in all the equations 1a–4d. The significance of the policy related variables varied throughout the 1960–2002 period, however (equations 3a–4e). The Chow structural break test shows structural stability for 1960–90/1991/2002 break. The test fails to accept stability of the parameters when including the 1980s as a separate break. We interpret these results as indication that the 1980s deviate from the long-term pattern observed and that this decade constitutes a special case for the drawing of general observations for the whole 1960–2002 period.

3.   Specific observations about the influence of the policy related variables through the period are: (a) inflation appears significant before the 1990s; (b) trade 'openness' becomes significant in the 1990s; (c) external debt appears significant before 1980 and after the 1980s; (d) government consumption shows significance before the 1990s; (e) FDI shows significance in the annual equation for the whole period and also before the 1990s; (f) infrastructure also shows significance in the annual equa-

tion for the whole period and before the 1990s; and (g) education loses significance after the 1990s.

Observation 5 The contribution of investment in machinery and equipment to per capita GDP growth is higher than the contribution from investment in buildings. Combined with some key policy related variables, inflation, the share of government consumption in GDP, the size of external debt in terms of GDP and education, per capita GDP growth is better explained overall.

In Table 7.5 we also show OLS regressions for per capita GDP growth on fixed investment divided between machinery and equipment, and buildings, and we include as control variables the same policy related variables that we used for the total investment equation estimates (we also used country fixed effects and corrected for heteroskedasticity as needed). This procedure allows us to compare across similar equations the robustness of the estimates. From the results, shown in Table 7.5, we found that when fixed investment is in the form of machinery and equipment the impact on growth is higher as compared to overall investment (see equations 1–4 compared to equations 5–11). The regression coefficients of machinery and equipment are higher than those for total fixed investment for equations that included the same additional explanatory variables.

We found that investments in buildings played a non-significant role as a factor explaining per capita GDP growth when considering the whole 1960–2002 period (see regressions 7,8, and 9 in Table 7.5). The primary role of machinery investments as a source of growth has been supported by the empirical evidence provided by De Long and Summers (1991 and 1993). The social returns of machinery investments are higher than investments in buildings because machinery (and equipment) investments embody new technologies that are more dynamically updated and spread through different activities and sectors. Buildings last longer and the direct and indirect impact on production processes is subject to higher inflexibility than machinery and equipment. In addition, imported machinery provides an effective vehicle to acquire modern technologies.

When combined with other key policy related variables the explanatory power of the estimated equations increased. The policy variables that were shown to matter the most when combined with machinery and equipment in the long-run equation benchmarks were inflation and government consumption (see equations 9, 10 and 11). The significance of education declined when combined with machinery and equipment, however. As new machinery and equipment is combined with upgraded labor, the impact of education could be captured by machinery and equipment investment.

The effect of machinery and equipment and buildings has varied across time, however. Investments in machinery and equipment were shown to be very significant as a factor explaining per capita GDP growth in all the sub-periods considered from 1960–2002 (see equations 4a–11e). The sizes of the coefficients of machinery and equipment rose in the 1980s and thereafter as compared to the previous years. The growth slump of the 1980s was reflected in lower shares of machinery and equipment investments (see Figure 7.4 and Appendix Table 7.B.2). The shares of machinery and equipment (as per cent of GDP) recovered after the 1980s to about the levels observed in the 1960s and 1970s triggering also a recovery of per capita GDP, though at a pace below the 1960s and 1970s. Mexico led the countries with higher shares of machinery and equipment in the 1960s, and Brazil and Venezuela led in the 1970s, likely reflecting the more advanced stage of import substitution reached in these countries.

The shares of machinery and equipment in GDP shrank across countries in the 1980s except in the case of Chile which managed to increase its share of machinery and equipment investment. Chile also led the six countries in terms of machinery and equipment investments (in terms of GDP) in the 1980s and 1990s (including the early 2000s). Despite the modest recovery after the 1980s, machinery and equipment were more effective as a factor contributing to growth (as indicated by the increase in the size of the coefficients observed in equations 4d, 6d, 7d, 8d, 9d, 10d and 11d, compared to the estimates for other sub-periods). It is likely that under the new outward looking development model the trade reforms and associated trade liberalization increased the productivity of machinery and equipment through new technologies acquired through imports.

Although, investment in buildings showed little significance (t-values) as a factor contributing to per capita GDP growth during 1960–2002, a slightly positive impact appeared to develop after the 1980s (see equations 8d, 9d and 10d). However, the shares of investment in buildings in GDP on average moved only slightly higher after the 1980s while per capita GDP moved from negative to positive growth rates. In other words, buildings did not play a leading role as a growth factor either in the 1980s or in 1990s (and early 2000s), though in the latter the social returns of investment in buildings as measured by the equation coefficients increased (see also Figure 7.4). It is likely that the increase returns of buildings emerged in part as a result of the reduced role of subsidized house building during the period of outward orientation and more reduced role of state participation.

Specific observations about the influence of the policy related variables are in general similar to the equations for total fixed investment: (1) inflation loses significance after the 1980s; (2) trade 'openness' becomes significant in the 1990s; (3) external debt appears significant before the 1980s and after the

Machinery and equipment rate   Buildings rate

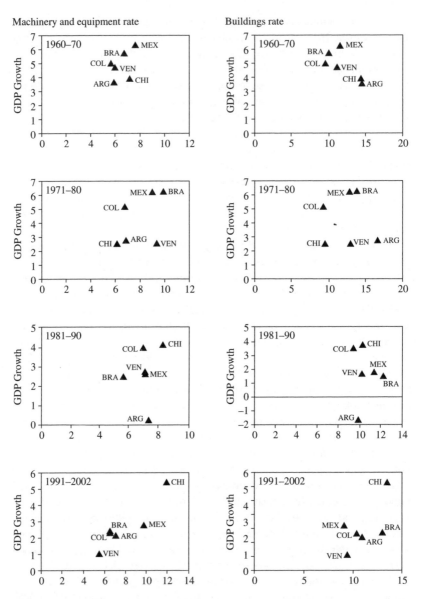

*Figure 7.4   GDP growth, machinery and equipment, and construction rates
              (constant prices, WDI)*

1990s; (4) government consumption shows significance before the 1990s; (5) FDI shows significance in the annual equation for the whole period and before the 1990s; (6) infrastructure shows significance in the annual equation for the whole period and before the 1990s; and (7) education shows significance before the 1990s. The replacement of total fixed investment by machinery and equipment investment changed somewhat the relative relevance of the different policy related variables but the overall long-run trends and structural qualifications remain almost the same.

Observation 6 Human capital as measured by secondary education appeared to be a key factor contributing to productivity growth, but lost significance after the 1980s.

Education appeared as a significative variable in most of the long-run equations that contained total fixed investment or machinery and equipment plus other key policy related variables. In three of the five equations in which education was included its coefficient was significative at least at the 10 per cent level (see equations 3, 4, 9, and 11 in Table 7.5). The effect of education on growth loses some significance when running with machinery and equipment investment instead of total investment (equation 10 compared with equation 3). As newer machinery and equipment requires increased training skills, part of the education effect could be captured by investments in machinery and equipment. This is, however, an hypothesis that would require further testing the educational requirements associated with the different types and vintages of machinery and equipment.

The three countries with the lowest secondary enrollment ratios in 2001 were Venezuela (66 per cent), Colombia (70 per cent) and Mexico (73 per cent). The other three countries had ratios above 80 per cent: Chile (85 per cent), Argentina (97 per cent) and Brazil (100 per cent). Although the potential for additional growth by raising secondary enrollment is stronger for the three countries having the lowest secondary enrollment ratios (Colombia, Mexico and Venezuela), the potential impact of education applies to all other countries as well if we interpret the indicator of education as a proxy for a broader measure of human capital. However, data on education (World Bank database (WDI), and Barro and Lee, 2003) provide indicators of education with a span of five years only and the data are not adjusted for quality. The quality component should add strength to the educational stock and therefore to the impact on growth, which becomes evident from the increasing demand for new skills to innovate in more efficient and competitive production processes and for adopting newer technologies incorporated in new machinery and equipment.[17]

Observations about the stability of the relationship between education and per capita GDP growth during 1960–2002 are also relevant. We have found evidence showing that secondary education was an important factor contributing to per capita GDP growth during the 1960s and 1970s but its role gradually lost force in the 1980s and further in the 1990s and 2000s (equations 3a–3e; 4a–4e; 9a–9e; 10a–10e; and 11a–11e):

Education appeared to be more significant in explaining per capita GDP growth in the 1960s and 1970s (see equations 3b, 4b, 9b, 10b and 11b). In the 1980s education appeared significant in the equations that included the most significant policy related variables: inflation and government consumption (these are the two variables that showed high significance in most of the equations in Table 7.6) When adding other policy related variables (in addition to inflation and government consumption) education loses significance in the 1980s (see equations 3c and 10c). This period was subject to many disturbances, however, induced by debt restructuring and adjustment programs, which make it difficult to interpret the declining significance of education during the 1980s.

What appeared interesting in the estimates, however, was the loss of significance of education as an explanatory variable during 1991–2002 (see equations 3d, 4d, 9d, 10d and 11d). To some extent the modernization of investment, especially of machinery and equipment, could have been capturing the use of additional educational skills, but most importantly, it may be reflecting the declining importance of encouraging secondary enrollments as they reach nearly 100 per cent of the population of secondary age. Our education variable measures the ratio of secondary enrollment (compared with the population of secondary age). As most of the population of secondary age becomes enrolled, the room for additional enrollments narrows. This is telling us that in the 1960s and 1970s the role of increasing the coverage of secondary education was very relevant for economic growth, but that this effect has gradually eroded. This does not mean, however, that education is no longer relevant. It means that other ways of expanding education are becoming increasingly more relevant such as improving on the quality of education and the supply of new forms of human capital formation. The evidence suggests that new impetus should be given to education as a force of growth, that first generation educational policies should be gradually replaced by a second generation of education policies which increasingly focus on strengthening the effectiveness of educational stock. Quality seems to be at the center of the international experiences with second generation educational policies (the importance given to education in the Asian countries is an example of the second generation type of education).

7.4   COMPOSITION OF INVESTMENT BETWEEN PRIVATE AND PUBLIC SECTORS

In this section we examine the incidence of the sectoral composition of investment on per capita GDP growth. We disaggregate fixed investment between private and public sector investment and obtained estimates for the role played by private and public investment in the process of economic growth. As for the decomposition of investment between machinery and equipment and buildings, some previous evidence has also been found regarding the effects of private and public investment on economic growth (see for example: Easterly and Rebelo 1993; Greene and Villanueva, 1991; Khan and Reinhart, 1990, and Schmidt-Hebbel et al., 1996a). In the literature there seems to be a consensus that these two components of investment may have a differential impact on growth depending on the context in which they take place and if public investment becomes a complement to or substitute for private investment.

Public investment that complements private investment appears to increase investment productivity and economic growth. Public investment in education and infrastructure show strong complementarities to private investment and have positive effects on economic growth. Public investment may on the other side become a substitute for private investment and reduce aggregate investment returns and economic growth. Public investment may crowd out private investment by using scarce resources and adversely affect growth through the implementation of investment projects of low or negative social returns. Thus, academics and policy makers have been increasingly aware that it is not only the level of total of investment that matters, but also its composition between private and public sectors.

Evidence of the impact of private and public investment on growth has important practical implications. It shows the need to rationalize public investment budgets and allocate public resources to projects that offer the highest social rates of return, seek opportunities for complementarities with private investment, and find room for counter-cyclical investment policies, when the macroeconomic framework permits. The implications for public investment policy are especially relevant for macroeconomic policy also if, as we show below, private investment and growth present mutual causality, opening the possibilities for the creation of virtuous and vicious cycles. In this section we show evidence for our six Latin American countries during the whole 1960–2002 period that private investment has had a positive impact on per capita GDP growth, that public investment has had (on average for the whole period and six countries) a non-significant effect on growth, and that the combination of private investment with other key policy variables helps further increase per capita GDP growth. The evidence leads us to draw our next observation regarding the investment–growth process in Latin America during 1960–2002:

Observation 7 The contribution of private investment to growth has been positive and strong. The contribution of public investment has not been very significant. Price stability appears as a leading policy related factor adding to per capita GDP growth.

In Tables 7.7 and 7.8 we show a selected number of OLS estimated equations for per capita GDP growth against private investment, public investment, and a selected set of key policy variables. In Table 7.7 we show our benchmark long-run estimates and in Table 7.8 the estimates used for the structural break analysis. As for the regressions in Tables 7.5 and 7.6, we also used country fixed effects, corrected for heteroskedasticity as needed. As in the previous estimates, per capita GDP growth has been approximated by the first differences of the natural logs of per capita GDP. However, for the private–public investment estimates shown in Table 7.7 we used data for the period 1970–2002 at current prices in local currencies and we used three-year averages (instead of the 1960–2002 period and five-year averages used in the previous long-run estimates).

The only publicly available series of investment figures divided between private and public investment are those compiled by the IFC (2001) and the WDI. The series are available for the period 1970 onward and are at current prices only. We found that the data for our six selected Latin American countries were the best available for Latin American countries. Data on public investment in other countries either did not cover public enterprises or the series had only a short history. We preferred to avoid mixing weak data with good data despite sacrificing a number of observations. Data from the United Nations on national accounts contain longer historic series but for central and general governments only, which exclude the public enterprises.

We reduced the averages of the variables from five to three years in order to compensate for the shortage of the estimation period. As for the estimates in Tables 7.5 and 7.6 we also obtained in this case similar results for the whole 1970–2002 period when using three-year averages (62 observations) and annual data (178 observations), which helps to reinforce the main conclusions contained in observation 7, which is based on the benchmark long-run estimates in Table 7.7. As for our previous observations, due qualifications are drawn from the structural break analysis based on the results shown in Table 7.8.

Our long-run estimates for the period 1970–2002 shown in Table 7.7 show that private investment was a main driving force of per capita GDP growth, with public investment playing a negligible role. We also found evidence that

Table 7.7 GDP per capita growth determinants: private and public investment (three-year averages)

	(1)	(2)	(3)	(4)	(5)
Private investment (% GDP)	0.0032	0.00417*	0.0042*	0.0038*	0.0036*
	(1.62)	(1.82)	(1.95)	(1.75)	(1.77)
Public investment (% GDP)		0.0024	0.0024	0.0017	0.0022
		(0.92)	(0.91)	(0.63)	(0.88)
Inflation (annual %)			−0.00002	−0.00002***	−0.00003**
			(−2.70)	(2.60)	(−2.46)
Government consumption (% GDP)					−0.003**
					(−2.28)
External debt (% GDP)				−0.029	
				(−0.93)	
Per capita GDP (ln of value at beginning of each sub-period)	−0.0004***	−0.0004***	−0.0004***	−0.0044***	−0.0005***
	(−3.01)	(−3.32)	(−3.23)	(−2.94)	(73.46)
R-squared	0.24	0.26	0.34	0.36	0.41
F stat	2.44	2.34	2.78	2.62	3.2

Notes:
t-statistics in parentheses; Asterisks mean: statistical significance at the 10% level (*), 5% level (**), and 1 % level (***)
Fixed effects; corrected for heteroskedasticity

Source: Author's elaboration.

Table 7.8   GDP per capita growth determinants: private and public investment (three-year averages annual data)

	(1) 1970–2002 3-year averages	(1a) 1970–2002 annual	(1b) 1970–1980 annual	(1c) 1981–1992 annual	(1d) 1993–2002 annual	(1e) 1981–2002 annual	(1f) 1970–1992 annual
Private investment (% GDP)	0.0032	0.0034***	0.0104***	0.0033	0.0109***	0.0052***	0.0036*
	(1.62)	(2.50)	(3.57)	(0.94)	(5.01)	(2.55)	(1.73)
Per capita GDP (ln of value at beginning of each sub-period)	−0.0004***	0.0017**	−0.0014	0.0011	−0.0001	0.0006	0.0018
	(−3.01)	(1.93)	(−1.01)	(0.64)	(−0.83)	(0.51)	(1.72)
R-squared	0.24	0.15	0.37	0.12	0.43	0.18	0.12
F stat	2.44	30.93	25.57	8.59	38.1	26.24	15.55
Chow tests:							
1970–80/1981–92/1993–2002	4.36						
1970–80/1981–2002	3.13						
1970–91/1992–2002	1.58						

	(2) 1970–2002 3-year averages	(2a) 1970–2002 annual	(2b) 1970–1980 annual	(2c) 1981–1992 annual	(2d) 1993–2002 annual	(2e) 1981–2002 annual	(2f) 1970–1992 annual
Private investment (% GDP)	0.00417*	0.0037**	0.01***	0.003	0.0139***	0.0047**	0.0035
	(1.82)	(2.41)	(4.08)	(0.82)	(5.85)	(2.09)	(1.62)
Public investment (%GDP)	0.0024	0.0008	−0.0073*	−0.0033	0.0120**	−0.0011	−0.0006
	(0.92)	(0.48)	(−1.90)	(−0.79)	(2.04)	(−0.38)	(−0.23)
Per capita GDP (ln of value at beginning of each sub-period)	−0.0004***	0.0014	−0.0025	0.0013	−0.0028**	0.0005	0.0018*
	(−3.32)	(1.63)	(−1.76)	(0.75)	(−2.41)	(0.44)	(1.74)
R-squared	0.26	0.15	0.44	0.13	0.51	0.17	0.12
F stat	2.34	14.03	16.69	4.63	23.01	11.36	7.74
Chow tests:							
1970–80/1981–92/1993–2002	4.86						
1970–80/1981–2002	3.10						
1970–91/1992–2002	1.65						

Table 7.8 continued

	(3) 1970–2002 3-year averages	(3a) 1970–2002 annual	(3b) 1970–1980 annual	(3c) 1981–1992 annual	(3d) 1993–2002 annual	(3e) 1981–2002 annual	(3f) 1970–1992 annual
Private investment (% GDP)	0.0042* (1.95)	0.0042*** (2.85)	0.0108*** (5.51)	0.003 (0.81)	0.0138*** (5.62)	0.0046** (2.09)	0.0044** (2.14)
Public investment (% GDP)	0.0024 (0.91)	0.0006 (0.36)	0.0044 (1.469)	-0.0036 (-0.89)	0.0111* (1.74)	-0.0006 (-0.20)	-0.0013 (-0.54)
Inflation (annual %)	-0.00002*** (-2.70)	-0.00002*** (-2.52)	-0.0003*** (-6.17)	-0.00003*** (-3.41)	0.00001 (1.37)	-0.00001* (-1.83)	-0.00003*** (-4.49)
Per capita GDP (ln of value at beginning of each sub-period)	-0.0004*** (-3.23)	0.0003 (0.31)	-0.0056*** (-3.58)	0.0009 (0.52)	-0.0027** (-2.27)	0.0003 (0.22)	0.0002 (0.15)
R-squared	0.34	0.18	0.73	0.21	0.51	0.19	0.21
F stat	2.78	11.01	28.19	5.15	15.32	-8.72	-8.94
Chow tests:							
1970–80/1981–92/1993–2002	5.38						
1970–80/1981–2002	2.99						
1970–91/1992–2002	2.33						

	(4) 1970–2002 3-year averages	(4a) 1970–2002 annual	(4b) 1970–1980 annual	(4c) 1981–1992 annual	(4d) 1993–2002 annual	(4e) 1981–2002 annual	(4f) 1970–1992 annual
Private investment (% GDP)	0.0038*	0.0039**	0.0116***	0.0017	0.0121***	0.0041	0.005***
	(1.75)	(2.66)	(8.64)	(0.40)	(5.41)	(1.60)	(2.36)
Public investment (% GDP)	0.0017	-0.00009	0.0052*	-0.0042	0.0137**	-0.0005	-0.0032
	(0.63)	(-0.05)	(1.81)	(-1.07)	(2.27)	(-0.19)	(-1.26)
Inflation (annual %)	-0.00002***	-0.00002**	-0.0003***	-0.00003***	0.000008	-0.00002*	-0.00003***
	(2.60)	(-2.44)	(-8.37)	(-3.62)	(1.29)	(-1.84)	(-4.21)
External debt (% GDP)	-0.029	-0.0414*	-0.0874***	-0.0565	-0.1081**	-0.0168	-0.0667***
	(-0.93)	(-1.83)	(-2.45)	(-1.47)	(-2.63)	(-0.63)	(-2.60)
Per capita GDP (ln of value at beginning of each sub-period)	-0.0044***	0.0001	-0.0057***	0.0009	-0.0031**	0.0003	-0.0003
	(-2.94)	(0.10)	(-4.36)	(0.55)	(-2.80)	(0.24)	(-0.26)
R-squared	0.36	0.2	0.76	0.23	0.55	0.19	0.26
F stat	2.62	9.4	24.39	4.38	13.37	6.58	8.81
Chow tests:							
1970–80/1981–92/1993–2002	5.25						
1970–80/1981–2002	2.49						
1970–91/1992–2002	2.80						

209

Table 7.8 concluded

	(5) 1970–2002 3-year averages	(5a) 1970–2002 annual	(5b) 1970–1980 annual	(5c) 1981–1992 annual	(5d) 1993–2002 annual	(5e) 1981–2002 annual	(5f) 1970–1992 annual
Private investment (% GDP)	0.0036*	0.0044***	0.0108	0.0049	0.0136***	0.0054***	0.0052***
	(1.77)	(3.13)	(5.32)	(1.27)	(5.34)	(2.51)	(2.62)
Public investment (% GDP)	0.0022	0.0011	0.0051	−0.0007	0.011	0.0007	−0.0007
	(0.88)	(0.62)	(1.65)	(−0.19)	(1.71)	(0.25)	(−0.27)
Inflation (annual %)	−0.00003**	−0.00002**	−0.0003***	−0.00003**	0.000009	−0.00002*	−0.00003***
	(−2.46)	(−2.31)	(−6.04)	(−2.44)	(1.30)	(−1.80)	(−4.49)
Gov. consumption (% GDP)	−0.003**	−0.0019*	−0.0028	−0.0033	−0.0005	−0.002	−0.002
	(−2.28)	(−1.69)	(−0.96)	(−0.93)	(−0.28)	(−1.51)	(−0.92)
External debt (% GDP)							
Per capita GDP (ln of value at beginning of each sub-period)	−0.0005***	0.0002	−0.0055***	0.0003	−0.0027**	0.0001	−0.000003
	(73.46)	(0.22)	(−3.35)	(0.18)	(−2.23)	(0.05)	(0.002)
R-squared	0.41	0.21	0.73	0.29	0.51	0.23	0.26
F stat	3.2	9.56	20.3	5.2	11.25	7.94	8.01
Chow tests:							
1970–80/1981–92/1993–2002	5.37						
1970–80/1981–2002	2.87						
1970–91/1992–2002	2.32						

Notes:
t-statistics in parentheses; Asterisks mean: statistical significance at the 10% level (*), 5% level (**), and 1% level (***)
Fixed effects; Corrected for heteroskedasticity

Source: Author's elaboration.

inflation was also very significant in explaining per capita GDP growth (see equations 3, 4 and 5). The coefficients appeared all significant at the 1 per cent level and improved the explanatory power of the equations when combined with private investment (see the R-squares and the F values). We also found that conditional convergence appeared significant in these estimates (we included in this case as a dependent variable the initial per capita GDP at the beginning of each three-year sub-period).

These estimates could be interpreted as showing evidence of some existing inefficiencies in the management of government finances of the six largest countries of the region when considering the whole 1970–2002 period. The results also help to understand the importance of appropriate economic policies as additional ingredients of the growth processes. Government consumption showed low significance in the long-run equations (but no significance in the sub-periods; see below). External debt was not significant as well as other variables not explicitly shown (openness, FDI and infrastructure). Education did not show significance in this exercise. Reasons for this result could include: (1) the shorter period used in this case (1970–2002 compared to 1960–2002 in the previous datasets); (2) that private investment may have been capturing some highly correlated impacts from other policy variables; and (3) that progress on increasing the ratio of secondary enrollments increasingly eroded through the 1960–2002 as the ratios were getting closer to 100 per cent (some evidence of this was shown earlier).

The countries that have promoted private investment and have reinforced price stability, reducing the associated vulnerabilities and uncertainties caused by high inflation, have enjoyed faster per capita GDP growth. Chile, Colombia and Mexico have performed better while Argentina and Venezuela on the other side have suffered from stronger price instabilities during 1970–2002, discouraging both private investment and economic growth. Price instabilities increase the exposure to vicious cycles and reduce the leverage for counter-cyclical fiscal policies.

Some qualifications regarding the stability of our long-run estimates are the following (see Table 7.8):

1. The structural tests show stability in the estimates when breaking the period into 1970–80/1981–2002 and 1970–91/1992–2002, but not when including the 1980s as a separate break (see last rows of equations 1a, 2a, 3a, 4a and 5a). As for the estimates for total investment and the composition of investment between machinery and equipment and buildings, the 1980s appeared to be 'different' as compared to the global period and the rest of the sub-periods. This should not be strange given the series of domestic and external shocks suffered by Latin American countries in the

1980s. In particular, the spread of debt restructuring, stabilization, and reforms combined with lack of external financing and negative per capita GDP growth made that period significantly different from the others. The estimates show that in the 1980s neither private nor public investment seemed to be leading factors contributing to the decline of per capita GDP growth. Inflation was shown to be the main explanatory variable of growth performance in the 1980s. The results seem consistent with previous estimates and also considering that Latin American countries entered a phase of strong monetary adjustment to cut inflationary expectations and re-establish domestic equilibrium. Stabilization was assigned priority in the

Private investment rate   Public investment rate

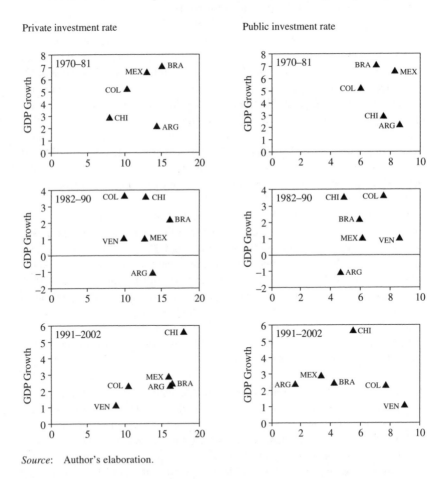

Source: Author's elaboration.

Figure 7.5   GDP growth and private and public investment rates (current prices)

1980s while structural reforms acquired an increasing role during the 1990s. After the 1980s, we observe higher shares of private investment in GDP along with a recovery of economic growth, though economic growth in the 1990s was on average below the rates observed in the 1970s, except for the case of Chile (see Figure 7.5 and Appendix Table 7.B.3).

2. In the case of public investment, we observe some dissimilar incidence within the 1970–2002 period. The contribution of public investment to per capita GDP growth acquired significance only in the 1990s. In the 1970s and 1980s public investment appeared not significant. It is likely the fiscal reforms and rationalization of public budgets in the second half of the 1980s and first half of the 1990s strengthened the complementarities between public and private investment and, thus, its significance as a factor contributing to per capita GDP growth. We also observe in the 1990s an increasing dispersion in the shares of public investment across the six countries (see Figure 7.5). Colombia and Venezuela reported the highest shares of public investment in GDP but also performed the poorest in terms of economic growth. Chile's economic growth was the highest with an average share of public investment in GDP nearly 6 per cent, more than 2 per centage points below that of Colombia and 4 percentage points below that of Venezuela. This tells us that the contribution of public investment to economic growth is more country specific and that aggregate conclusions could be misleading. In the case of Chile public investment did not appear to have been a major constraint on economic growth.

3. Some specific observations about the influence of the policy related variables emerge from the structural analysis: (a) inflation loses significance after the 1980s; (b) government consumption does not show significance in any of the sub-periods used for the structural tests; (c) external debt appears significant before the 1980s and after the 1990s. The nonsignificance of government consumption when combined with private investment helps to strengthen the evidence of the reduced direct role of the government in contributing to per capita GDP growth, though country specific exceptions could also apply.

Observation 8 Private investment and economic growth show mutual causality, inducing virtuous and vicious cycles between private investment and economic growth.

Table 7.9 shows a series of estimates for private investment rate (percentage of GDP; based on data at current prices) during the 1970–2002 period. We follow the same statistical approach applied in the previous estimates (panel OLS estimations with fixed country effects). From the larger set of equation trials we selected the five best equations (in terms of explanatory powers and economic and statistical significances of the control variables). In Table 7.10 we show the annual estimates for the whole period and the sub-periods used to qualify the long run estimates. Similar results are obtained for the annual equation and the equations using the three-year averages for the whole 1970–2002 period (our benchmark long-run equation) (178 and 62 observations, respectively, reinforcing the conclusion stated as observation 8. Some additional results are provided from the structural break analysis based on the estimates shown in Table 7.10.

From the results of Table 7.9 we observe that per capita GDP growth appeared as a positive and very significative factor contributing to the private investment rates (at the 1 per cent level) (equations 2–5). Combined with observation 7 the estimates show a mutual causality between private investment and growth, which opens the room for virtuous and vicious cycles. An increase (decline) of private investment induces an acceleration of per capita GDP growth, and an acceleration (decline) of per capita GDP growth induces an increase of private investment. This mutual causality between investment and growth has been addressed in some previous studies.

Servén and Solimano (1992a and 1992b) found a positive correlated cyclical interaction between private investment and growth in the context of the 1980s and early 1990s. They mentioned the possibility of using public investment to attenuate the mutual reinforcing phase of both private investment and economic growth at times of economic contraction, and supporting growth stability factors to stimulate private investment and induce a virtuous cycle of recovery and growth. They remarked that growth recoveries took longer when, in the declining phase of the cycles, public investment was cut excessively and when uncertainty about the policy framework delayed the recovery of growth and private investment. We agree with these findings but we would stress that our evidence showed that public investment was not a key constraint on economic growth and that the use of counter cyclical public investment policies would depend on the existence of an appropriate policy framework.

Our evidence suggests that the 'package' of policies matters a lot for economic growth as well as investment (especially policies reinforcing price stability), and that the effectiveness of public investment is crucial. As shown in Figure 7.5 for the case of Venezuela during 1991–2002, high public investment did not guarantee an acceleration of economic growth. In equations 1–3 of Table 7.9, we found a negative correlation between private and public investment for the whole 1970–2002 period, indicating that public investment was crowded out rather than crowding private investment during 1970–2002.

We also found that other key factors contributing to private investment during the whole 1970–2002 period were foreign direct investment (FDI) and

Table 7.9 Private investment determinants (three-year averages)

	(1)	(2)	(3)	(4)	(5)	(6)	(7)
Public investment rate (% GDP)	−0.2363* (−1.83)	−0.233** (−2.14)	−0.2035 (−1.52)				
Per capita GDP growth (%)		26.43*** (3.07)	34.04*** (3.31)	26.5*** (3.04)	35.42*** (3.70)		
Foreign direct investment (% GDP)	0.901*** (4.29)	0.9608*** (5.71)		1.0758*** (6.79)		1.014*** (4.94)	
Infrastr. (ln teleph. lines per cap.)			2.5217*** (3.49)		2.8867*** (4.88)		2.2830*** (3.61)
R-squared	0.65	0.71	0.67	0.71	0.67	0.65	0.57
F stat	14.05	16.26	13.11	19.02	15.8	17.01	12.23

Notes:
t-statistics in parentheses; Asterisks mean: statistical significance at the 10% level (*), 5% level (**), and 1 % level (***)
Fixed effects; corrected for heteroskedasticity

Source: Author's elaboration.

Table 7.10 Private investment determinants (three-year averages, annual data)

	(1) 1970–2002 3-year averages	(1a) 1970–2002 annual	(1b) 1970–1980 annual	(1c) 1981–1992 annual	(1d) 1993–2002 annual	(1e) 1981–2002 annual	(1f) 1970–1992 annual
Public investment rate (% GDP)	-0.2363* (-1.83)	-0.2993*** (-3.55)	-0.2265 (-1.15)	-0.1171 (-0.92)	-0.6502* (-2.81)	-0.2855*** (-2.59)	-0.2354** (-2.19)
Foreign direct investment (% GDP)	0.901*** (4.29)	0.6275*** (4.19)	0.2312 (0.28)	0.3598 (0.74)	-0.0643 (-0.53)	0.3362** (2.23)	0.8300*** (2.55)
Infrastr. (telephone lines per cap.)							
R-squared	0.65	0.51	0.65	0.50	0.77	0.57	0.5
F stat	14.05	177.06	90.15	60.86	154.43	152.21	114.07
Chow tests:							
1970–80/1981–92/1993–2002		9.70					
1970–80/1981–2002		5.17					
1970–92/1993–2002		6.23					

	(2) 1970–2002 3-year averages	(2a) 1970–2002 annual	(2b) 1970–1980 annual	(2c) 1981–1992 annual	(2d) 1993–2002 annual	(2e) 1981–2002 annual	(2f) 1970–1992 annual
Public investment rate (% GDP)	-0.233**	-0.2856***	-0.0298	-0.0792	-0.7223**	-0.2437***	-0.2254**
	(-2.14)	(-3.72)	(-0.18)	(-0.60)	(-2.85)	(-2.38)	(-2.21)
Per capita GDP growth (%)	26.43***	17.34***	25.13***	8.98	29.81***	16.06***	11.24**
	(3.07)	(3.49)	(3.19)	(1.42)	(4.79)	(2.99)	(2.13)
Foreign direct investment (% GDP)	0.9608***	0.623***	0.2743	0.236	0.0081	0.3336***	0.7377***
	(5.71)	(4.66)	(0.42)	(0.46)	(0.09)	(2.48)	(2.38)
Infrastr. (telephone lines per cap.)							
R-squared	0.71	0.55	0.72	0.52	0.85	0.61	
F stat	16.26	105.36	60.72	32.02	122.87	88.06	
Chow tests:							
1970–80/1981–92/1993–2002		10.32					
1970–80/1981–2002		5.1					
1970–92/1993–2002		5.9					

Table 7.10 continued

	(3) 1970–2002 3-year averages	(3a) 1970–2002 annual	(3b) 1970–1980 annual	(3c) 1981–1992 annual	(3d) 1993–2002 annual	(3e) 1981–2002 annual	(3f) 1970–1992 annual
Public investment rate (% GDP)	−0.2035	−0.1672**	−0.1293	0.0554	−0.6957***	−0.1249	−0.1803**
	(−1.52)	(−2.20)	(−0.57)	(−0.45)	(−3.05)	(−1.20)	(−2.00)
Per capita GDP growth (%)	34.04***	21.39***	23.98***	5.39	24.7***	15.25***	15.72***
	(3.31)	(4.44)	(3.02)	(0.87)	(4.40)	(3.09)	(2.94)
Infrastr. (telephone lines per cap.)	2.5217***	2.5421***	1.2122	3.5042***	−2.6842***	2.1942***	2.231***
	(3.49)	(6.39)	(0.88)	(2.32)	(−2.39)	(3.80)	(3.56)
R-squared	0.67	0.59	0.72	0.55	0.86	0.64	0.53
F stat	13.11	122.54	61.18	36.18	139.77	101.23	64.83
Chow tests:							
1970–80/1981–92/1993–2002	9.52						
1970–80/1981–2002	4.69						
1970–92/1993–2002	4.71						

	(4) 1970–2002 3-year averages	(4a) 1970–2002 annual	(4b) 1970–1980 annual	(4c) 1981–1992 annual	(4d) 1993–2002 annual	(4e) 1981–2002 annual	(4f) 1970–1992 annual
Per capita GDP growth (%)	26.5***	18.07***	25.5***	9.34	30.79***	17.81***	11.60**
	(3.04)	(3.64)	(3.46)	(1.54)	(4.34)	(3.51)	(2.16)
Foreign direct investment (% GDP)	1.0758***	0.7473***	0.3019	0.2063	0.0754	0.4041***	0.8383***
	(6.79)	(5.53)	(0.46)	(0.42)	(0.64)	(3.03)	(2.76)
R-squared	0.71	0.55	0.72	0.51	0.8	0.61	0.5
F stat	19.02	209.75	123.93	64.73	200.34	187.88	117.00
Chow tests:							
1970–80/1981–92/1993–2002	11.74						
1970–80/1981–2002	6.76						
1970–92/1993–2002	6.15						

Table 7.10   continued

	(5) 1970–2002 3-year averages	(5a) 1970–2002 annual	(5b) 1970–1980 annual	(5c) 1981–1992 annual	(5d) 1993–2002 annual	(5e) 1981–2002 annual	(5f) 1970–1992 annual
Per capita GDP growth (%)	35.42*** (3.70)	23.13*** (4.79)	25.85*** (3.47)	5.4 (0.87)	29.86*** (4.07)	17.33*** (3.59)	16.54*** (3.04)
Foreign direct investment (% GDP)							
Infrastr. (telephone lines per cap.)	2.8867*** (4.88)	2.7964*** (8.32)	0.7591 (0.74)	3.3653*** (2.32)	−0.3993 (−0.32)	2.336*** (4.69)	2.5422*** (3.93)
R-squared	0.67	0.60	0.72	0.55	0.80	0.65	0.52
F stat	15.80	259.52	123.29	73.37	199.28	221.32	125.2
Chow tests:							
1970–80/1981–92/1993–2002	8.96						
1970–80/1981–2002	5.62						
1970–92/1993–2002	3.70						

	(6) 1970–2002 3-year averages	(6a) 1970–2002 annual	(6b) 1970–1980 annual	(6c) 1981–1992 annual	(6d) 1993–2002 annual	(6e) 1981–2002 annual	(6f) 1970–1992 annual
Foreign direct investment (% GDP)	1.014*** (4.94)	0.7556*** (4.96)	0.4584 (0.57)	0.3225 (0.68)	0.0449 (0.29)	0.4204*** (2.78)	0.9384*** (2.92)
R-squared	0.65	0.5	0.64	0.5	0.71	0.57	0.48
F stat	17.01	28.94	17.63	10.18	20.81	26.07	17.73
Chow tests:							
1970–80/1981–92/1993–2002		10.64					
1970–80/1981–2002		6.53					
1970–92/1993–2002		6.33					

Table 7.10   concluded

	(7) 1970–2002 3-year averages	(7a) 1970–2002 annual	(7b) 1970–1980 annual	(7c) 1981–1992 annual	(7d) 1993–2002 annual	(7e) 1981–2002 annual	(7f) 1970–1992 annual
Infrastr. (telephone lines per cap.)	2.283***	2.5677***	0.9204	3.8529***	−2.0325	2.4198***	2.2747***
	(3.61)	(6.69)	(0.86)	(2.88)	(−1.47)	(4.35)	(3.39)
R-squared	0.57	0.52	0.64	0.54	0.72	0.61	0.47
F stat	12.23	31.65	17.34	12.15	22.19	30.83	17.00
Chow tests:							
1970–80/1981–92/1993–2002		10.75					
1970–80/1981–2002		7.33					
1970–92/1993–2002		4.90					

Notes:
t-statistics in parentheses; Asterisks mean: statistical significance at the 10% level (*), 5% level (**), and 1 % level (***)
Fixed effects; corrected for heteroskedasticity

Source: Author's elaboration.

infrastructure (equations 4–7). These results could imply that government policies that have encouraged privatization sales and concessions have been effective in promoting private investment (and economic growth). The significance of FDI and infrastructure seem inconclusive, however, when adding the structural qualifications (see below).

A further exploration within the whole 1970–2002 period adds relevant qualifications to the 'long-run' 1970–2002 benchmark estimates:

1. The structural break tests (Chow tests) show a clear instability in the coefficients obtained in our long-run 1970–2002 estimates. In the last columns of Table 7.10 we show the Chow tests for three different breaks (1970–80/1981–92/1993–2002; 1970–80/1981–2002; and 1970–92/1993–2002) under the annual estimates equations corresponding to each set of similar equations. The results in all cases point to the rejection of the null hypothesis of stability of the coefficients through 1970–2002. These results could be expected taking into consideration the shorter period considered and the structural changes that have affected both the incentives and the composition of private and public investment. Liberalization of capital flows, privatization, and the rationalization of public budgets have become major structural factors affecting private investment incentives through the 1970–2002 years not only for the whole region but also with different emphasis across countries in the region.

   In the 1970s FDI was highly restricted in most Latin American countries and most infrastructure investment was public. This situation gradually changed in the 1980s amid a process of strong fiscal and monetary adjustments. In the 1990s, FDI gradually gained acceptance in most countries, infrastructure policies focused increasingly towards the participation of the private sector and public investment was seen increasingly as adopting a role of a complement rather than a substitute for private investment. Progress on privatization and public sector reforms have also varied across countries. Chile and Mexico have been ahead in implementing the reforms affecting capital flows and the public sector. Argentina, Brazil and Venezuela have remained behind in improving their public finances.

2. The instability of the estimates shown in the structural Chow tests implies that our 'long-run' observation about the specific form of the mutual causality between private investment and per capita GDP growth appears to hold except in the 1980s.

3. The estimates in Table 7.10 confirm the negative correlation between public and private investment through the various sub-periods shown (equations 1a–3f), implying that public investment has been more a substitute rather than a complement to private investment.

4. The estimates show that FDI and infrastructure showed as main forces driving the slump of private investment during 1981–2002 but were not main factors contributing to private investment in the 1970s (see equations 1e, 2e, 3e, 4e, 5e, 6e and 7e, compared with equations 1b, 2b, 3b, 4b, 5b, 6b and 7b). The 1970s was still a decade under the previous import substitution model for most countries in Latin America with significant participation in the economy from the state, which is likely to have contributed to reduced significant private investment in infrastructure and FDI, though this conclusion is tentative given the instability of the equations through the different breaks. For the 1990s we found a non-siginificative correlation between FDI and private investment (equations 2d, 4d and 6d). We also found an unstable correlation between infrastructure (telephone lines per capita) and private investment, and a negative correlation during the 1990s (equations 3d, 5d and 7d).

The interpretation of the results for FDI could lead to the conclusion that FDI did not contribute directly to private investment. It could have contributed indirectly through the attraction of new technologies, though specific research could allow the drawing of more precise conclusions regarding the interactions between FDI and private investment in Latin America. Specific research on this subject is contained for example in the work of Lim (2001), Borensztein et al. (1998) Olofsdotter (1998).[18]

The same applies to the association between infrastructure and private investment given the sensitivity of the association. In a case study about investment and reforms in Latin America, Moguillansky and Bielschowsky (2000) provided a detailed structural analysis of the incidence of infrastructure investments on economic growth for eight Latin American countries during 1960–2000. Calderón and Servén (2004) also studied the role of infrastructure in Latin America during 1980–2001.[19] Although not included in Table 7.10 a separate estimate of the equation for the private investment rate against per capita GDP growth and our infrastructure proxy for the period 1991–2002 instead of 1993–2002 (that is an equation of type 5) yielded a strong and positive coefficients for both per capita GDP growth and infrastructure as factors explaining private investment (significative at the 1 per cent level).

7.5   CONCLUSIONS

In our research we obtained evidence about the contribution of investment to economic development in Latin America during the period 1960–2002 based on a sample of six Latin American countries (Argentina, Brazil, Chile, Colombia, Mexico and Venezuela), representing the region's aggregate trends. These six countries are the largest of the region and produce about 90 per cent of total Latin America's GDP (WDI, 2004, World Bank). The selection of countries was also guided by the availability and reliability of the data we required. We divided the whole 1960–2002 period into several sub-periods and disaggregated fixed investment by type of asset (machinery and equipment, and buildings), and also by sectoral origin between private and public investment. In Section 7.2, we examined the contribution of physical capital to Latin America's economic growth. In Section 7.3, we examined the contributions of machinery and equipment, and buildings and in Section 7.4, the contribution of private and public investment to per capita GDP growth to per capita GDP growth. A shorter period was used in Section 7.4 (1970–2002 against 1960–2002) given the limited availability and reliability of the data on private and public investment.

The growth accounting exercises in Section 7.2 provided evidence of the primary role played by total factor productivity in explaining the difference between fast and slow growth experiences, with physical capital factors playing a secondary role on the growth process of the six largest Latin American countries during 1960–2002. Extending the traditional growth accounting approach through the incorporation of additional elements (adjusting physical capital by its rate of utilization, expressing physical capital in terms of GDP basket units, and decomposing labor between its raw and human capital components) did not change the evidence found in other growth accounting studies regarding the key role played by total factor productivity in driving economic growth. From the evidence we concluded that aggregate fixed investment per se did not explain the difference between fast growth countries and slow growth countries and that total factor productivity made the difference. Total factor productivity reflects all types of cost reductions raising efficiency in the use of production factors, including those induced by the composition of investment and the macroeconomic framework.

In Section 7.3 we found that fixed investment was significant in explaining per capita GDP growth during 1960–2002, but that key policy related variables were also main factors contributing to growth, helping to mark the difference between fast and slow growth experiences. We found that main policy related variables contributing to growth were: inflation, trade openness, external debt, the size of the government, and education. Inflation, a proxy for price stability, showed the most consistent significance during 1960–2002, however.

We found that machinery and equipment formed the main part of fixed investment contributing to per capita GDP growth, with the role of buildings playing a secondary role. The stability analysis confirmed the significance of total fixed investment and also of machinery and equipment investment as factors contributing to per capita GDP growth. Although, investment in buildings showed little significance (t-values) as a factor contributing to per capita GDP growth during 1960–2002, a slight positive impact developed after the 1980s.

We also have found that secondary education was an important force contributing to per capita GDP growth during the 1960s and 1970s but its role declined in the 1980s and further in the 1990s and 2000s, as the coverage of secondary education increased. The evidence suggests that education policies should incorporate new forms of expanding the human capital stock, mainly through efforts to improve the quality of all types of education and other training that facilitates a dynamic adoption of new technologies.

In Section 7.4, we examined evidence about the influence of investment on per capita GDP growth from a sectoral perspective during 1970–2002. We decomposed fixed investment between private and public investment. A shorter period was used in this case given the limited availability and reliability of the data. As for the estimates in Section 7.3, we obtained estimates for the whole period and supported the conclusions with qualifications drawn from a structural break analysis. We found that the contribution of private investment to growth was positive and strong, that the contribution of public investment was not significant, and that inflation was also the main key variable contributing to per capita GDP growth that showed systematic and consistent significance. We found that public investment was not a key constraint on economic growth. As for the implications drawn from of Section 7.2, the structural tests showed the 1980s as 'atypical' compared to the rest of the period.

We also found a mutual causality between growth and private investment, which helps to understand the formation of vicious and virtuous cycles in Latin America. A contraction (increase) of private investment induces a reduction (increase) of per capita GDP growth, which in turn, induces a contraction (increase) of private investment. Per capita GDP growth showed consistent significance as a main factor explaining private investment rates during 1970–2002. The evidence also indicates that a precondition for the use of active counter cyclical public investment policies would be the prevalence of a stable macroeconomic framework (mainly price stability). Finally, we did not find general conclusive evidence about the incidence of FDI and infrastructure on private investment or growth in Latin America. Specific case by case observations seem required to appreciate the influence of FDI and infrastructure.

APPENDIX 7.A

Data Sources

Variable	Description	Source
GDP	Current and constant prices local currency units	World Development Indicators (WDI), World Bank
Potential GDP	Seven-year centered average of GDP at constant prices	WDI and own calculations
GDP Deflator	Index of GDP current prices/ GDP constant prices	WDI
Gross fixed capital formation	Current and constant prices	WDI, United Nations Statistical Office
Factor shares	Annual labor and capital shares in national income. Capital shares excludes land and other assets not part of the national accounts' concept of fixed capital formation	Economic Commission for Latin America (ECLAC), United Nations Statistical Office
Capital stock	Fixed capital derived from the series of gross fixed capital formation at constant prices (K) and at current prices (K^*)	WDI and own calculations
Labor	Employment series	ECLAC, United Nations Statistical Office
GDP growth	$\ln GDP_t - \ln GDP_{t-1}$ (data at constant prices, local currency)	WDI
Total investment rates	Percentage of GDP at constant and current prices (data in local currency)	WDI and national sources (data for 2000–2002)

Variable	Description	Source
Machinery and equipment, and construction rates	Percentage of GDP at constant and current prices (data in local currency)	WDI and national sources (data for 2000–2002)
Private and public investment rates	Percentage of GDP at constant and current prices (data in local currency)	WDI and national sources (data for 2000–2002)
Inflation	Percentage annual change in the consumer price index	WDI
Openness (exports + imports)	Percentage ratio of exports + imports on GDP	WDI
Government consumption	Percentage share of government consumption on GDP	World Bank database and data compiled by N. Loayza
External debt	Percentage ratio of external debt on GDP, at average market exchange rate	WDI
Foreign direct investment	Percentage ratio of FDI on GDP, at average market exchange rate	WDI
Infrastructure (ln telephone lines per capita)	Ln of average annual per capita telephone lines	WDI and N. Loayza database
Education (ln ratio secondary enrollment)	Ln of the ratio of secondary enrollment calculated over secondary school age group	WDI and own calculations
Population growth	Annual percentage rate	WDI

Table 7.A.1 GDP growth and investment rates

	1961–65	1966–70	1971–75	1976–80	1981–85	1986–90	1991–95	1996–02
Argentina								
GDP growth	4.0	4.0	3.1	3.0	-2.4	-0.3	6.7	-0.3
GDP per capita growth	2.4	2.5	1.4	1.4	-3.9	-1.6	5.5	-1.2
Investment rate (current LCU)	22.3	22.4	24.1	28.1	20.6	17.0	17.7	16.8
Investment rate (constant LCU)	21.7	21.9	23.3	25.1	18.7	16.2	18.1	17.8
Brazil								
GDP growth	4.6	7.8	10.3	6.7	1.2	2.1	3.2	2.0
GDP per capita growth	1.5	5.0	7.7	4.2	-0.9	0.3	1.6	0.7
Investment rate (current LCU)	19.8	19.7	23.6	22.9	19.2	21.8	20.8	21.0
Investment rate (constant LCU)	19.3	19.7	23.6	22.9	19.2	21.8	21.2	18.4
Chile								
GDP growth	3.7	4.6	-1.1	7.3	1.1	6.8	8.7	3.8
GDP per capita growth	1.2	2.5	-2.8	5.7	-0.4	5.0	7.0	2.5
Investment rate (current LCU)	17.4	18.7	16.8	19.2	14.9	22.8	24.6	24.2
Investment rate (constant LCU)	33.7	21.7	18.5	17.5	18.7	23.7	29.9	31.5
Columbia								
GDP growth	4.7	5.9	5.7	5.4	2.2	4.9	4.1	1.1
GDP per capita growth	1.6	2.9	3.2	3.0	0.1	2.9	2.1	-0.7
Investment rate (current LCU)	18.5	20.2	18.7	18.4	19.8	18.9	21.1	17.1
Investment rate (constant LCU)	18.5	18.9	18.8	18.6	20.2	17.8	20.7	17.2
Mexico								
GDP growth	7.2	6.3	6.3	7.1	2.0	1.7	1.6	4.0
GDP per capita growth	4.0	2.9	3.0	4.3	-0.2	-0.2	-0.2	2.5
Investment rate (current LCU)	18.3	20.3	21.8	24.4	22.4	21.3	21.8	23.2
Investment rate (constant LCU)	24.7	27.2	26.4	26.5	21.0	17.3	20.0	22.0
Venezuela								
GDP growth	6.2	4.0	3.0	2.5	-0.9	2.8	3.5	-0.4
GDP per capita growth	2.4	0.7	-0.5	-0.9	-3.4	0.1	1.2	-2.3
Investment rate (current LCU)	22.7	27.8	31.1	36.5	20.1	19.3	18.7	18.8
Investment rate (constant LCU)	19.5	21.9	23.2	29.9	19.6	15.9	16.2	16.3

Note: Total investment rates: data correspond to total gross capital formation.

Source: World Development Indicators.

Table 7.A.2   Machinery and equipment and construction shares, percentages of GDP

	1961–65	1966–70	1971–75	1976–80	1981–85	1986–90	1991–95	1996–02	1961–02
Argentina									
Total investment	19.94	20.70	22.15	24.72	18.46	15.95	18.23	17.81	19.65
Mach. and equip.	5.93	5.82	6.44	7.26	7.62	7.13	7.13	6.99	6.80
Construction	14.01	14.88	15.70	17.45	10.84	8.81	11.10	10.81	12.85
Brazil									
Total investment	15.31	17.96	23.52	23.71	18.31	17.17	17.41	19.30	19.09
Mach. and equip.	5.96	7.41	10.27	9.53	5.70	5.45	3.33	7.01	7.13
Construction	9.35	10.55	13.25	14.17	12.62	11.72	14.08	12.29	11.97
Chile									
Total investment	22.37	20.30	16.26	15.03	15.87	21.24	26.46	24.64	20.48
Mach. and equip.	7.16	7.04	5.39	6.96	6.35	10.33	14.85	9.76	8.54
Construction	15.21	13.26	10.87	8.07	9.52	10.91	11.61	14.88	11.94
Colombia									
Total investment	14.47	15.74	16.08	15.89	17.24	15.49	18.28	15.82	15.74
Mach. and equip.	5.52	5.66	6.50	6.98	7.34	6.66	7.26	5.87	6.31
Construction	8.95	10.08	9.58	8.91	9.90	8.83	11.02	9.96	9.43
Mexico									
Total investment	17.50	20.37	21.46	22.25	20.03	16.95	18.58	19.07	19.50
Mach. and equip.	6.99	8.12	8.82	9.20	7.71	6.62	9.39	10.00	8.43
Construction	10.52	12.24	12.63	13.05	12.32	10.32	9.20	9.07	11.07
Venezuela									
Total investment	16.12	18.02	17.91	26.60	19.03	15.66	16.18	14.12	17.77
Mach. and equip.	5.48	6.39	7.23	11.50	8.09	6.24	6.02	5.21	8.27
Construction	10.64	11.63	10.68	15.11	10.94	9.42	10.15	8.91	9.50

Notes: Averages of annual shares. Shares are on the basis of data in local currency at constant prices.

Sources: ECLAC/UN Statistical Office and national sources (1990–2002).

Table 7.A.3 Private and public investment rates, percentages of GDP

	1970–72	1973–75	1976–78	1979–81	1982–84	1985–87	1988–90	1991–93	1994–96	1997–99	2000–02	1970–2002
Argentina												
Total investment	20.90	21.10	26.10	23.60	20.90	18.20	16.10	16.80	18.70	19.00	14.00	19.60
Private investment	12.80	13.40	14.50	16.70	15.40	13.80	12.00	15.20	17.00	17.10	13.10	14.60
Public investment	8.10	7.70	11.60	6.80	5.40	4.40	4.10	1.60	1.70	1.90	0.90	5.10
Brazil												
Total investment	19.60	22.90	21.90	23.60	20.60	20.40	24.70	19.90	20.10	19.40	21.00	21.30
Private investment	13.80	16.30	14.30	15.40	14.50	14.70	18.90	14.60	16.00	16.20	19.10	15.80
Public investment	5.80	6.60	7.50	8.20	6.10	5.70	5.80	5.30	4.20	3.30	1.90	5.50
Chile												
Total investment	14.40	14.30	15.00	17.70	12.90	17.80	22.20	22.40	24.00	24.00	22.00	18.80
Private investment	6.80	4.30	7.90	12.40	7.80	13.60	17.00	16.90	19.20	18.00	16.60	12.80
Public investment	7.50	10.00	7.10	5.30	5.10	4.20	5.20	5.60	4.80	6.00	5.30	6.00
Colombia												
Total investment	17.20	15.80	15.30	16.60	18.10	17.00	17.10	16.30	22.40	17.30	14.30	17.20
Private investment	11.30	10.50	9.40	10.00	9.20	10.10	10.40	9.20	14.70	8.80	6.90	10.20
Public investment	6.00	5.30	5.90	6.60	8.90	6.90	6.70	7.10	7.70	8.50	7.40	7.00
Mexico												
Total investment	18.80	20.20	20.60	25.00	19.50	19.10	17.90	19.00	17.80	20.50	19.10	19.80
Private investment	13.10	12.10	12.50	13.90	11.70	12.90	13.60	15.10	13.90	17.90	16.20	13.90
Public investment	5.80	8.00	8.10	11.10	7.80	6.20	4.30	3.90	3.90	2.60	2.90	5.90
Venezuela												
Total investment	na	na	na	na	16.00	19.60	17.90	19.80	16.60	17.90	15.40	17.80
Private investment	na	na	na	na	10.50	11.40	8.10	8.50	7.40	9.60	9.40	9.20
Public investment	na	na	na	na	5.50	8.30	9.80	11.30	9.20	8.20	6.00	8.60

Notes: Simple averages of annual shares. Shares are on the basis of data in local currency at current prices.

Source: World Development Indicators (2004); International Finance Corporation (IFC) (2001).

231

NOTES

*   Research commissioned by the Economic Commission for Latin America (ECLAC/CEPAL – United Nations.

   I appreciate comments from Victor Elías, Andrés Solimano, Andrés Rodriguez, and Norman Loayza. I am also grateful to Subika Farazi and Ayhan Cil for their assistance.

1.   A further decomposition of the human capital component, between the part due to human capital maintenance and the part due to human capital upgrade, is given by:

$$\omega \Delta L = \omega^* \Delta L + \omega^* \frac{(L^* - L)\Delta L}{L} + \omega^* \left(\Delta L^* - \frac{L^*}{L} \Delta L \right).$$

2.   This proxy is also used by Harberger (1996). Using his words: ' … those who earn two thirds of a year's GDP are overwhelmingly poor, low skilled, and with relative low levels of human capital'.

3.   The total labor share presents some important variations though time and between countries. The ranges for the period 1960–2002 are: Argentina (40–60 per cent); Brazil (60–80 per cent); Chile (60–65 per cent); Colombia (50–67 per cent); Mexico (36–60 per cent); and Venezuela (44–75 per cent). Data on shares were obtained from Hofman (2000) and the ECLAC/UN national account statistics. The labor share has been adjusted to include own account workers. The capital share (1 – total labor share) assimilates to the national accounts concept of physical capital (which excludes land and other non-reproducible or intangible assets).

4.   A similar procedure is used in Loayza and Soto (2002) and is based on the Baxter and King work on business cycles (1999).

5.   In our capital equation (6) we use $I_t(1-\delta/2)$ instead of I_t as we are measuring capital at the beginning of each year and gross investment depreciates through the year. We assume fixed investment depreciates at half the annual depreciation in each year. However, this modification has a negligible impact on the capital stock series (about 0.2 per cent difference in the annual percentage change in the capital stock series obtained using our equation against the traditional equation). For estimates with no depreciation applied to the investment series, see for example, Loayza et al. (2005), Nehru (1994) and Gutiérrez (1983).

6.   The gross fixed capital formation series we use are in national currency units. The source are ECLAC and the UN Statistical Office. We updated the last seven years of the series using the most recent national account data obtained directly from the original country sources.

7.   The 1970s is also called a period of debt-led growth as Latin America's foreign indebtedness rose significantly induced by the oil shocks of 1973 and 1979, negative real interest rates, weakened commodity prices by the mid-1970s, and deteriorated economic conditions reflecting the agony of the old import substitution and state dirigisme model (see Thorp (1998)). The lending boom and 'herd' related effect induced a debt-led growth in the 1970s that was also seen in the 1990s, but with less systematic negative effects than in the 1980s.

8.   Solimano and Soto (2004) concluded that most of the evolution of GDP growth is the result of changes in the efficiency and rate of utilization in the use of capital and labor (TFP).

9.   From the EA growth accounting calculations, the implicit net returns to physical capital in Chile rose from about 10 per cent annual rate in the early 1980s to about 15 per cent by the mid 1990s. From the mid-1990s onward, the rate declined to slightly below 10 per cent by 2002, reflecting the negative TFP trend that developed after the mid-1990s.

10.   Solimano and Soto (1994) use the growth rates of TFPs (computed through growth accounting) for a panel of 12 Latin American countries for the period 1960–2002 as the dependent variable instead of per capita GDP growth. They showed evidence, however, of

a 'striking similarity' between changes of total factor productivity and per capita or per working age GDP. Both approaches should yield similar results as long as the regression estimates takes account of fixed investment as an additional control variable.

11. High inflation episodes have been generally associated with more expansionary monetary and fiscal policies. A high share of government consumption in GDP has reflected fiscal policies that have assigned the government a more predominant role in the growth process. A higher share of trade in GDP reflects commercial policies that have reduced trade barriers. Higher shares of FDI in GDP and of infrastructure are reflecting policies that have deregulated FDI and have been more aggressive in the privatization processes (including concessions). And, changes in the coverage of secondary enrollment reflect the strength of educational policies, although as we mention in the text, existing education variables are imperfect measures of human capital formation. Measures of education levels do not account for quality or on-the-job training factors.

12. We applied White's diagonal method that has proven to be robust to observation-specific heteroskedasticity in the residuals.

13. These observations are representative for the six countries as a whole, however. The debt crisis events of Argentina, Ecuador and Uruguay in the 2000s (to which Brazil was close in 1999) are indicative that policy disparities across countries continued after the 1980s making some countries more sensitive than others to the different factors affecting growth.

14. We also examined some additional variables such as the fiscal balance (percentage of GDP) and the current account balance (percentage of GDP) but the series were short, truncated or of questionable reliability. We also examined more disaggregated fixed investment data from Penn World Table 5.6, but the series were also truncated and we could not obtain reliable documentation explaining the data sources. National accounts data from the United Nations and national sources in Latin America do not include data for our countries on disaggregated fixed investment except for the broad categories between machinery and equipment, and buildings.

15. Per capita GDP growth in the right side of the equations has been computed as the first difference in natural log terms between consecutive periods ($\ln y_t - \ln y_{t-1}$). Thus, a 3 per cent rate is measured as 0.03. This is relevant for an appropriate interpretation of the estimated coefficients and the derived elasticities.

16. Servén and Solimano (1992b) also remarked on the investment slump during the 1980s and the slow recovery during the early 1990s as a factor contributing to the slow growth recovery after the 1980s.

17. We use the data on gross enrollments in secondary education from the WDI 2004 (World Bank), measured as the ratios of total secondary school enrollment to the population of secondary age group. See also Appendix 7.A for a description of variables and sources. Series measuring the quality of secondary education should add insights to the impact of education on growth. This is a line of statistical development that would enrich future research on economic growth.

18. Lim (2001) provides a survey showing that the literature provides substantial support for positive spillovers from FDI but that there is no consensus on the causality from FDI to economic growth. Borensztein et al. (1998) found that the level of human capital helps to determine the ability to adopt foreign technologies and that FDI may crowd out domestic investment. Olofsdotter (1998) found evidence showing that the beneficiary effects of FDI depend on institutional capability, which varies between countries.

19. Moguillansky and Bielschowsky (2000) studied eight countries: Bolivia, Brazil, Chile, Colombia, Costa Rica, Mexico and Peru. They analyzed the effects of the structural reforms on investment decisions in the 1990s, covering macroeconomic, sectoral and microeconomic aspects, and found that weak institutions and regulations have limited the benefits from the privatization of investments in infrastructure (including the concessions). Calderón and Servén (2004) show that Latin America lags behind the international norm in terms of infrastructure quantity and quality and that infrastructure investment has fallen in Latin America, induced by the retrenchment of public investment and the limited response of the private sector. They also observe considerable disparities between countries.

REFERENCES

Barro, R. (1999), 'Notes on growth accounting', *Journal of Economic Growth*, **4**, June.

Barro, R. and J.-W. Lee (1993), 'International comparisons of educational attainment', *Journal of Monetary Economics*, **32**.

Barro, R. and J.-W. Lee (1994), 'Sources of economic growth', in *Carnegie–Rochester Conference Series on Public Policy*, **40**.

Baxter, M. and R. King (1999), 'Measuring business cycles: approximate band-pass filters for economic time series', *Review of Income and Statistics*, **81**.

Blomstrom, M., R. Lipsey and M. Zejan (1996), 'Is fixed investment the key to economic growth?', *Quarterly Journal of Economics*, February.

Borensztein, E., J. De Gregorio and J. Lee (1998), 'How does foreign direct investment affect economic growth', *Journal of International Economics*, **45**.

Calderón, C. and L. Servén (2004), 'Trends in infrastructure in Latin America: 1980–2001', World Bank working paper 3401.

De Long, B. and L. Summers (1991), 'Equipment investment and economic growth', *Quarterly Journal of Economics*, **106** (2) (May).

De Long, B. and L. Summers (1993), 'How strongly do developing economies benefit from equipment investment?', *Journal of Monetary Economics*, **32**.

Easterly, W. (2001), *The Elusive Quest for Growth: Economists' Adventures and Misadventures in The Tropics*, Cambridge, MA: MIT Press.

Easterly, W. and R. Levine (2001), 'It's not factor capital accumulation: stylized facts and growth models', *World Bank Economic Review*, **15** (2).

Easterly, W. and H. Pack (2001), 'Is investment in Africa too low or too high? Macro and micro evidence', World Bank policy research working paper 2519.

Easterly, W. and S. Rebelo (1993), 'Fiscal policy and economic growth', *Journal of Monetary Economics*, **32**.

Economic Commission for Latin America (ECLAC) (2003), *Foreign Investment in Latin America and the Caribbean. 2002 Report*, Unit of Investment and Corporate Strategies, United Nations, April.

Elías, V. (1992), *Sources of Growth: A Study of Seven Latin American Economies*, San Francisco: ICS Press.

Elías, V. (1990), 'The role of total factor productivity on economic growth', background paper prepared for the World Development Report 1991, World Bank.

Fajnzylber, P. and D. Lederman (1999), 'Economic reforms and total factor productivity growth in Latin America and the Caribbean (1950–95), an empirical note', World Bank working paper, 2114, World Bank, November.

Greene, J. and D. Villanueva (1991), 'Private investment in developing countries: an empirical analysis', IMF *Staff Papers*, **38** (1).

Gutiérrez M. (1983), 'Savings and economic growth in Chile', Serie de Estudios Económicos, 18, Central Bank of Chile economic research series.

Harberger, A. (1996), 'Reflections on economic growth in Asia and the Pacific', *Journal of Asian Economics*, **7** (3).

Harberger, A. (1998), 'A view of the growth process', *American Economic Review*, **88** (1) (March), 1–32.

Hofman, Andrè (2000), 'Standardized capital stock estimates in Latin America: a 1950–94 update', *Cambridge Journal of Economics*, **24**.

International Finance Corporation (IFC) (2001), 'Trends in private investment in developing countries: statistics for 1970–2000 and the impact on private investment of corruption and the quality of public investment', IFC discussion paper 44, Washington, DC.

International Monetary Fund (IMF) and Organization for Economic Co-operation and Development (OECD) (2003), 'Foreign direct investment statistics: how countries measure FDI', Washington, DC.

International Monetary Fund (several issues), *International Financial Statistics Yearbook*, Washington, DC: IMF.

Kahn, M. and M. Kumar (1997), 'Public and private investment and the growth process in developing countries', *Oxford Bulletin of Economics and Statistics*, **59** (1).

Khan, M. and C. Reinhart (1990), 'Private investment and economic growth in developing countries', *World Development*, 18, January.

Klenow, P. and A. Rodriguez-Clare (1997a), 'Economic growth: a review essay', *Journal of Monetary Economics*, 40.

Klenow, P. and A. Rodriguez-Clare (1997b), 'The neoclassical revival in growth economics: has it gone too far?', *National Bureau for Economic Research Macroeconomics Annual*, vol. 155, pp. 000.

Lim, E. (2001), 'Determinants of, and the relation between, foreign direct investment and growth: a summary of the recent literature', International Monetary Fund working paper no. 01/175, November, Washington, DC.

Loayza, N. and R. Soto (eds) (2002), *Economic Growth: Sources, Trends, and Cycles*, Santiago: Central Bank of Chile.

Loayza, N., E. Fajnzylber and C. Calderón (2005), *Economic Growth in Latin America and the Caribbean: Stylized Facts, Explanations, and Forecasts*, Washington, DC: World Bank, June.

Lucas, R. (1988), 'On the mechanics of economic development', *Journal of Monetary Economics*, **22**.

Moguillansky, G. and R. Bielschowsky (2000), *Inversión y reformas económicas en América Latina*, Santiago: Fondo de Cultura Económica-Cepal.

Nehru, V. and A. Dareshwar (1994), 'A new database on physical capital stock: sources, methodology and results', *Revista de Análisis Económico*, **8** (1).

Olofsdotter, K. (1998), 'Foreign direct investment, country capabilities and economic growth', *Weltwirtschaftliches*, **134** (3).

Pack, H. (1994), 'Endogenous growth theory: intellectual appeal and empirical shortcomings', *Journal of Economic Perspectives*, Winter.

Pindyck, R. and A. Solimano (1993), 'Economic instability and aggregate investment', National Bureau for Economic Research working papers, 4380.

Schmidt-Hebbel, K., L. Servén and A. Solimano (1996), 'Saving, investment, and growth in developing countries: an overview', in A. Solimano (ed.) *Road Maps to Prosperity: Essays on Growth and Development*, Ann Arbor, MI: University of Michigan Press.

Servén, L. and A. Solimano (1992a), 'Private investment and macroeconomic adjustment: a survey', *World Bank Research Observer*, **7** (1) (January).

Servén, L. and A. Solimano (eds) (1992b), 'Striving for growth after adjustment: the role of capital formation', World Bank Regional and Sectoral Studies.

Solimano, Andrés and Raimundo Soto (2004), 'Economic growth in Latin America in the late 20th century: evidence and interpretation', ECLAC.

Thorp, R. (1998), *Progress, Poverty and Exclusion: An Economic History of Latin America in the 20th Century*, Washington, DC: Inter-American Development Bank.

United Nations Conference on Trade and Development (UNCTAD) (2000), *Cross-*

border Mergers and Acquisitions and Development, New York and Geneva: UNCTAD.

United Nations Conference on Trade and Development (UNCTAD) (2003), *FDI Policies for Development: National and International Perspectives*, New York and Geneva: UNCTAD.

World Economic Forum (2004), *The Global Competitiveness Report 2003–2004*, Geneva: WEF.

World Bank (database), *World Development Indicators*, Washington, DC: World Bank.

Young, A. (1994), 'Lessons from the east Asian NICS: a contrarian view', *European Economic Review*, **38** (3–4) (April).

Index

244   *Vanishing growth in Latin America*

Smith, A. 1
social structure 4, 91
socialism 232
Solimano, A. 1, 6–7, 11, 44, 72, 74,
    90–91, 98, 158, 161–2, 182–3, 214,
    232–3
Solow, R. 44, 89, 98, 128–9
Soto, R. 6, 11, 14, 44, 90 ,161, 182, 232,
    233
South Africa 68, 141
South America 133
Southern Cone 4–5, 7, 67
Southern countries 46, 48–52, 54–5,
    57–9, 63–5, 67–8
Spain 21–3, 29, 32–3, 38–9, 43, 68
Sri Lanka 68
stabilization 66, 74, 135, 161, 169, 195,
    212
  economic 46
  macroeconomic 4, 9, 133–4, 157
  policies 12
stagnation 2–3, 5–6, 11–12, 15, 17
state-dirigisme 3–4, 232
steady-state 2, 17, 89–90, 98, 188
stylized fact 2, 6, 12–15, 101, 133
Sub-Saharan economies 3
Summers, L. 97, 117, 161, 182–3, 198
Sweden 68, 141
Switzerland 68
Syria 68

Taiwan 44, 86
Tarling, R. 149
Tavares, J. 158
Taylor, L. 148–9, 152
technical progress 81, 89, 98, 103–4,
    127–9
technological
  frontier 54
  progress 34, 54, 66, 125, 129
terms of trade 1, 11–12, 40–41, 59–60,
    62, 69, 75, 92, 94–6, 98, 115, 117,
    125–6, 130, 133, 135, 145, 156,
    169
TFP 1, 6–9, 12, 24–6, 28–37, 39–43, 52,
    54–9, 62–8, 71–2, 82, 86–9, 96,
    102–4, 110–13, 124–6, 131,
    178–82, 233
  see also productivity
Thailand 21–3, 29, 32–4, 38–9, 43–4, 68

TMA 164, 166, 168, 170, 175–7, 179,
    180
  see also 'traditional modified'
    approach
Togo 68
Tornell, A. 143
tourism 8–9, 101, 138
trade 2, 46–7, 72, 101, 104, 106,
    114–15, 119–21, 126–7, 133–4,
    138, 143, 149, 157–8, 184, 196–7,
    199, 225, 233
  barriers 233
  deficit 136, 154
  foreign 107, 109, 144, 158
  free 106, 127, 157
  international 40, 90, 103, 143, 145
  liberalization 146, 157, 199
  openness 121, 149, 184, 225
  protection 184
  reforms 196, 199
  regime 5, 104
  shocks 11–12, 40–41, 59, 62, 96, 135
  specialization 138, 147, 158
  'traditional modified' approach 164,
    175
  see also TMA
Trinidad and Tobago 141
Tunisia 68
Turkey 21–3, 32–3, 43

UN Commodity Trade Statistics
    Database 69
UNCTAD 147
UNDP 112, 136, 141
United Kingdom 68
United Nations 204, 227, 232–3
United States 2, 17, 24, 68, 76–7, 81,
    96, 98, 101, 105–7, 120, 122, 124,
    129–31, 134–6, 138, 141, 145–6,
    148, 158, 182
  see also US; USA
Uruguay 6–7, 13–14, 16, 19–21, 26–9,
    31, 37, 43–4, 46–51, 54–5, 57–8,
    68, 72, 141, 233
US 9, 78, 106–7
  see also United States
USA 13, 35, 44, 51, 75–8, 81
  see also United States

value-added contribution 144, 146–7